THE
TEACHERS
OF ONE

Living Advaita
Conversations on the
Nature of Non-Duality

PAULA MARVELLY

WATKINS PUBLISHING
LONDON

This edition published in the UK in 2002 by
Watkins Publishing, 20 Bloomsbury Street, London, WC1B 3QA

Cover design by Echelon Design
Cover photograph © Contexture
Interviewee photographs © Paula Marvelly
Designed and typeset by Echelon Design
Printed and bound in Great Britain by NFF Production

British Library Cataloguing in Publication data available

Library of Congress Cataloguing in Publication data available

ISBN 1 84293 028 1

For my family

Paula Jane Marvelly was born in London in 1967. She read English at Royal Holloway College, University of London, where she was awarded the Mary MacPherson essay prize for journalistic writing. She then went on to complete a postgraduate research degree in European Studies at Selwyn College, University of Cambridge. She has been interested in the philosophy of non-dualism for many years and is a member of the Ramana Maharshi Foundation in London.

ACKNOWLEDGEMENTS

First and foremost, I owe everything to my family – Mum, Dad and Colin – who have always offered me immeasurable love and support.

My gratitude and appreciation also go to the following: to Alan Jacobs for writing the Foreword to this book, as well as his philosophical guidance over the years; to Jane Adams Jacobs for her editorial advice; to Anne Irwin for her meticulous proofreading and her unceasing encouragement; to Gill Please for her literary guidance; to Nathan Gaydhani for his photographic tutelage; to Neill Bartlett for his insights into Western philosophy; to Philip Guillermond for his advice on the 'Advaitic Shuffle'; and to Mick Brown for inspiring the writer within.

I would also like to thank Mr Ramanan, President of the Ramanasramam, for kindly giving me permission to quote from Sri Ramanasramam publications in the final chapter.

I am also indebted to Arthur Osborne, whose books, *Ramana Maharshi and the Path of Self Knowledge*, *Ramana Arunachala* and *Buddhism and Christianity in the Light of Hinduism*, all published by Sri Ramanasramam, formed the factual basis for the material on the life and teachings of Sri Ramana Maharshi.

Finally, I would like to thank all the publishers who have agreed to give permission to quote from their publications in *The Teachers of One*.

CONTENTS

FOREWORD

The best English translation of the Hindu term, 'Advaita' is 'non-dualism', which means simply 'not two but One'. This fundamental philosophic principle has been latent in the ancient wisdom of India since time immemorial. The seeds of this realization by the rishis that all is One are found scattered in the hymns of the *Rig Veda*.

In the later Upanishads, the principle was analogously stated over and over again. The Aryachara Shankara cogently elaborated this whole teaching in his *Commentaries on the Principal Upanishads* and the *Brahmana Sutras*. This tradition has been maintained for over 1,000 years by numerous enlightened sages who have refreshed the teaching by their lives and writings, yet never altering it in any progressive way. It was, and is, for the Advaitin, the final truth.

The Western world, however, had to wait for Advaita as the Indians have proclaimed it in detail until 1801 when Duperan, a French scholar, translated the first collection of Upanishads into Latin. In 1882 these were translated into German and attracted the interest of scholars and philosophers.

It is true that since the time of ancient Greece, which had important links with India, the mystics of Christianity, Judaism and Islam had also penetrated the veil of separation and made similar declarations as to the essential unity of the universe. Plato and the Neoplatonic philosophers had come to metaphysical conclusions similar to those reached by the ancient rishis, albeit in different metaphorical and cultural languages and settings.

When, however, the German philosopher Arthur Schopenhauer discovered the Upanishads he found that, along with early Buddhist teaching, it coincided with his own post-Kantian philosophy that the world was 'will' (a numinous self and empiric ego) and 'representation' or 'idea' – an illusion in consciousness presented by the human sensory apparatus and then interpreted by the brain (maya). Later his principal pupil, Paul Deussen, went further, explaining the Upanishads in books of systematization and translation. Then in the late 19th century, the teaching of Advaita Vedanta (the ending of the Vedas) became widely known in academic circles and available for those in the West who searched for such knowledge.

A German Doctor and Oxford University Professor, Max Müller, then oversaw a gigantic literary project – the translation of the 50 most important sacred books of the East. Ramakrishna, a *bhakti* saint and Advaitin, founded his monastic order and Vivekananda, his disciple, visited London and America, a living example of the teaching. Furthermore, the Theosophical Movement was founded by the Russian occultist, Madame Blavatsky, and in 1889 Annie Besant joined the Society, which eventually led to the discovery of Jiddu Krishnamurti as the future world teacher.

Now the West could study the wisdom of the teaching of non-dualism for its own intrinsic value, not as a superstitious set of beliefs inferior to the dogmatism of Christianity. With the advent of Sri Ramana Maharshi, the world could also now witness in actuality the living truth of this great teaching. From the 1930s until Maharshi's death in 1950, many Westerners visited his ashram at Arunachala. He taught that the way of *jnana* or Self Knowledge, combined with *bhakti*, devotion, was a possibility for all in life, if they earnestly studied the teachings and were willing to apply them in their daily life.

After Ramana's death, his disciples H L Poonjaji in Lucknow, and Robert Adams in the USA, brought a few of their Western pupils to the point at which they were permitted to teach the Maharshi's way of Self Enquiry and Self Surrender, as well as explain its metaphysical basis. With their deaths, another similar devotee of Ramana and pupil of the Mumbai sage, Nisargadatta Maharaj, Ramesh S Balsekar continues to write and teach daily, and has brought a few more of his pupils forward to teach.

This fascinating and beautifully written book of Paula Marvelly's gives in detail the intimate stories and teachings of the leading contemporary Western Advaita teachers active in the world today. Her series of interviews and photographs, taken by her, demonstrate that the same principles and practices with different flavours, emphases and delineations are available to earnest seekers today.

There are now many thousands of young, middle-aged and old men and women greatly benefiting from this wisdom, the keynotes of which are unconditional love, freedom, the whole-hearted affirmation of 'what is' and Self Knowledge.

This book forms a fine introduction to this whole movement. Many people discover a teacher with whom they strongly resonate and thus a process of ever deepening intellectual and emotional understanding commences.

I would advise Western seekers to study this book well and then go deeper and deeper into the source of their own being. They will be following the ancient Socratic injunction to 'Know thyself', the culmination and consummation of a useful life on our dear planet Earth.

Alan Jacobs
Chairman, Ramana Maharshi Foundation (UK)
June 2001

INTRODUCTION

When I first read about Aldous Huxley's taste of *satchitananda*, I was jealous. His description of 'visionary experience', recounted in *The Doors of Perception* and published in 1954, was the very thing I had been chasing after for most of my life. Nevertheless, Huxley's expansion of consciousness, and subsequent merging with his surroundings, was precipitated through chemical means – it was mescaline that had unleashed the 'gratuitous grace' from within. Timothy Leary, an American academic psychologist, who was also looking to 'turn on, tune in and drop out' with hallucinogens, was however to proclaim that lysergic acid diethylamide (LSD) was the cheaper and more accessible alternative. LSD, he declared, could also unlock the potential cellular memory of the beatific vision. Indeed, such was the invitation that it spawned a counter-cultural revolution of people searching for that most elusive of Holy Grails – spiritual enlightenment. But by the late sixties, the vision was losing its lustre as the effects of sustained drug abuse were becoming more and more apparent. The use of LSD was therefore criminalized – a new elixir of life was needed.

In 1967 the Maharishi Mahesh Yogi arrived in Los Angeles, offering a technique that would bring personal fulfilment, spiritual enlightenment and world peace, without any harmful side effects. Transcendental Meditation (TM) had come to the West. Indeed, the one time devotee, John Lennon, was to remark: 'We aren't sorry that we took LSD, but we realize that if we'd met the Maharishi before, we would not have needed to take it.'

But the TM movement needed no iconic proselytizers. During the sixties, it attracted more new followers in the West than any other religious domination, apart from Christianity. A technique merely entailing the twice-daily repetition of a mantra, TM was initially seen as an attractive alternative to LSD. But then the rumours began to circulate – discrepancies involving money and devotees – and thus, by the early seventies, the Beatles, as well as many others, had disassociated themselves from the Maharishi's movement.

The quest for self-understanding and divine illumination is not new. Since the beginning of history, through religious ritual and worship, people have sought the meaning of their existence and intimate contact with their Creator. But it was Socrates, born in 469 AD, who launched formal philosophy in the West. His pupil, Plato, who recorded and developed Socratic thinking, postulated that the world around us is merely phenomena, representations or 'Forms', in a never-ending process of 'becoming'. That which motivates this world of 'Forms', he stated, is the underlying realm of 'Ideas' – archetypal blueprints embedded in the consciousness of the universe. Plato believed that these 'Ideas' – like 'Beauty', 'Wisdom' and 'Truth' – were changeless and eternal; that they were in fact synonymous with the absolute reality of 'being'. Moreover, Plato said that mental enquiry could take man's attention away from the external world of the senses to the internal world of the intellect, in order to awaken within him a deeper and more profound level of reality, the 'gratuitous grace' from within.

But, as the centuries passed, revolutions and reformations in every field of knowledge and understanding were shaking people's belief systems right to the core. It was René Descartes who, against this backdrop of rising scepticism, set out to discover, once and for all, infallible truth. With mathematical precision, he deconstructed every philosophical premise, until he was left with one piece of information that he could not go beyond and of which there could be absolutely no doubt – the fact of his own doubting. Descartes concluded that the 'I' who was doubting, the conscious thinking subject, exists. *Cogito, ergo sum* – I think, therefore I am.

Inasmuch as he also deduced that something cannot come from nothing – believing that the dualistic world of mind and matter was a manifestation of God – his most important conclusion was that God's existence was not known to man through divine revelation but that it was through man's reasoning that God revealed himself to man. It is only when the thinker 'I' exists that God then comes into existence. In other words, in Descartes' view, existence precedes essence; 'I' comes before God.

Some people might think that to enquire into the nature of Oneself is an indulgent hobby reserved only for those with time on their hands. But for others it can be the only worthwhile pursuit in life. Indeed, it is not difficult to follow a line of Self Enquiry: I think therefore I am – but if I think not, am I not? In other words, do I still exist if I am not thinking? Will I know that I exist if I do not have the capacity to think about whether I exist or not? Obviously something exists when I am not thinking – I can prove this when I start to think back to the time when I wasn't thinking and the fact that I survived it. So what exists when 'I' am not there to think about it? Does this mean that I am something other than 'I'? And who is this 'I' which seems to exist only when it is thinking about something? In short, who am I?

Descartes set the ball rolling in the hunt for the elusive 'I', but as a separate, self-subsistent entity. Indeed, as the centuries passed, God or consciousness or the underlying reality, faded more and more out of the philosophical picture. Moreover, reflecting the contemporary existentialist view, Friedrich Nietzsche was to declare, 'God is dead'. Furthermore, as theories grew progressively more reductionist, even the 'I' nearly became obliterated. And although the work of Freud and Jung turned their focus of attention to the unconscious in the search for the individual self, by the middle of the 20th century it seemed that the post-modernist mind had deconstructed itself, and the universe, into nothingness.

The prevailing belief was that there were no beliefs – all knowledge is subjective and in flux and no human understanding is final. The only certainty was that reality is something that is an unfolding process – it is ambiguous, indefinable, differentiated; a complex amalgam of cultural and psychological conditioning, but with no recourse to an objective truth.

What this unveiling of belief systems brought to the West nonetheless was an exposure of religious dogma and philosophical ignorance. By stripping human knowledge of every one of its foundations, there then arose the potential for something else to emerge. People were now turning to a new intellectual vision. They were no longer seeing the universe as a fragmentation of opposites but seeking to bring about reintegration and relationship, the synthesis of complementary opposites; to move away from linear thinking and to turn to a more lateral form of intuition.

But, whereas Western philosophy had deconstructed the 'I' to the point where it was able to declare what it was not, it could not provide the answer as to what it was. Moreover religion, predominantly represented in the West by Christianity – a faith steeped in ritual and dogma – was not able to provide any adequate answers either, postulating that what man is, at best, is a miserable sinner. Thus, in an age when anything went, more acceptable and practical methods of self-discovery were being sought to understand the nature of consciousness and the answer to the ultimate question – Who am I? Through more diverse forms of spirituality, in particular those from the East, people were learning ways of getting back in touch with their inner selves, discovering who they were in relation to this new holistic universe.

And now, in the 21st century, the emphasis is on self-investigation – not blind adherence to a philosophical or religious party line. And inasmuch as the essence of Eastern teaching is still the transience of 'I' – an inconsequential bundle of rising and falling thoughts and perceptions – the invitation is to transcend the veil of 'I' and go beyond it. What lies beyond is not a meaningless emptiness but the very consciousness of the universe itself. Self-realization, the ultimate goal and end of ignorance, is the understanding that 'I' is not a separate identity but merely a filter of mind, that God or consciousness is the animating life force in which the 'I' arises. Consciousness therefore comes before 'I'. And if I am not intrinsically this 'I', I must be the consciousness in which the 'I' manifests. Thus essence precedes existence; I am consciousness. I am God.

To know that 'I am consciousness' is the basic tenet of Advaita, non-dualism – I am One, existing without a second. Indeed, it is the fundamental principle of all Eastern teachings, its source being found in the ancient texts of the Indian Vedas, the oldest scripture known to mankind. And it is this teaching that has become available once more in the 20th and 21st centuries, initiated through the life and teachings of Bhagavan Sri Ramana Maharshi, and now made available through teachers in the West. Using the method of Self Enquiry, it is possible to see through the veil of illusion and find an answer to the most elusive question of all – Who am I?

This book is a record of that enquiry – a voyage of self-discovery, taking me through all the ideas that I think I am, in the hope of discovering that, ultimately, all I am is consciousness and consciousness is all there is.

The writer and journalist, George Orwell, said that writing should be like a windowpane. These interviews, which took place between the spring of 1999 and the autumn of 2000, are arranged in chronological order and presented as spontaneous conversations rather than sanitized questions and answers. Transcribed from the spoken word, the interviews have been lightly edited in collaboration with the interviewee (with the exception of Ramesh Balsekar, who was happy for me to write his interview without seeing it for himself).

I am; yet what I am none cares or knows
My friends forsake me like a memory lost,
I am the self-consumer of my woes —
They rise and vanish in oblivious host,
Like shadows in love's frenzied, stifled throes —
And yet I am, and live — like vapors tossed

Into the nothingness of scorn and noise,
Into the living sea of waking dreams,
Where there is neither sense of life or joys,
But the vast shipwreck of my life's esteems;
Even the dearest, that I love the best,
Are strange — nay, rather stranger than the rest.

I long for scenes, where man hath never trod,
A place where woman never smiled or wept —
There to abide with my Creator, God,
And sleep as I in Childhood sweetly slept,
Untroubling, and untroubled where I lie,
The grass below — above the vaulted sky.

'I Am'
John Clare

Satyananda

CHAPTER ONE

ALL MY TROUBLES SEEM SO FAR

AWAY

As I enter the empty Unitarian church behind the turban domes and lofty pinnacles of the Brighton Pavilion, I see a young man, with his back towards me, seducing the keys of an old and out-of-tune piano. 'Who's the composer?' I ask by way of introduction as I approach. Satyananda's playing trails off into silence; meditatively he turns around and smiles. 'Don't you recognize it?' His Hispanic cadences have their own song-like quality. 'It's "Yesterday" by the Beatles.' I blush at my ignorance as he returns to play the concluding chords.

This is the first interview upon which I am about to embark. Tacking between excitement, fear and an intense headache, my mind feels like a precocious child, begging for attention to its preferences, its dictates and its grand unifying theories of everything. And, of course, all those intelligent and provocative questions, learnt like a script the night before, are now disintegrating into a stream of words and confusion.

Who am I? Who am I indeed. Over the past decade or so, I have asked the question so many times it is beginning to lose its meaning – and pretty much boring me to death in the process. But here is the opportunity to ask someone who claims to really *know* the answer. This is the moment when I can see the living proof of someone who professes to understand the ultimate reality of their own being, having transcended their sense of individuality and merged with consciousness to become One with the universe.

The final notes from the piano resonate through the dank and musty air with a psychedelic twang. We wait for the pulsating sound to fade into nothingness. I dare not move for fear of disturbing something – though what I might disturb I am unsure – and I stand as if lost in a trance.

Satyananda is very gracious in his manner and shows me to a seat where I can sit next to him. He is wearing a brilliant white T-shirt and grey sweatpants;

multi-coloured braids are tied around one wrist. His shoulder-length brown hair is swept back into a ponytail, accentuating his feline countenance that tilts ever so slightly as a cue for me to ask about the spiritual understanding which I have come in search of. As we start our conversation together, I notice that there is a distinct lack of homiletic phrases in his speech – the only theoretical references he does make being to the process of Self Enquiry, which he discovered on silent retreat a few years previously at Osho Leela (UK base of the 'Osho Experience'), where he also assumed the name of Satyananda, meaning 'truth-bliss'.

Bernardo Lischinsky Arenas was born in Uruguay in 1964 to a Jewish father and a Catholic mother, though there was never much talk of religion at home. He felt that his relationship with God was very much a private affair, engaging in Holy Communion well beyond the protective gaze of his parents. His mother still had, nonetheless, a profound influence on his life. Working as a doctor, she often experienced difficulties adapting to the pressures of life in an ever modernizing society, and this led eventually to a nervous breakdown – an event that was to teach Satyananda about the potentially destructive nature of the mind.

Moving to Venezuela at the age of 12 for 'political reasons', he then travelled to Europe in 1987, settling in Amsterdam where he worked as a puppeteer, making dolls and performing with them in the streets and at local art festivals – a fitting occupation given the familiar metaphor of the world as a play in the hands of a divine string-puller. While based in Europe, Satyananda holds meetings throughout the year, most specifically in Holland and the UK, where he has recently moved to a converted barn in Worcestershire in the Midlands. There are also plans to set up a commune in the Andes – Alahcanura is a strip of land bought specifically for holding retreats for three to four months at a stretch. Far removed from technocracy, it would be a return to the life of the land.

A handful of people is slipping into the church behind us. Their anticipatory chatter makes the surrounding world re-emerge and I momentarily lose my concentration as I look to see who has arrived. Satyananda senses my distraction and rises from his seat – he has something to show me. We step outside the church and he points to a large plaque hanging majestically on the outside wall:

> *This church seeks to encourage and support each person on their spiritual and religious journey and does not ask for commitment to any one particular creed or doctrine.*

As I reflect on the words, he disappears back inside to prepare himself for the meeting. A few more people arrive, enthusing over life in general, eager to be in the presence of truth.

Satyananda's satsang is always low-key. There are no pictures of great teachers, no flowers, no religious relics — just a beeswax candle effortlessly burning and minding its own business. Raised on a platform at the front of the congregation, Satyananda sits on a chair positioned on top of what appears to be an animal skin rug and he carefully puts on a headset microphone. A beaming young devotee sits in the corner behind a display of recording gear, preparing tapes to capture the words, and the silence, of the meeting.

We sit for many minutes in the quietness of the church. Satyananda closes his eyes and I follow suit. I try to witness my bodily sensations — the tightness around the muscles in my stomach, the tension in my shoulders and neck. And then I observe the mental chatter — a stream of animated consciousness, dancing and performing in front of me; a riveting drama of conversations, opinions and pious acts of good will.

Satyananda clears his throat and I start, emerging from the dream. He looks around at each person in turn — with some he rests his eyes on theirs, lingering intently; with others he simply smiles and moves on. Then Satyananda looks at me, pausing awhile — I smile in return, hold his gaze but then, abashed, look away. A microphone is then handed around the small gathering. Technical problems make the first questioner anxious; Satyananda just sits very still. Finally, it is my turn to ask — I feel disconcerted and embarrassed as I hear a metallic voice grating out from the loudspeaker — alien and unrecognizable as my own. This is one moment that I am perfectly happy to believe that the voice I hear is not me.

Could you speak about the moment when you realized that you were free of your sense of individuality?

When I was seven, coming back from school, I knew I was late and going to be punished. I was totally in a panic and almost couldn't walk into the house. And suddenly there was this voice but it wasn't in the way we are speaking now — it was all at once. It was just a direct knowing that what was about to happen wasn't important. Somehow I knew that it was fake — the punishment, the pain, everything.

In that knowing, I simply allowed myself to go through the punishment, realizing that in the future I would laugh. I remember that — it was so clear. So the fear was gone. I went into the house and confronted my father and remember that he saw in my eyes that I wasn't scared. I remember his expression in that moment. So during the punishment I was in a state of presence — I wasn't touched by it. It was like finding a safe place where I could hide every moment when I was scared or suffering.

We rationalize this process of being present but all we need to do is relax into this state. How does this happen?

I don't know how it works. I asked my father what he had remembered about that moment and he said, 'You are the only son that wasn't scared of me!' I had been scared of him for a long time. I don't know how it happened but I do know that since that moment I couldn't take anything seriously any more.

I wasn't able to adapt to my studies, I didn't want to follow a career. But that inner place never left me. I was in trouble many times but, if I could be alone for a moment, I would click in and stay at peace and nothing touched me. From then on, there was a feeling of going in and out of that inner place. Sometimes I would catch myself suffering and then I would suddenly see that it was over. But it wasn't an intellectual process.

Did you have a spiritual master, so to speak?

When we speak about masters, one of my biggest masters when I grew up was Bob Marley and he still is because he is speaking about the nature of the mind. He's not just talking about revolution in a political way – his words are very deep and I could always catch what he meant. 'We are coming in from the cold,' he used to say. There are many songs I still like – it's pure wisdom. So my master was always appearing in different forms, in different bodies, when it wasn't clear that it was within. Music, my mother – there was always a way of remembering.

You know, I never read much and didn't get to learn about meditation or spiritual paths. I started going to satsang about two and a half years ago. I was at the end of a very long process of suffering. It was very deep – I have never suffered so much in my life. It was great! I couldn't have been more down – I was married to a lady and we were in the process of getting divorced. I couldn't work it all out for a long time. But I had an instinct to go into myself.

When I was in Amsterdam during the time of my divorce, there were advertisements for courses in meditation. I did a course, which lasted for three days, and then I joined a meditation group and sat in silence with them, twice a week. It used to give me a lot of peace. But I was still living with my wife – we were in the process of separation, so being with the group was the only place where I could be in silence! I was so grateful to them – they taught me some mantras including *Om*. Then I went to Brazil and stayed on the beach and I would sing it almost all the time, particularly in the morning when I woke up. It was very helpful to calm down my mind. It became a deep obsession.

I have often heard of people who have reached a peaceful state speaking about a period before that of intense suffering. It's not necessarily a prerequisite but it is very common.

Yes, for me I knew it was misery but I also knew it was because of something I had caught, if you like. I began to believe all the bad things I was telling myself and so I suffered for it. Somehow I was blaming myself. But somewhere in the corner was silence. It's difficult to explain – the outside expression of it was suffering but inwardly there was peace.

When I went on a silent retreat at Osho Leela at the beginning of September 1997, I was at the end of that suffering – I was feeling much better within myself. I sat down in satsang and the first things that were talked about I recognized as being true. There was nothing new. I was on retreat for 10 days, I think, but I didn't speak a word while I was there. It was just a reconfirmation, a deep reconfirmation – like drinking water when you are thirsty. The answers were in the same place in the same moment. After the retreat I lived by myself all through the winter in a wooden wagon in the Dutch countryside. I stayed all that time deep within. I knew it was all over.

Is it like a process where the mind dissolves?

No, the mind does not dissolve. In my experience there is a new arrangement of things – the things that were in the front go to the back and the things that were on one side go to the other. It is not that you throw away things or gain new things but, somehow, there is a rearranging of the structure. The quality of the mind changes. And then, the mind returns to itself, to its own nature, which is calm, which is silence.

There seems to be some confusion about silence. You once mentioned something that really struck me – silence is not 'no-speech', not 'no-thought'. It's not like that.

No, it's not like that. To be silent is your true state and it is not absence of noise or absence of thought. Actually when a thought arises, *you* don't have it – it is nothing to do with you. It's not something you own – it just comes from the same source. If you decide to have a thought, then you are not in silence. Realize the distance between you and the thought. If you can see that, then you realize that you are in silence. From that moment you can investigate the mind and the patterns of thought.

The transmission that I received while on retreat, for which I am eternally grateful, is Self Enquiry. That for me was enough to break the cycle of patterns. It's like if you find out exactly where the problem of an illness is, you go directly to the point that is the cause of the problem. I realized the importance of Self Enquiry as a process in which we totally neutralize the mind. Instead of finding out what 'I' feels or what 'I' wants or what 'I' learns, I found out that 'I' is not real and all that happens to that 'I' is irrelevant. That is the transmission I received. Now I want to offer myself in any way for the service of truth. That's what happens. That's all.

There seems to be a new generation of teachers. A couple of decades ago there were masters, let's say, like Ramana Maharshi, Nisargadatta, Papaji, and now we have these troubadour teachers who don't have any teaching necessarily or any masters whom they refer to. Could you speak about this generation? Why it's come about?

No, I cannot say anything about it. You see, it's been a long time since I asked why! And if I do answer it, I will never know if it is right, so it's kind of wasting words. It all just manifests. It seems like we live in times when religion has collapsed. We don't want to believe in anything, we don't want to follow anybody. It's a new expression. Maybe that's why there are now masters without lineage. We live in different times — technology and communication have allowed us to know what happens in the same moment on the other side of the planet. We have a lot of information and a common feeling that there is emptiness in all that information, so this is why it is happening. That's my impression.

Why is there always a pull to find happiness outside of us? The obvious example that comes to mind is relationships — the desire for sexual and emotional intimacy with other people. We hear the theory that truth is within but there is such a difference between actually knowing that and experiencing it.

Yes, we never experience what we know. What we call knowledge is always relative — it's just intellectual. You see, a child knows that the iron burns so it doesn't touch it. There has been very strong conditioning in our minds, not by teaching but by direct example. The people who brought you up — they have also been conditioned and those who brought them up too. And that conditioning is based on a belief that is transmitted beyond words, through their example. It's a sense of individuality. When you are a baby, you don't have it. The baby starts to learn about objects. It sees a flower, a tree and if you put a mirror in front of it, it will say 'baby'. The first way in which we call ourselves is 'baby'. We don't say 'I', we say, 'Baby wants this, baby wants that.'

But the baby listens to his father and mother saying, 'I, I, I' and it starts to create an identification with the body. Instead of seeing an object in the mirror, it starts to see itself as 'I'. He learns this concept and that moment is extremely powerful because there is now a belief in the limit of 'I'. So there is a direct identification – 'I am this body'. From that moment, all information is reinforcing that idea – 'I am fat', 'I am old', 'I look like my father', and so on. So this separate identity continues creating itself and, as a result, there is a deep feeling of separation.

There is from then on a longing to go back to what the baby was before the feeling of being a separate form. There is a longing because in that moment there was freedom, there was happiness. There is a memory of boundlessness. So the baby grows up, becomes a child and still it continues to learn the example, the sense of 'I', the separation. It sees its parents and brothers and sisters and friends at school – everybody's also missing something. But there is a natural inclination to go back, there is always a promise. That is why we keep searching outside through the senses. We grow up and never really question ourselves – what is the motivation behind all the desires? All that we want is to be ourselves. That's what we all want. We don't want anything else.

The thoughts arise pulled by the centre of the mind – that sense of 'I', that image of you. It leads your life. I like the example I've read from Poonjaji – you think, 'When I buy my new house I will be happy.' So then you buy the new house and you are actually happy but it is not because of the walls that you are happy, it's not because of the material house that you are happy. The happiness is in the absence of the thought, 'I want a house'. That thought has gone. And there, you're happy!

But then another thought will come – you want something else because you want happiness. And so on. I want a boyfriend, I want a relationship – just to find what we already have. So with any thought, if we could simply look for a moment what is beyond it, if we can see what is in between two thoughts just for a second, we can experience happiness. When we are in deep sleep we are happy. We like to go to sleep because we find happiness. It's the most simple thing. We are happy because we get rid of thoughts.

There seems to be a very pure impulse when love arises for certain things or people. But then very quickly possessiveness comes in – wanting to hold on to those things or people to sustain the happiness. And then the fear of loss and jealousy and all those other connected emotions also arise. So then you shut down and try not to experience love at all to prevent all of that.

Yes, we don't see the source of this happiness. We don't see the real source of that love – we think it is coming from outside. The real love is recognition. Even the expression of beauty is recognition. When we see something beautiful, it resonates within us. But there is a belief system in which we think it is coming from outside.

You think that if you lose that object or that person, the happiness is going to be gone. If you try to solve all that 'I' feels or knows or thinks, it's endless. If you simply try to understand that you are not that 'I', if you look directly into that 'I', you will see that it is just a thought, a story, and that you are already free. Then you can recognize, then you can experience without the need for an object. So, basically, that is what is called to 'Know thyself' — to see that you are the source. This possession — desire and jealousy — it happens in the level of mind, to the ego. So if it happens . . . OK. You are not going to punish yourself because of it. It happens because it happens — it's a good sign because it's showing you that you are suffering. It is showing you attachment.

So who am I?

Who am I? is the question that the mind cannot answer. In that impossibility it stops. You know, it's like computers — when you put something in that they cannot handle, they just crash. It's the same with the mind. If the mind asks itself, Who am I? it cannot solve it. It cannot solve it because all that it knows is name and form. That which is the source of the mind is completely beyond name and form, so it cannot put it into a box. In that impossibility, the mind just stops. That which remains as consciousness is the real you. That is the way home, cutting through everything that is there — passion, fear, pain, whatever. The real you is all that remains.

[Today, satsang is an 'intensive' — an initial session of questions and answers, a short break and then an invitation to experience 'oneself' more deeply. Satyananda explains that he simply wants to invite anyone on stage to sit in his chair and see what he experiences and sees.]

Each one of you is welcome — it's not an obligation. You can come and I will sit in front of you and we will go deeper into the experience of yourself.

[After a number of people have had this experience, I too go up on stage and sit in Satyananda's chair. Paralyzing fear arises. I look around at each person in the room, starting from the left and then over to the right. My body is violently trembling. I look desperately at Satyananda but am unable to hold his penetrating gaze for long. I feel completely unable to relax. Oh God, I'm starting to cry.]

It's just fear. Let it be here, the fear. Let it be.

[I smile, laugh, cry again.]

Yes, this is good. The fear is not the problem but your not accepting it is the problem.

It feels like a vice that grips. There's a lot of tension and anxiety.

Umm . . .

But I know it's just fear . . .

That's very good. So don't be scared of fear and see what happens.

[I want to let go but am unable to do so – I feel that I'm about to become hysterical and lose it (and in front of all these people) . . . I look around again, seemingly on the edge of letting go and yet holding back even more tightly. I then look into Satyananda's eyes, this time holding his gaze, falling in and out of their focus . . .]

There is such a desire to want to be still and I'm not still so it creates even more anxiety.

OK, right.

[I look again into his eyes. My eyes smart and my heart pounds . . . Several minutes pass . . . Thoughts arise, subside. Fear arises, subsides. My body starts to relax. Now I feel I am dropping into something I know not what. I momentarily surrender and drop over the edge.]

What are you thinking?

[I shrug my shoulders, laugh.]

There was so much fear to come and sit here. When I sat down, the fear was strong and yet it seems to have temporarily subsided.

You want it back?

No way!

[I look around the room again at everyone.]

This is your experience. Every time you look into the face of fear it disappears but, if you keep looking to the shadow, it grows and grows.

[I put my hands in the traditional Indian prayer position and bow, ready to get up and leave the stage.]

Not yet . . .

[I laugh nervously, slightly disconcerted that it's not quite over yet . . . I look into Satyananda's eyes and then at everyone else. I start to laugh again.]

Let it go.

[Time slows down almost to a standstill . . . I rest my eyes in his.]

Yes, that's much better. Are you still now?

[I nod.]

Every time you want to be still, just be as you are. Just look within, into that which you don't know but which you just need to remember. Yes, now you can go! Thank you.

[I put my hands in *namaste* once more and return to my seat.]

Satsang comes to a close. People get up from their seats and leave, others gather around Satyananda to continue with a specific question or discuss a more intimate matter. Friends of Satyananda gather outside the church as a meal has been arranged in a local vegetarian restaurant near the seafront. Everyone is burbling with excitement and well-being. I too emerge into the sedative twilight but I am starting to get another headache. And yet, somehow and somewhere, I feel incredibly free. It is as if something has relaxed, has been released inside. The muscles around my chest have yielded their vice-like grip and I breathe deeply the balmy air.

When I came to Brighton, my only wish was to interview Satyananda, to be a passive observer. I did not expect to participate, to publicly expose my weaknesses and fears. Papaji spoke of walking like an emperor through this life – 'Throw away your begging bowl', he would tell his devotees, 'for everything belongs to you.' And here, in the backstreets of an English coastal town, I too am experiencing a surge of infinite and ultimate confidence, a shedding of some innate insecurity and an unfamiliar feeling that I somehow belong to the world around me. Can freedom be this easy, I think? Can all my troubles really dissolve away if I face them head on? After all, haven't I just proved that they could?

In the restaurant we order tea and light snacks. I sit next to Satyananda. 'Perhaps you would like to continue the interview?' But what can I ask? I grope around in the recesses of my brain for queries and observations, only to be left feeling I am clutching at clouds. Satyananda grins knowingly at my attempts. 'Let them go. Soon there will be no more questions left. Let them all go.' I realize that in one way there are no more questions that I can ask him as, intuitively, I know what the answers will be. As the familiar mental turbulence lurks in the background of my mind, like a formless mass, an insatiable frustration, just for once, I remain unmoved.

As we all say goodbye under the neon lights of Brighton Parade, the laughter and pop music filtering out from the bars and cafés along the seafront, it strikes me how surreal everything is. As I walk away, I hear the sea fizzling on the pebbles and smell the stench of seaweed in the air. All my senses are alive. I feel alive. I get into my car and start on my journey home. Everything seems so effortless; the roads are no longer a competitive racetrack but an organic flow of fellow human beings. Even the fact that I have driven in the wrong direction for nearly an hour seems like a minor error of judgement rather than the end of the world. Wouldn't it be amazing to always live like this, I reflect — free from fear, anxiety and pain; free from the tyranny of mind.

Q: What is the nature of the mind?

A: The mind is nothing other than the 'I'-thought. The mind and the ego are one and the same. The other mental faculties such as the intellect and the memory are only this. Mind [manas], *intellect* [buddhi], *the storehouse of mental tendencies* [chittam], *and ego* [ahamkara]; *all these are only the one mind itself. This is like different names being given to a man according to his different functions. The individual soul* [jiva] *is nothing but this soul or ego.*

Be As You Are: The Teachings of Sri Ramana Maharshi

Wayne Liquorman

CHAPTER TWO

THE DHARMA
BUM

Ram Tzu knows this . . .

You clever ones
Are always looking for a way
To beat the system.

You want Enlightenment
You want eternal bliss
You want the ultimate orgasm
You want it all . . .
And
You want to be around
To enjoy it.

This renders you
The ultimate sucker.
You are fair game.

You get baptized and analyzed.
You get rolfed and ESTed.
You meditate and vegetate.
You're rebirthed and realigned.
You're fucked and sucked.
You chant, you rant,
You heal the child within.
You collect money in airports.
You get in touch with your feelings.

You have your palms, your cards,
Your auras and your chakras read.

If you're very clever
You go to India, Tibet,
Thailand, China . . .

In your heart
You know the Truth is incompatible
With indoor plumbing.

You humbly contract dysentery or hepatitis.
You pretend that Sai Baba
Is different from Oral Roberts.

It's a wonder Ram Tzu hasn't died laughing.

'No. 23', No Way for the Spiritually "Advanced"
Wayne Liquorman

Wayne Liquorman swears a lot. And he's unimpressed by most things. He has also asked what could be more boring than having a conversation about the truth. Somewhat daunted, therefore, I meet him in a friend's house in West Hampstead, London, to discuss, at least I hope, something of interest.

Dorothy, his wife, opens the front door – a stunning woman in her early forties with piercing blue eyes and short blonde hair, who greets me like a lifelong companion. She beckons me through the house into a small patioed garden, where Wayne is sitting, drinking in the late afternoon sunshine. He slowly stands up, his gargantuan six-foot-five frame animating into life, his egg-shaped head cushioned in a nest of hair, tipping over to one side. Casually dressed in a petrol-blue shirt, stone-coloured wool waistcoat and slacks, he fixes me with a wry grin, moving his head in a circle as I explain who I am, as if to say, so what?

Wayne has a chequered past. Teacher of truth he may be and better known as the 'spiritual son' of Ramesh Balsekar, Wayne's early life was associated more with hanging around bars, living in a narcotic haze of drugs and booze and blackjack.

Through a guttural Californian growl, he tells me that he was born in 1951 in the Los Angeles suburb of San Fernando Valley and was raised nominally as Jewish. His father was an office furniture salesman and his mother an artist and housewife.

He was bar mitzvahed at Sunday school but soon 'ditched' it, deciding instead to drag off his companions to the local bar to play cards with a marked deck. Considering himself to be a little too smart to believe in God, he wasn't buying that 'big guy up in the sky' deal, choosing instead the more epiphanic effects of alcohol, marijuana and cocaine. That, he says, was the apex of his religious education.

After leaving school he went on to study creative writing at the University of Hawaii, where he attempted to write a fictional account of the legalization of marijuana in the United States with two characters – one an idealist hippie, the other a calculating businessman. 'They were two sides of my own personality that I was trying to reconcile, so that conflict was played out within the novel,' he explains. That inner struggle having ended, Wayne still felt the need however to publish his satirical observations on life. *No Way for the Spiritually "Advanced"* is a collection of short poems under the pen name of Ram Tzu – a pink, though hardly blushing, volume of expletives, lambastings and more expletives. He has also established the Advaita Fellowship, an organization dedicated to promoting Advaitic teachings, based in his home town of Redondo Beach, California.

As I listen to his picaresque past, Wayne punctuates his sentences with a gravelly chuckle. I cannot tell whether his sardonic humour is just all part of the performance or he really is that entertained by this tragicomedy of life. As I unravel the lead for my clip-on microphone, Wayne watches me intently – again, half bemused, half couldn't-care-less. Meanwhile, I am half-scared. It is Dorothy who appears in the garden again, bringing us some tea. She throws me a knowing glance, puts the tea things on the table and disappears inside. Wayne nods, 'Shall we begin?'

So, to get to that night at the end of a four-day drinking binge – you were lying on your bed and suddenly there was some kind of understanding . . .

Yes, there was a moment when it was absolutely clear that the obsession was over. The thing about drinking and drug abuse addiction is that at some point it crosses over from a lifestyle into a compulsion – one where there is no longer any control. There's no means of controlling it with will power or intention. It has very much a life of its own. And there isn't even the pretence of being able to control it as a separate 'me'.

The other part of the condition was that for me there was complete denial, even though I was in desperately bad straits. Physically, I had alcoholic oedema, I had lost bladder control, my wrists and ankles were swollen. I had a slow urine leak that wasn't very lovely, requiring a change of great wads of toilet paper every half-hour or so. Despite that condition, I would tell you that I didn't have a problem, there was nothing wrong with me – this was a lifestyle choice on my part. The physical aspects were completely ignored, they weren't even seen. And if you pointed them out to me, I would get very upset.

In that moment back in 1985 at the end of that four-day binge, I felt that obsession go. It was a palpable experience of feeling it leave my being. It was very extraordinary. Up to that point, I had considered myself absolutely to be the master of my own destiny. It was up to me to do whatever I wanted and anything that happened, I was responsible for it. But this was so clearly outside my intention and my capacity that I was then stuck with a very difficult intellectual dilemma. What had done this to me? If I hadn't done it, then what, how or who was there in the universe that could do this to me?

Did that make you angry?

No. It didn't make me angry – it made me astounded more than anything. I was just astonished. It was sort of like waking up and looking around and saying, 'My God, I was killing myself and didn't even know it!' Suddenly, there was clarity and vision – I had been insane and then sanity was restored. After this seeing came, the compulsion went away and those blinders were taken off – and that happened in an instant.

So you realized that something else had made your life the way it was. Did you then equate that with God?

Well, I was still hesitant to use that word because of all my negative associations with God as being essentially a Santa Claus-like character with a book, recording whether I had been naughty or nice, and then bringing me presents or punishing me. I wasn't comfortable with that. I felt more comfortable in the Eastern traditions as I had far fewer prejudices since I didn't know much about them. I wasn't too comfortable with the notion of karma either though, in that there was some kind of justice in the whole system for the individual. It took me a few years to really find out about the Eastern traditions, to develop a healthy prejudice against those as well!

Which texts did you look at?

Well, I looked at them all but I was immediately attracted to the mystical. I first got attracted to Taoism. One of the first books I ever read was the *Tao Te Ching* –

I didn't really understand it but it was incredibly potent to me. I was still very immature as a spiritual seeker but I intuitively knew that there was something deeply profound there. I read Alan Watts' book, *Tao: The Watercourse Way*, and that introduced me to t'ai chi and I so started doing t'ai chi on the beach every day. I was also introduced to Thich Nhat Hanh and Ram Dass.

When did you meet Ramesh?

16 September 1987 in Hollywood, California. He was brought there by a fellow called Henry Dennison who ran a spiritual salon. Back in the fifties and sixties, Krishnamurti came through his place and also Christopher Isherwood, who was living down the hill with Swami Prabhavananda and also Alan Watts who was often drunk, howling at the moon. Dennison went to see Ramesh in Bombay and was very taken with him and decided to bring him to the States.

And then you went along to meet him.

I was there at his first talk. I was not particularly impressed – he didn't know what the hell to do. The only thing he had ever done before was have a few people show up at his house, even though he had several books in print at that time.

But you went back . . .

I did go back. When I got back from a business trip it was as if I had been bitten by something that had incubated and festered. And you know, it was something about that little guy . . .

'That bespectacled banker from Bombay'.

That's the one! So I went to see him again. And then it was a very powerful, very dramatic and intense kind of connection that I experienced with him.

What exactly was it? His words?

No, just being there. What I today call 'resonance' – that deep and intense connection between the disciple and the guru or, more precisely, the body-mind mechanism of the disciple and the body-mind mechanism of the sage. When there is this deep connection, there is a resonance in the space between the two – the guru is made manifest. The guru is then experienced by the disciple and, to a lesser degree, is experienced by the body-mind mechanism of the sage as reflected in the disciple. However, there is no aspect of the experience of sagacity or sagehood or guruhood that has any particular import for the sage.

It's a relationship isn't it, like two ends of the same stick — you can't have one without the other.

Right. In the absence of a disciple, there's no guru. There's just simply, in the most profound sense, a body-mind mechanism through which totality functions without even the sense of personal doership overlaying it or a thinking that anything that's happening is his doing. So, in the absence of that, there's simply pure doership, simply the body-mind mechanism functioning according to its nature, its programming.

I'm trying to understand all of this. I believe that I am the doer. You believe that you're not doing anything.

That's one way of saying it.

I'm trying to get away from all those dreadful phrases like 'Self-realized', 'enlightened' or whatever . . .

It is tricky.

So what's happened to you essentially?

Well, the pointer is that the sense of personal doership has gone. The subjective experience was that *nothing* happened. There was an event in phenomenality like any other event in phenomenality that happened through this body-mind mechanism. But the thing about that event was that it removed the sense of personal doership, it removed that which would identify that event as being significant for me because there is no one left for it to be significant for. Therefore, in the most profound sense, nothing happened from the standpoint of the 'you' that is seeking to know the difference between 'you' and 'me'.

But can you possibly describe it for 'me'?

I can describe the event — just as I can describe my meal that I had a couple of hours ago because it was an event in phenomenality. The waitress came and brought the menu and I picked it up and looked at it and the thought came, 'This chicken dish sounds attractive.' So, I ordered the chicken dish and the waitress brought the chicken dish . . . so all of those kinds of aspects of the experience are describable. But they aren't any more significant in a causal relationship than my lunch.

But for the seeker, that's the Holy Grail, the description of that experience . . .

It is.

So, could you describe the experience of 'having your lunch'?

Sure. The experience was that I was in love with two women — one of them being my present wife and the other, another very lovely woman whom I also knew. And I loved them both, which certainly creates all kinds of social problems . . .

You should have moved to India then you could have had as many wives as you wanted!

Well, that creates it's own kind of social problems! The fact was that in the same week both of them came to me and said, 'Wayne, I love you very much but I can't do this . . . I'm out of here!'

That's terrible!

Yeah, that's what I thought! So, when the second one came, who was Dorothy, and she was telling me all this and started crying, I started crying and it seemed very sad and such a shame that it should happen. And as these tears were welling up, I felt the sobbing growing stronger and my reaction growing more intense and soon my body was just wracked with sobs. Then my visual field closed out and I was falling into this blackness, this horrendous, horrendous suffering. It was really awful. It was in a sense like Alice falling down the rabbit hole in an endless freefall. But as I was falling, the intensity and the pain were growing and becoming more acute — the sense that I was approaching the source pool of all suffering. My body was just heaving. I was in a terrible state.

And then there was a very dramatic kind of cessation to it. It just stopped and there was a clarity that all that suffering, all of that horrendous and excruciating pain, couldn't hurt me because there was truly no 'me' to be hurt by it and it all just was.

And I say that now — as it was happening, it all just was. The most profound sense of it was that nothing had happened. There was an event and people would be interested in this event, as this was what I and everybody else who was a seeker was looking for — the Holy Grail of seeking. But the amazing thing was that I didn't find myself convulsed with laughter at the big joke of it all. What surprised me so much was that this was it! And nothing had happened, then or ever, and this event in phenomenality was just another aspect of the one total happening.

You once said it was like having a toothache and then suddenly the pain was gone.

Right. That's another analogy that I use to describe the change in perception. But with a toothache, when the toothache is eliminated, very quickly there is no longer a perception of the world through the absence of pain. In the moment that the pain goes away, you are now seeing the world through the absence of pain. It's so dramatic that the pain has gone, the clarity of your vision is because there is a point of comparison and it's fresh. But a few days later you are no longer perceiving things through this absence of pain – it is now perceived directly.

This isn't a secondary perception that what you see is dramatically there – it's just there. It's only dramatically there because your vision was obscured before and now you can see how amazing it is in the moment. But the amazement of it quickly disappears and it just is. And such is the case of the perception of the body-mind mechanism after the sense of personal doership goes.

There are a number of teachers who talk about a shift from a 'state' of a sense of personal doership to a 'state' of non-personal doership and this process can oscillate back and forth – in other words, there can be degrees of 'enlightenment'.

You'll find this a lot in modern teachings that are trying to pass themselves off as Advaita in which a spiritual experience is characterized as enlightenment. The thing about an experience is that an experience is defined by the start and the end. For something to be an experience, it has to be encapsulated. For enlightenment to be 'experienced', it has to have a beginning and an end. Now enlightenment, in its true sense, has no end therefore there is no experience of it.

Now what is usually being described is mystical experience – you can move in and out of mystical experience. What is happening is that you have a mystical experience, which is profound and clear and there is a sense of having looked over the fence but you only know that it is true *after it's over* and you've come back to experience it. While it's happening you are not there. The only point where it has any relevance for you is when you come back – otherwise there is no one for whom it has any relevance.

The sudden explosion in 'enlightened beings' has to do with the redefinition of enlightenment so that anyone now who's had a mystical experience is saying to others, 'You're in the fourth dimension, you've moved over. Make no mistake, you're enlightened now! You've got the certification. The reason why you're moving in and out of it is that source is not through with you yet. You're only partially cooked!' That's all a lovely notion. You go, 'Well shit, I'm already enlightened. Great! I like this a lot!' And you can go out and give your own satsang. You get to do the whole deal. And then you can help other people to gain what you have gotten. So it's like a pyramid marketing scheme.

So mystical experience is a red herring?

I wouldn't say it's a red herring. What I would say is that it is the highest, the most wondrous of states that the identified human can experience. And if you have the choice – which you don't – but if you did have the choice between that and enlightenment, take that because if you have that, then there's someone there to enjoy it. When enlightenment comes, things get very ordinary.

How can one know a good guru from a bad one?

You can't. The understanding is that the good ones and the bad ones are a product of the same consciousness – that in order for some people to be left on the path they will encounter false gurus. And of course nobody says that they are a false guru – everyone claims to have the truth. 'I have the truth – follow me!' All the rest of them are full of shit. 'Stick with me, baby, and we'll go far together and you'll get all the benefits!' The problem is, of course, that eventually you have so many gurus that you run out of disciples!

There does seem to be a league of teachers. Do you know what I mean?

Oh, I do! It makes me want to go and find honest work!

I suppose in the eyes of totality, it doesn't really matter.

That's right. All of the body-mind mechanisms, not only the guru-body-mind mechanisms but also the disciple or devotee-body-mind mechanisms are all exactly where they are supposed to be at every instant. There's no mistake here.

It seems like there is no free will, there's no choice – just behave as everything is . . . and that's it and . . . well . . . that's it.

That's it.

But . . .

It's very simple actually.

But what I don't understand is . . .

Yes . . .

This lottery system — you are where you are and I'm over here and I envy you because I want to be where you are. If that's God's will, should I just accept that? Should I just enjoy my ignorance?

Well, any sentence that has the word 'should' in it should be a flag. The 'should' presumes that you have some say in the matter. Should I do this? It is pointing back to the question of what is it that 'you' as a separate doer are supposed to do or *should* do which may be different from what you *want* to do.

If all this is as God wants it, is it that God wants that I think I am separate from God?

Very definitely.

So I am going to carry on thinking this way until God decides that I start thinking like you?

Yes, but the way I think is structurally identical to the way in which you think, with the one exception that there is no ego there to claim credit or blame for any of the actions that happen to the organism.

So ego is God's making?

Very much so.

This is where I lose it.

OK.

I accept that all there is is consciousness.

OK.

But I don't understand why there is this apparent seeking or the thought, 'If only I could just lose the sense of personal doership, then all would be well.'

But the point is that all *is* well. And there is a desire in this body-mind mechanism for something . . .

You're telling me . . .

And so we call this one here a 'seeker' body-mind mechanism because what it is desiring is this spiritual connection, this Oneness, this completeness, this wholeness, that it has tasted in those moments of knowing. There is a desire to have that all the time. That is what characterizes this particular body-mind mechanism. Others have a desire for power in which they are moved to actions and to go places and do things in accordance with this seeking of power. Others seek fame and others will seek money and are moved in accordance with this kind of seeking. So this particular body-mind mechanism is infused with the characteristics and qualities that move it to seek spiritual Oneness, spiritual connectedness.

But the Holy Grail I cannot get?

Yes.

So I might as well give up seeking. Or is it that my programming is making me seek whether I like it or not?

Yes.

It's a ridiculous kind of paradox. It's a conspiracy! I can't get my head around it.

Well, actually, you can't get your head around it. The paradox inherent in the whole thing is that that which is seeking is seeking something that it will never get. The seeking may culminate in the dissolution of the seeker . . .

May?

May — obviously it's not assured. There have been billions of seeker body-mind mechanisms over time and relatively few in which the seeking has culminated. But the same is true for all kinds of seeking — there have been billions of writers seeking fame, artists seeking recognition, millions of them.

Something in me says it's not fair — why you and not me!

Well, hell, you're probably a much nicer person than me! You've probably worked harder, done more to get it, though I'm not so sure that you've necessarily suffered as much. Who knows? The fact is that it isn't a meritocracy. Maybe you've noticed!

Ramesh talks about going into a state of limbo. There's an understanding of the teaching in a theoretical, intellectual way, but something within is not making that transition from having my head in the tiger's mouth to having my head completely ripped off.

The whole point of the image of your head being in the tiger's mouth – the jaws have closed and there is no escape – is that you don't have any say about it or when the tiger's jaws are going to snap. And through beseeching or any other number of methodologies, you're not going to be able to induce the tiger to do things your way and to give you what you want.

But, for many, there is a belief that years and years on a meditation cushion are going to give some kind of reward, lead to that final snapping of the jaws.

Yes, but the teaching says that if you are to spend years on a meditation cushion then there's nothing on earth that you can do to avoid those years on a meditation cushion. If you're attracted to someone at some time in your life and what they say rings true for you and makes sense to you, then those years on a meditation cushion will be spent as such. You can say they will have an effect – what that effect is may be very profound or it may be that 20 years on a meditation cushion is not going to produce for you that which you had expected it to 20 years ago.

Most people coming to Advaita are those people who have spent a great number of years doing various spiritual practices, have worked their way through all of the psychological and many of the spiritual methodologies that promise, one after another, to produce and deliver. The practices are ultimately found to be empty promises. So when this pure message of Advaita comes – not the one that says you can get there just by witnessing your thoughts and letting go, that is the Advaita of subtle doership, but rather pure Advaita in which it is unequivocally put forward that you as a separate individual have no power to do anything and in fact do not exist – then it is simply seen as a projection of consciousness and as such is subject to whatever consciousness determines is going to happen.

This is the crux of the issue. There seems to be apparent paradox inherent in the Advaita teaching. On the one hand, 'I' am being asked to control the mind, to disassociate from attachment, to engage in Self Enquiry. On the other hand, there is nothing that 'I' can do because when you look at it from pure Advaita, there really is nothing that I can do. 'I' cannot control the mind, 'I' cannot disassociate from attachment, 'I' cannot engage in Self Enquiry, because 'I' do not exist. That 'subtle doership' you were talking about – that's where people get stuck.

Yes, that's right. You have to understand that all teachers, including Ramana Maharshi and even Ramesh, when pressed and in an individual case, if somebody were to say, 'Look, I hear what you're saying but I consider myself to be the doer.

I am suffering — what *do* I do?' they'll say out of compassion, 'OK, do this.'
Ramana would say, 'Enquire as to who it is that is experiencing this, who it is that
wants to know'. That can have a profound impact in the moment. Ramesh would
say in that situation, 'OK, this is the *sadhana* that you can do.' And he would
qualify it. If you were to say, 'But I thought there is nothing that I can do,' he
would say, 'Well, if it's God's will for you to do this, this might be productive.'
So he would get out of it that way. For someone at that level of understanding, it
is something for them to do. They are not ready yet to hear this message. For
Ramana, he had a full range of people coming to him and for some he would give
very specific instructions and *japa* to do — 'OK, repeat the name of God 10,000
times.' Pure Advaita was not going to be of benefit to them.

So even Self Enquiry is just a little game?

Even Self Enquiry! Ramana would just say willy-nilly to all those who came, 'Well,
just enquire into the Self.' He would see who was there and if there was some
receptivity he would then draw them back to this very basic kind of question. Who
is it that is asking the question? Who is it that is really operative here? And so
this is the path of *jnana* — this is the setting back of the mind. I mean, he didn't
make this up. This notion has been around a long time. Utilizing the mind to
look back in on itself, various things can happen. The mind can essentially exhaust
itself in the search.

Ramesh talks about a divine hypnosis — that the ignorance is divine.

Yes, that's right. If all there is is consciousness, then the ignorance has to be
divine. Pure Advaita is not your doing — the ignorance is not your fault and will
not be removed. The very term 'ignorance' has a very pejorative quality to it. It is
this sense in the seeker that it is something that has to be gotten rid of.

The other term that is often used is that there is 'understanding'. What I have
observed in many cases, mine being one of them, is that the intellectual
understanding of this teaching, of these concepts, has had an impact on the life
of this organism. When there is involvement by the ego — fear, worry, remorse and
all of those associated, involved processes — this teaching can rise up in mind as
concepts to cut off the other conceptual stream of involvement. So, you could call
it a counter-conditioning. But you can't choose to impose it on yourself. You can't
say, 'OK, now I am going to accept, now I'm going to cut off the conditioning.'
But the teaching, as it deepens, will more and more often arise in the moment and
cut off the involvement, so the effect very often is the increased sense of peace or
well-being, comfort, ease.

Inevitably what happens is that the 'me' comes in afterwards and says, 'Oh, I accepted and therefore all I need to do now, in the next situation when this happens, is accept again. And then I won't feel as involved.' You have very clever people who see this, particularly ones who have some kind of psychological practice or body-work practice, who say, 'OK, I can weave this into my existing teaching and all you have to do is accept and by accepting you'll experience more peace.' And they'll develop methodologies and other things in order to help you accept. But the fact is that this pure teaching just happens. The understanding just arises.

What is the function of the mind therefore? Does it have a purpose?

It's an aspect of the organism.

And the emotions?

The emotions are an aspect of the mind. They come with the apparatus and they have different weights and combinations that are unique to each organism. It makes for this incredibly rich and diverse life and living.

How should I live my life?

Is this a rhetorical question?! How do 'I' live my life? How should 'I' live my life? What's the question?

I don't know anymore! How does one live one's life in order to be at peace?

OK . . . How do I get what I want? What must I do to get what I want? There are countless teachers out there, each with a formula. If you just do this you'll get what you want. As I'm an ex-business man, I see it all as a great business. You've got a need here. They need something to do and you are over here and you can supply that need so you say, 'OK, you want to know what you can do – sit on your arse on the snow until your genitals freeze!' You know, someone was telling me the other day that he was actually doing this! Can you believe that! He would sit naked in the snow. God. And people are willing to do that. Another girl told me that her guru made her eat the ashes of corpses in order to make her see the impermanence of the body. In order to get this, people will do all kind of things. Now you can look into your own heart and realize that it isn't so far-fetched in comparison with what you have also done!

So there's no answer to my question.

The point is, if you want to know what you can do, what I will say is that you can do a virtually endless number of things, none of which will necessarily provide that which you are seeking, but it may. If it happens, you causally link the two, you ignore the 10,000 other cases in which it didn't. You say, 'But I did that and then I got this — therefore I am living testimony! I did this and then got that, therefore there's a connection!' The connection's notional of course.

Why do you give satsang then?

People call. My guru said, if people come, talk to them. And that's how all this thing started. At the end of one of his talks back in 1996, Ramesh said, 'You should all come back tomorrow, Wayne's giving the talk.' And I said, 'What! I am!' I figured he thought I just needed a job — my business had failed six months earlier. I was exporting and importing motors to and from the Far East. It had grown quite lucrative but it died. I was a middleman and I got unmiddled one day and I was out of business.

What do you do now — you manage the Advaita Press?

Actually Dorothy runs Advaita Press. Basically I talk. I have a very heavy schedule now. And that's my life, that's what I do. I don't call it satsang because the word has got a nasty connotation for me. Anybody who's flown over Lucknow is giving satsang. 'Oh, there's Lucknow down there — oh great, I feel it, I think I've had the experience. Come to me. You are already that! You are enlightened! All you have to do is wake up! Ha ha ha!'

I look at all this and I think, 'What the fuck am I doing? How did I get into this?' It's so ludicrous. But it's what I do. Somebody's got to do it. Actually, it seems quite a lot of people are doing it! For whatever reason, for as long as people show up, I suppose I will continue to talk, as my guru has asked me to do. I have no agenda — I'm not trying to bring about world enlightenment or bring on the next evolutionary step of mankind or right all the perceived wrongs in the universe, shining my light of truth on what is or any of that stuff. I just show up and talk to people and whatever happens, happens. And some people are incredibly moved and others go away thinking that guy's an arsehole.

Particularly when you start quoting Ram Tzu.

Yes, 'Ram Tzu knows this — you're fucked!'

By the end of the interview I really warm to Wayne. There is something almost, dare I say it, endearing about his couldn't-give-a-damn bravado. I feel at ease and realize we have been chatting and laughing for nearly three hours. He is now due to hold a meeting in the Holloway Road in north London. I offer to drive him there and we make our preparations to leave. As everyone busies around, Wayne becomes noticeably quiet. I am somewhat disconcerted by this – the banter of the afternoon is no longer appropriate, it seems. The show is definitely over.

I consider what Wayne had to say. Every action, every thought, every spiritual endeavour is all part of my mind-body programming. That's a relief – I don't have to feel guilty for anything 'I' have supposedly done, even if we are delayed for Wayne's meeting by the rushhour traffic. But is that it? Is that who I truly am – merely a functioning organism, pre-programmed to behave and respond in this world according to some divine blueprint? Something in me cannot quite accept this. What about my feelings, my emotions – surely they have more validity than being only some aspect of this particular mind-body machine?

On the one hand, pure Advaita makes perfectly logical sense – that all there is is consciousness, so everything that arises must be an expression of God's will. But what about my innate sense of a personal self, a unique manifestation of gross and subtle attributes freely existing within the context of something greater – in short, what about *me*?

Q: Is there such a thing as free will?

A: Whose will is it? So long as there is the sense of doership, there is the sense of enjoyment and of individual will. But if this sense is lost through the practice of vichara *[Self Enquiry], the divine will will act and guide the course of events. Fate is overcome by* jnana, *Self Knowledge, which is beyond will and fate.*

Q: I can understand that the outstanding events in a man's life, such as his country, nationality, family, career or profession, marriage, death, etc., are all predestined by his karma, but can it be that all the details of his life, down to the minutest, have already been determined? Now, for instance, I put this fan that is in my hand down on the floor here. Can it be that it was already decided that on such and such a day, at such and such an hour, I should move the fan like this and put it down here?

A: Certainly. Whatever this body is to do and whatever experiences it is to pass through was already decided when it came into existence.

Be As You Are: The Teachings of Sri Ramana Maharshi

In other words, even the practice of Self Enquiry for an individual was already decided at the moment when that individual came into existence. Argh, this infernal paradox.

I drop Wayne off at the Resource Centre where the meeting is to take place. I am exhausted by the flow of philosophical conundrums flowing through my mind. The only thing I want is to be free – but the more I think about it, the less available it is to me.

Pratima

CHAPTER THREE

THE SMELL OF BURNT ALMONDS

I feel I am trapped in a weird and wonderful movie. I arrive for our interview in a backwater of Crouch End in London and am met by the choice of four doors with no numbers to identify one from the other. Suddenly, one of the doors swings open. A middle-aged man wearing jeans, a T-shirt and daubed in building-dust dashes past. 'Paula?' he taunts over his shoulder as he disappears down the street. 'You are expected. Go on up.' Stupefied but relieved, I enter and thread my way past rubble, plasterboard and relics of a former architectural empire and weave my way up and up the back staircase.

Finally I am greeted by a petite and attractive-looking woman in a long white linen dress, the seemingly modern equivalent of religious attire. Pratima's face is open and relaxed. 'Please excuse the mess!' There is a touch of irony in her Antipodean intonation, which masks a deeper Liverpudlian nostalgia. She leads me to the kitchen at the back of the house, overlooking a suburban garden basking in the scorching July heat. Torches of sunlight ignite the room and suffuse it with white light. All my senses are overwhelmed. From the cooker, a vegetarian supper is seething – the air is a melange of tamari, ginger and garlic. As we start talking together, a soundtrack of building maintenance from the outside hall sets up an underlying pulse – at first cacophonous but softened into melody by its droning beat.

Michèle Mumford was born in Liverpool in 1952. The daughter of two professors – her father of dentistry, her mother of sociology – the atmosphere at home was one of liberal agnosticism but by the age of 15 she had started yoga classes and developed an interest in Hinduism and Buddhism. It was also around this time that she had her first LSD experience. Taking drugs, she muses, made her realize that it was possible to live a life that was free from desire and that was not limited by other people's concepts and ideas – she felt, she says, like a free being. 'You know, it was Liverpool, the Beatles – it was very much a happening kind of place. I was number 54 in their fan club. And, of course, the Beatles had gone to India and had their gurus.' She smiles coyly, 'Whatever they did, I had to do!'

By 21 Michèle knew, however, that there was still something missing in her life. Despite her seemingly existentialist upbringing – tolerant parents, plenty of boyfriends, a good academic career leading to a degree in philosophy from the University of Nottingham – she wanted something different. 'I knew that I was incomplete because I hadn't known what the rest of the planet was experiencing – struggle, poverty, suffering. I needed to experience the depths of life so I had to leave.' So her parents drove her as far as the motorway and then she took to the road.

Michèle first hit Rishikesh and Hardwar in India in 1973 and started meeting sadhus and gurus, ending up in Puri in Orissa State, where she stayed for about four months. Visiting the area of the main temple, she bought puffed rice, as was the tradition, to give to the local beggars gathered on the steps outside. As soon as she had finished one bag she bought another, but soon beggars started to appear from everywhere, pulling on her clothes wailing, 'Mataji, Mataji,' demanding to be fed. In that moment, she realized that no matter how much rice she gave them, it could never alleviate their misery. 'It touched me on such a deep level that I burst out crying and ran down to the beach where I stayed for hours deeply, deeply sobbing. I didn't want to speak to anyone for days – it just felt so frivolous in the face of this incredible suffering.'

From India, she hitched to Laos, ending up as a private student to an Indian monk on the run from a radical religious sect. 'I was like Nivedita, the English personal assistant to Ramakrishna,' Michèle grins. From there she travelled to Pakistan, then over to the USA, Canada and Peru. Next a trip to Fiji, from where she sailed the South Pacific, got into raging storms and landed finally in Bali, which has been her home ever since. Beadwork she learnt from the South American Indians has become her trade – she now employs some 300 Balinese women in five local villages, supplying beaded bags, shoes and jewellery to shops in the USA and Italy as well as such stores as Liberty's and Harrod's in London.

In 1992 Michèle's long and eventful spiritual search came to an end when she met Hariwansh Lal Poonja, or Papaji to his devotees, in Lucknow, in India. Knowing that she had met her true master, she remained in his presence until her transformation was complete. It was Papaji who gave her the name of 'Pratima' meaning 'in the image of God'. She now regularly tours the world, spreading her master's message.

I notice a stack of small pieces of paper on the table beside us – a quote for the day to hand around at the end of satsang. But this is not some sentimental keepsake; it is an extract from Nelson Mandela's inaugural speech in 1994, in which he quotes from *A Course in Miracles*:

> *Our deepest fear is not that we are inadequate. Our deepest fear is that we are powerful beyond measure. It is our light, not our darkness, that most frightens us. We ask ourselves, 'Who am I to be brilliant, gorgeous, talented, fabulous?' Actually, who are you not to be? You are a child of God. Your playing small does not serve the world. There is nothing enlightened about shrinking so that other people won't feel insecure about you. We were born to manifest the glory of God that is within us. It's not just in some of us; it's in everyone. And as we let our own light shine, we unconsciously give other people permission to do the same. As we are liberated from our own fear, our presence automatically liberates others.*

I meditate on the words' healing power. The fear is not of my weaknesses, I think, but of my own divinity. A quote from the *Book of Psalms* drifts into my mind, 'Be still, and know that I am God.' Be still, and know that I am God.

Pratima moves towards the window to check whether her clothes are dry that hang precariously over the sill – the symptoms of living out of a suitcase for the past couple of months. Builders wander in asking for more cups of tea. The rice boils over. Pratima offers me almonds.

Tell me about the time when you first met Papaji?

When Papaji walked into the room, I just knew that I had met the master of my life. Having had many masters before, I knew this man was something different. He had this incredible, all-encompassing love that just radiated out of him. When he looked into your eyes, it was as if he were looking right into your very soul. He could see everything about you in that moment – he could see every personality trait, every weakness, every positive aspect about you. And he loved all of us. He loved me so much that I felt totally accepted for who I was and loved unconditionally. I had never experienced such unconditional love before. My parents were very loving but I had never known such a depth of love like this.

So, at every opportunity, I would go up to him in satsang and ask him questions, spend hours and hours waiting at his home to see if I could go in and sit with him, eat a meal with him, watch television with him, anything . . . It was absolutely an obsession. Every other interest I had in my life just dropped away. All interest, even for men – and as a young lady this had been a dominant interest in my life – totally became a distraction. I didn't want anything to do with anything that would take a moment of time away from the love of my life, which was Papa.

Satsang was the opportunity to ask any questions, air any doubts and just go up and be close to him and look into his eyes. I still had a lot of spiritual questions, so slowly over the next 18 months, I asked him all the questions I possibly could. Sometimes I would go up a lot, which took a certain amount of courage – there would be between 60 and 200 people in the room and later 300 or more. So you would go up to the front and actually sit in front of him and occasionally he would let you sit next to him on the podium. Usually you would end up laughing so much or crying so much – but usually tears of joy.

Papa was such a tease! You never knew when you went up to ask him a question whether he was going to shower love on you and praise you and say, 'Yes, very good, this is it,' or whether he was going to cut your head off with a metaphorical knife. Sometimes you would go up and think that you had asked this great, simple, innocent question and he would just scream at you because in some way you were being stubborn or your ego was getting in the way. He had many devices and tricks to wake you up. So whatever you individually needed, he would find some way to help you to get out of your stuck concepts and rigid ego identification. He could somehow sense just what you needed and he would just say the right words that would cut through all the nonsense. Sometimes he would be ruthless, shocking, terrifying. To go up was absolutely nerve-wracking because you didn't know what was going to happen.

I went to Lucknow whenever I possibly could but it was about a year and a half before I actually felt like I didn't have any questions left. Finally the questions dried up. There were a series of wake-up calls or perhaps one could call them 'realizations'. There was never one single moment when it was like, 'Wow, this is it!' It was like one day he would say something and then one whole load of concepts would be kicked out of the door and then the following week there would be something else – again I would realize that I couldn't hold on to any firm ground any longer. It was like the ground was kicked from under my feet. In the end, I was struggling to dig up some vague doubt or something I could ask him and of course, after a while, I didn't have any anymore. But many people by that time were also not having any doubts — we'd all started changing. One person would ask a question and that would answer something for someone else as well. So slowly there was a large group of us who were there regularly and we just had all our doubts cut at their roots. Slowly we started asking whether we could sing him a song, read a poem or dance for him. The whole thing loosened up a lot.

From when I first arrived in January 1992, it was quite a strict group and satsang was quite formal. But as we all melted and really started living his message, Papa seemed to loosen up too and he became very funny and joked all the time, twisting around our serious questions. So new people would come with these terribly serious questions and ask, for example, 'How can I get out of my pain and suffering?' and he would twist the sentences and words around to mean something quite different and make us all crack up laughing. He would say that, as long as there is laughter, you can't think and when mind is quiet, there is no problem. Laughter was a wonderful aspect of his satsang. It was the best comedy show on earth! It broke through all mental barriers.

He could still be ruthless and occasionally very angry but he would never hang on to his anger — it came up and it went again very quickly. For example, once he screamed at someone to get out of satsang because they were asking some kind of intellectual question and Papa got totally impatient and furious with them and yelled for them to be taken out. Drastic! You could have heard a pin drop! Then as soon as the person was out of earshot, he burst out laughing and the whole place cracked up — it was devices all the time. He could even work miracles but he was like Ramana Maharshi, his master before him, in that he didn't want anyone to come to him because of miracles or siddhis, as they are called in Sanskrit.

He didn't want to attract people who weren't sincerely, deeply interested in freedom. If he had started doing miracles openly, the deeply sincere seekers might have been lost in the crowds. So he would work these miracles but in such a subtle way that someone new could easily miss what was happening. But those of us around him, we could see what he was up to.

Once somebody was attacked with an iron bar, his head was cracked open and he had multiple cuts and bruises. Papa was no longer very agile and had difficulty walking but when he heard of the attack he went immediately to the man's house, strode up two flights of stairs unassisted and, upon meeting the man, gazed at him slowly from toe to head and then said, 'He looks good. In two days he will be well.' And he was! Master loved this man so much and this man was totally devoted to him. They hardly needed to share any words. Their inner silence united them as consciousness itself. It was easy for my master to heal such open loving emptiness.

He would also set people up to be in the right place at the right time. For example, he would say, 'No, you mustn't go on the plane to Madras, you must fly to Bangalore!' And the person would say, 'Papa, Madras is much closer and I have already got my ticket!' and he would say, 'You must go to Bangalore!' He'd make up some excuse. 'There's a man in Bangalore that you must go and see and take this letter for me.' And then they would find out that the plane to Madras had crashed while they had gone to Bangalore. So he would actually save people's lives but he would never say directly – of course, that person would be so eternally grateful that their master had intervened and that their trust and love for him had made them change their ticket.

This is the nature of the *sadguru* or true teacher – Papa was such an empty bamboo that the power of existence could work through him. Often I think even he didn't know what he was doing. I saw many occasions when he didn't seem to be aware of what he was doing. But what he did was absolutely perfect because he was so empty that existence could create through him these cosmic synchronicities which really helped his devotees to somehow recognize the nature of their true Self. It can take a lot for someone to break through years of conditioning but with the help of a master like Papaji, it can happen in an instant. This is the miracle.

To return to you and your own experience with Papaji – I know that essentially nothing has happened to you but could say what has apparently happened?

Ha! No, nothing really has happened. Papa used to tell me that nothing needed to change. There has been the simple recognition that who I am is not this body or this mind, not these emotions or these feelings. That who I am is untouched by any of these quickly changing phenomena. That who I really am is the place from which all phenomena arise, which is consciousness itself. There is the recognition that there is no separate individual here to be free. That which lie here and everywhere are just manifestations of consciousness, unquestionably perfect just exactly as they are. With that, all doubts and fears disappear.

There has arisen this acceptance of everything just as it is and so mind has become quite silent. I find I'm not interested in its ramblings, so there is not much there to concern me. This gives a simple, warm contentedness that's very ordinary and very loving, a naturalness. You refreshingly being you! When the mind is quiet we are *satchitananda* – truth, consciousness and bliss. It's our birthright but it's just shrouded over with concepts and beliefs. Somehow they have lost their hold and life is blissfully ordinary and gets on with itself without me doing anything about it. It is such a blessing. I am eternally grateful to my beloved master for this.

Is there then a point in time when this understanding arises?

There may be a certain point in time or there may not be. Every individual's awakening is totally unique to them. There are no rules. This is the danger that many people come up against when they believe that there must be a sudden moment of realization – a thunderclap and bells ringing. It wasn't my experience. My experience was a very gradual flowering, a very gradual falling away of all the identifications with things and people that I had before. I once asked Papaji about this in satsang. I said, 'Papa, you say that realization only takes a second but could it also be a gentle flowering?' And he said, 'Up to you! Whatever you want.' So if you are waiting for some drastic thing to occur like the difference between night and day – one minute you're like this, the next you're different – this may never occur. The belief that some kind of phenomenal change has to happen is actually a postponement, preventing you from allowing yourself to just rest in who you are already.

I have heard that personality and ego still operate but there is another level of perspective.

There are no levels. It's just that you no longer identify with your personality, your ego, as who you are – that's the difference. As long as you've got a body and a mind, personality and ego will always be there in some form. If you didn't have an ego, there might be a truck coming and I would yell, 'Paula, watch out!' and you wouldn't turn around. This is ego. It is required, it is necessary. The difference Ramana Maharshi said, between an ordinary man's ego and a sage's ego, is rather like with the remnants of a burnt rope. The rope still looks like a rope but when you kick it, it just falls apart – it looks the same but it's got no substance.

For me, it was rather like all the identification with this personality slipped gradually out of the back door without me really noticing. I might look back after a month or two and notice that my personality had not reacted in the same way as it would have done previously. Sometimes it hadn't reacted at all. Mind had not activated any thoughts, so I hadn't bought into it and made a whole story around it and slotted it into a particular hole that meant 'this' about me.

So personality and ego are still here and you may react as you always have done but the mind isn't interpreting situations in the way that it used to. It is quiet. So anger may arise, sadness may arise, but you're not feeding it, you're not picking it up and entertaining it in the same way as you have been conditioned to do. Ego, which is mind, starts losing its weight, so thoughts arise – but who's bothered about them in this moment? There's no one here judging it or believing the mind's ramblings to be true.

Ramesh Balsekar defines it by calling it the 'working mind' and the 'thinking mind'. The working mind is the one that books the tickets two months in advance. The thinking mind is the one that spends the next two months wondering whether they've booked the right day, whether they should have tried to get a cheaper ticket.

That's where the problem arises. Working mind is our tool – it's a wonderful tool. It is our servant. It is not for us to be the servant of the mind and have it rule us as if it speaks the unconditional truth. The thinking mind is just subjective, illusory nonsense taking us away from life as it is and into our imaginations.

So, it's really just about dropping the discussion that goes on in the mind about what is arising in life. Simply allow the moment to be as it is, don't interpret it. Don't move the mind, don't activate ego. It leads only to confusion and suffering. When the mind is quiet you are peaceful and just very ordinary and content inside. Personality and ego become almost redundant. Quietness prevails.

But where are those thoughts coming from? If everything is consciousness, everything is God, everything comes from God, where does the thinking mind come from? Isn't thinking mind just doing its job by thinking, as God deems it so?

Yes, even if you are involved in thought that is judgemental, still you know that the essence of your being is not this thought. It is just another manifestation of existence and existence wouldn't be complete without every single manifestation that arises.

So the thinking mind is OK. You don't have to feel guilty therefore about thinking badly of someone, for example?

No, the thinking badly may just arise. It's a conditioned reflex. If thoughts arise, they arise, but really Papa's message is to be quiet and not to entertain a single thought. As soon as you notice them, drop them. But you know, in some way we enjoy them – we somehow feel alive when we are miserable. We spend hours commiserating with our girlfriends, joining with them in their misery and subtly supporting them in it and, in a way, relishing it. So, it's a question of what we really want in our lives. If we really want freedom and a quiet mind, 100 per cent, it will be ours.

Papaji once said that truth is very simple – it's the attachments that are hard to give up. That's the real issue.

The truth is so simple we miss it. Yes, we are attached to our desires and our cravings but it may well happen to you, as a sincere enquirer, that slowly freedom takes over more and more. You find that you don't want to read about anything else, that you do want to go to satsang as often as possible and just share in that association with the truth – that's the meaning of the word satsang. Other things start losing their interest. It's not that you have to consciously give anything up, it's just that something else takes over.

And that's all God's will?

Yes, it's all grace, just grace. You can't do anything. It seems there is nothing you can do towards this except relax because you are already free. It is your true nature. It's just some ideas and concepts that are clouding that over. All we are doing is removing concepts and beliefs and ideas about not being free. So the only thing to really doubt is the doubter. If you notice yourself doubting, doubt that. Don't doubt anything that's happening. It's just happening, it's out of your control anyway.

I really liked something you recently said about fear. You spelt out the word with initials . . .

False evidence appearing real . . .

Fear is so paralyzing sometimes. It doesn't appear to arise in mind – it arises somewhere in your guts.

Appears to arise in your guts. But if you notice very carefully, you will see that prior to every gut-ripping experience, there is a flash moment of thought. It is always the mind that precedes any emotion. So all emotion and feeling and anger and sadness are secondary to the mind. That is why it is very important not to indulge in thought. If you start looking carefully, there is a moment when the thought arises and you start to feel that sadness welling up. Catch it there as soon as you can, catch it at its root. In the beginning it may take a little bit of vigilance. You have to say, 'No, there's that thought again, I don't want you, I'm not interested – get out!' Sing a song, read a book, put the television on – whatever it takes. Don't allow yourself to go into that thought. You will see that after a few minutes, even a few seconds, it does go. If you leave it alone, if you don't indulge in it, it goes very quickly. All thoughts are like that – totally transitory.

The same thought may arise again a few moments later and so you ignore it again. Just be vigilant. Say, 'I don't want you, I'm sick and tired of you, I've thought this thought a million times before, it gets me nowhere, it doesn't serve me in any way, it just makes me miserable!'

THE TEACHERS OF ONE

In fact, the very nature of the mind is pain. You can say that ego is the same as mind and mind is the same as pain. They are synonymous. Whenever a thought arises, even if it starts out as a really rosy thought, if you follow it to its natural conclusion, you will see that it deteriorates into some sort of painful thought after a while. So don't entertain any thoughts. Don't give them landing space. They are going to come in and they are going to want to land, so cut them as soon as you can.

However, ultimately, you have no control over even that. The noticing of the thought being there occurs when it occurs. Sometimes you might have been locked in thought for five minutes before you even notice – it happens all the time. So be forgiving of yourself, be gentle with yourself. The possibility of recognizing your true nature only occurs when you are relaxed and accepting of yourself and of the circumstances that come along. As long as you are fighting and trying to improve yourself, you're postponing. This is because of the conditioning from our parents, our teachers and so on. But we're not children anymore. We've already done the work upon ourselves that is required. We don't need to improve ourselves anymore. We need to accept ourselves as we are.

This seems to be very much the message that modern teachers are bringing. Nothing to do, nowhere to go . . . The whole 'tradition' of seeking the truth seems to have gone and has been reduced to something very simple.

Papaji's message is simplicity itself. Nothing to attain anew, only a thin veil to be removed. He is totally revolutionary in this. The traditional paths of seeking the truth all seem so laborious and painstaking . . . maybe in 10 or 20 years or so or at the moment of death we will realize who we are all along! So why not wake up now! Why waste time?

We do not need to 'seek' the truth anymore. We have matured beyond complicated rites and rituals, grown out of meditation, prayer and superstition. Mankind has done enough of this. It is clearly time for something totally simple, something that can be grasped equally by all people from all walks of life. Enough of wars over religion and particular belief systems. After all, we are all consciousness itself, inseparable, undivided. One throbbing beingness! It is time for us to wake up and roar this from the rooftops.

Who are Papaji's messengers?

The very first one that Papaji sent out to take his message to the West was Andrew Cohen but Andrew misinterpreted his message by believing that to be totally free it requires you to have immaculate behaviour. This was not Papa's teaching nor was it Ramana's. Freedom does not depend on anything that comes and goes such as behaviour. So Papa's and Andrew's ways parted.

Then Gangaji came along and he said to her, 'You are the teacher I have been waiting for. You have the purity of spirit and the warmth of heart, go out and share my message.' She now has several hundred people at any public satsang. She has maintained Papa's teaching in a very pure form. After Gangaji, there were a few men he told to do it. First was Hanuman from San Francisco and then Deva Prem from Germany, then Bharat from the USA. Arjuna was next – he is English, living in Seattle. Then came Isaac Shapiro, a South African, who also shares this gem with very large groups of people all over the world. Then I think I was next. We were all living in different areas of the planet and so Papa wanted us to go and spread the message wherever we resided.

For me, it happened at the end of his birthday party in October 1993. We had had a big celebration and I had sung and danced for Papa with all my heart. At the very end, he waved me up to the podium and I thought that maybe he wanted me to take a photo of someone – I used to take photos in those days. But he called me up really close to him and he said quietly, 'Yes, you'll be good!' And I said, 'What, Papa?' and he said, 'Yes, you will be very good!' and so I said again, 'What, Papa?' and he said, 'Yes, you'll be very good!' with his voice getting louder each time. At this point I realized that he was up to his mischief. He said, 'Tomorrow you will give satsang'.

So an announcement was made – there were over 300 people in the room. I just fell into this deep silent space. Everything became quiet and still and I just couldn't say a word to anyone! I couldn't believe my ears! It totally amazed me and yet my love of my master gave me the devotion to trust him totally. Instead of taking me into his room as he had done with other people, he had made a kind of proclamation of it. I had a feeling it was because people like Gangaji and Isaac have such dignity – they're older, they are so eloquent and obviously perfect for sharing satsang – whereas I was just an ordinary girl from Liverpool with no particular attributes. He may have realized that there were a few strong male egos around, who had been with Papa longer than me and who wouldn't believe it if he had said it to me in private. I can never know why he did it that way. But one thing for sure was it pushed me into it immediately. There was no time to think about it!

So then I did 11 satsang in Lucknow. Papaji's sister died and he had to go to Delhi. When he came back he was presented with a tape of one of my satsang and he didn't listen to it at first. He waited until I was sitting next to him for dinner one evening at his table. At the end of the meal, he said to someone,

'Where is that cassette of Pratima?' and a tape recorder was put on the table and he played it. I was just dying — I could have crawled under the table! Then gradually an immense quietness descended over me and we listened together in silence. At the end he just said, 'Very good!' and that was it. After that there was no stopping me!

All of his messengers have different ways of sharing this gift. As Arjuna put it, we are the same wine out of different bottles. Most of us travel around the world quite a lot so that people can hear the same message expressed in different ways. One person may be touched by one of us and not by another. You never know when the ignition spark will be triggered! The more of us that share this gem the better, as long as the teaching remains uncompromising in its pure simplicity.

The Dalai Lama said in his recent book, Ancient Wisdom, Modern World: Ethics for a New Millennium, *that his exile in India had made him realize that religion was something we possibly could do without. Isn't that an amazing thing to say? He said that all we need are the qualities of love and compassion. You don't need to be a Buddhist or religious. You don't even need to believe in God.*

That's wonderful. He is a very wise man. I met him in Dharamsala when I made him a huge beaded *thangka* of the White Tara, the goddess of compassion, which hangs in his palace today. I had a private interview with him and I asked him whether it was possible to awaken instantly to one's true nature. He said that looking at it from the absolute standpoint, yes, it is possible for someone to wake up in this very instant. However, looking at it from the relative perspective, we need teachings and practices and so on because it is too difficult for most human beings to awaken without guidelines and a path to follow. *Dzogchen* in Tibetan Buddhism is almost identical to Advaita — simply freedom now. But he has clearly stated that for those people who feel that they need to do something, Tibetan Buddhism provides carefully delineated steps for the process.

He talked for several minutes, occasionally asking his translator to assist. He said he wanted to be very precise in his use of words. I asked him a second question but again my mind became so still in the presence of such a master that I can't remember what it was!

Why is there this de-systemization happening now, making the truth seemingly more available to everyone?

Why? I really have no idea other than to guess it's like the 100th monkey story where all of a sudden the 99th monkey understands how he can wash off a sandy banana in the ocean. As soon as the 100th monkey gets it, simultaneously on other islands many monkeys get it. It's like the theory of evolution that says we develop in exponential leaps and bounds. On our planet there have always been a few individuals who have woken up in every period throughout history. I speculate that there may be many more in our lifetime.

Do you think there is a place for women teachers in the world? I have seen men in tears in satsang in the presence of a female teacher. Maybe there is a greater need for femininity right now. It is a very masculine age that we live in.

Much to my surprise, a man cried tears of joy in my very first satsang but ultimately it doesn't make any difference at all — the female or the male. The nature of the recognition itself is the same. However, as you say, because we are coming from such a male-dominated society, I feel it's a great treasure to have women teachers. For example, Gangaji was especially helpful and inspiring for me as a female teacher. I could ask her things I never dared ask Papa!

In another 10 years we may even find that there will be more female Advaita teachers than men! Women are less removed from their natural God-given birth-right. We are more in tune with ourselves as pure being, we are more receptive to life as it is. We are not so much in the mind. It is dangerous making generalizations but for me personally, I'm delighted that there are more women speaking their truth out loud. There's such a tradition of teachers being male that to get it back in balance again would be very helpful for the planet.

There have always been women teachers throughout the ages who have recognized the truth of their being but mostly, for the last 2,000 years or so, they have just shared it quietly with their family and dear ones. If it risked being burnt at the stake, I might be a little quieter about it too! But maybe not, sometimes it's hard to contain it! It is an exciting time to be alive, especially for women in the Western world.

So absorbed are we in conversation, the vegetables have overcooked, the rice has burnt. Somehow, though, it doesn't seem to matter. The sun continues to blaze through the window. I feel very much at peace.

Pratima dishes up the supper. I start to wish that I had met Papaji, that I'd had the opportunity to sit next to him and look into his eyes. Perhaps I could have received some kind of transmission through his presence and would now know the true nature of myself. 'Yes, I was very lucky to have met him,' empathizes Pratima, 'but his message lives on. He may have left his body but for me his presence is more alive than ever. If you want freedom, it can be yours right now.'

I wonder if that is true. I really want freedom but it is becoming a more and more elusive goal. Perhaps I really don't want it, I surmise – that's what the real problem is. I like Paula's idiosyncrasies, all her neuroses, all her desires. They are so familiar to me that I can't imagine life without them. Indeed, isn't it all pre-programmed anyway? And yet I never feel truly happy, never feel truly satisfied.

Pratima gets ready to leave to give satsang, like Wayne Liquorman, at the Resource Centre in the Holloway Road, north London. Although I am calm, I feel saturated by our conversation and the heat of the day. I long to return home.

That evening, I take down a book of Papaji's satsang from my bookshelf. Ceremonially, I light candles and incense and settle down on my meditation stool. I close my eyes, breathing deeply and focusing my mind on the mantra *Ram*. The sound fills my mind like an intoxicating perfume, anaesthetizing my whirling and spinning mind. I open the book and turn to the chapter, 'Relationship to the Teacher':

> *Traditionally, the student goes to the teacher in the forest and says, 'Please Master, save me. I am suffering. Tell me, who am I?' With all love the teacher says, 'My dear son, come sit here and I will tell you.' Then enquiry starts. The student asks, 'Who am I?' and the teacher tells you the truth, 'You are THAT!' He speaks the truth, and the student understands, 'I am THAT!' And it is finished.*

> *What is a teacher?*

> *A teacher is a raft to ferry you across to the other side of the ocean. A true teacher carries you across the ocean of samsara.*

> *Does one need a guru?*

> *Your Self is your guru, but you have not seen him within you. You do not understand the language of this guru within you. If you are very serious, if you have a longing, a burning desire to see him, what He does is introduce you to someone who has your same tongue to speak to you. The inner Self takes the form of the guru without, to speak to you in your lisping tongue. He*

tells you, 'I am within you.' When this outer guru is recognized as your Self, you will understand.

Wake up and Roar: Satsang with H W L Poonja

Please, I pray, I do so want to understand.

Tony Parsons

CHAPTER FOUR

THE SECRET
GARDEN

The first time I saw Tony Parsons, I was somewhat taken aback. An average-looking, late-middle-aged man, wearing beige corduroys and a neutral-coloured sweater, he lacked all the mystique that I usually associate with purveyors of the truth. Indeed, the most striking characteristic about Tony is how incredibly 'normal' he is – his manner being very ordinary, his perspective very direct. 'Mug in hand, bum on seat,' is his jovial catchphrase for a metaphor of what is. Wherever Tony goes, a small crowd always tends to gather around him, sharing in his good humour and *joie de vivre* – his deep, resonant voice, always seemingly deadpan, suddenly erupting into a hissing giggle.

We meet on a weekend retreat at Tekels Park in Camberley, Surrey – an hour or so's drive from London. The beauty is breathtaking: huge emerald firs bow in the light afternoon breeze, pink and red flowers blush in their beds. People mill about chatting and sipping tea. Tony greets me with a bear hug, enquiring of my journey and offering me refreshments. I get the impression his concern is very genuine – but it's not for the Paula with her itinerant tales of frustration and angst; rather something deeper within me, something way beyond my personal mask. I almost feel unworthy of the attention and momentarily reflect on how many of my own friendships I have turned into conditional arrangements, contracts of love.

Tony was born in Brixton, London, in 1933 though he was brought up in nearby Streatham. The son of a builder, life at home was nothing out of the ordinary. He started to attend Catholic School, but at the age of seven had 'the experience of the omniscient presence of God,' prompting him to decide at 18 that he wanted to become a Christian. Realizing that the Church however, 'hadn't got a clue about the secret of Christ,' Tony turned to a new interpretation of Christ's words in a book, *The New Man* by Maurice Nicholl, a contemporary of Gurdjieff.

'There was one word in his book that completely opened my eyes. It was an interpretation of the word "repent", which up until then I had been taught to mean "be sorry for your sins". But the word in Christ's local language meant "to turn around and see everything anew". And I suddenly saw when He talks about how He healed the blind, it wasn't that they were actually blind but that they had only seen or believed that they were separate. And that was it, bang!' Three days after that, Tony walked across Norwood Grove, a park in London where, he says, there came the understanding that there was 'no one there'.

I join the afternoon session – about 20 or so people sit silently on an assortment of wooden chairs and plastic seats. Tony looks placidly at the floor. A question is asked. Tony looks up, as if aroused from a deep sleep. There are no complicated answers, no philosophical riddles to resolve. The theme is always simple – presence. And judging by the look of contentment on people's faces, that's all that they have come to hear.

At the end of the session, Tony and I stroll into the garden. I feel strangely at rest. Pratima has come to join us for the interview as we sit down on a bench overlooking the lawn. And it is not long before more gather around us to hear Tony speak – some have pulled up chairs, others are seated cross-legged on the grass. So engaged am I in our conversation, I don't even notice the throng until I am momentarily distracted by the need to change the cassette on my recording machine.

Tony's svelte sea-blue volume, *The Open Secret*, rests on the table next to us. 'I really enjoyed your book,' Pratima smiles. Another great misconception down the drain, I think – that teachers no longer need to read spiritual books, let alone the works of their contemporaries. I scan its glossy pages, resting on a chapter entitled 'Presence':

> *Presence is our constant nature but most of the time we are interrupting it by living in a state of expectation, motivation or interpretation. We are hardly ever at home. In order to rediscover our freedom we need to let go of these projections and allow the possibility of presence. Its real discovery, or our access to it, can only be made within the essence of what is. This is where spontaneous aliveness resides and where we can openly welcome the unknown.*

> *Only here, in present awareness of simply what is, can there be freedom from self-image. To live passionately is to let go of everything for the wonder of timeless presence. When we are courageous enough to allow this we suddenly rediscover that we*

are the sole source of all and everything. Presence is not to be confused with 'being here now' which is a continuous process of the separate self and has no direct relevance to liberation.

Presence is a quality of welcoming, open awareness which is dedicated to simply what is. There can still be someone who is aware and there is that of which they are conscious . . . the sound of running water, the taste of tea, the feeling of fear, or the weight and texture of sitting on a seat. And then there can be a letting go of the one who is aware, and all that remains is presence. All of this is totally without judgement, analysis, wish to reach conclusion or to become. There is no traffic and no expectation. There is simply what is.

Tony invites Pratima and me to join everyone for supper. A sumptuous vegetarian buffet awaits us in the dining hall. I engage in conversation with my neighbours and we talk about Advaita and the current sociological trend of modern-day teachers — all journeying around the world, simply teaching the nature of what is. As we reflect on this present phenomenon, we all nod and thank God it is presented in that way.

I am then asked why I am here and I explain about the interviews and the book, so suddenly people want to know what I think about all the teachers I have met. For a moment, I am flattered that my opinion is worth something; then I feel disturbed about committing myself to any opinion at all. What, ultimately, do I know about anything, I think? It is beginning to dawn on me that my aspirations of being a 'spiritual journalist' demand a certain price. My vanity is reaching new heights — though I am always, of course, masquerading under the guise of seeker of truth; and my mental capabilities seem to be touching new depths. In the quest for some kind of relief from my ego, I find that Paula is getting more and more in the way.

So, you walked across Norwood Grove . . . then what happened?

Well, I can tell you. I walked across the park and I was aware that I was in the future, that I was going towards something and I wasn't really walking across the park. And I became aware of my feet and with each footstep I realized it was totally new. It had never happened before — it was unique and then it died on the spot. It was there and then it wasn't. Then the next footstep was there and then it wasn't. This was stunning, you know. Right at this moment, this was the first time this had happened. And it will never be like that again. Isn't that *amazing*! And then there was no one walking, there was just walking. Then after that, well, I'm sorry, I'm lost for words.

Well, possibly we could just talk a little more!

Ha . . . OK!

In your book, you say, 'I made the choice . . .'

I know, I know.

I always keep asking this question of everyone I meet but you did say, 'I chose to watch my feet.' Now, me sitting over here in this state where I believe that I am the doer, I latch onto a sentence like that which includes, seemingly, an act by an individual called 'I'.

Yes, 'I' must choose to watch my footsteps, I know. It's OK. As far as I'm concerned, I have no problem with that. I think the problem is generated by people overemphasizing the importance of who chooses. The mind then grabs hold of the idea of looking for a non-chooser and a non-doer. This begins another search, which is actually another avoidance. The end answer to who chooses is that it doesn't matter because whatever's chosen, whatever happens, doesn't matter either. So I say to people, live as if you choose. Be aware of your footsteps and then forget all that. It'll happen if it's going to happen.

I have heard it said that enlightenment is something that can be won like a jackpot in a national lottery.

I don't believe that but a lot of people do.

So if enlightenment is not a lottery system, it implies that there is some active decision within the individual to make the passage through the gate, as it were — do you see what I am saying?

Hmm, it seems like that but it isn't.

I recently had a conversation with another teacher who said that 'grace' was just a fancy word for 'good luck'. So that implies that it is like a lottery.

No, it isn't like that for me, or at least that's not how I see it. For me, all I can say is now I see that there wasn't anyone that achieved it. But I also see that there was someone there who was innocent. There was a sort of innocence and a readiness for that to happen. I can see people who have an innocence and a readiness for it to happen. I know very clearly that it is nothing to do with luck. It's something else. There's a readiness and there it is. Even in people who aren't conscious of being aware. But what I'm saying to people is that there's no particular way. So, all I can sense with myself is I can see that guy who was walking across that park and there was a sort of innocence and a readiness to wonder, to be in wonder. It's a childlikeness that's there.

So what's the purpose of coming to satsang, for example?

Oh, none at all. It's just that somebody says, 'Let's do a retreat in Camberley,' and then you're on a train and it's happening. I can't come here and have a purpose about that guy over there you know. The moment I have any purpose about it, there's some expectation, and he can have an expectation from me too.

Well, I have an expectation, very much.

You can go on having the expectation but I'm only going to respond to what happens here from the reality of presence. I am not going to play any of your games. I am not interested in your expectations or your so-called life story. At the same time I love what you are.

I have another burning question about the issue of presence rather than 'be here now', which has almost become a mantra — holding on to this moment with all my might. Can you speak about presence and how it is to be in presence rather than to be clutching at presence?

The only thing that I could say is, that after I had walked across the park, there was still this thing about the watcher, or the watching, which isn't me but there's watching of what is. So, for quite a while, there was Tony Parsons and then the switching on to watching. In a way, for me, it seemed that there was a watcher, just here about a foot behind the back of my head, in a sort of concentrated form. I am describing what I remember as an experience and for a while it was like that.

So there's the watcher and there's Tony Parsons. And then after a while, that watching was totally suffused into everything. So, there isn't anything concentrated, there isn't really a watcher, there's only being. And I can't describe that. All I can say is that there isn't anywhere that isn't home. There isn't anywhere that isn't love, unconditional love. But that doesn't mean that it's all beautiful — it just means that there's a presence, that everything contains this 'isness', this ground of being. It's so inexpressible, it's just so . . .

Certainly my sense of being in the park and afterwards is that you are being made love to by everything. That's another way of getting somewhere near it. But it may not be like that for other people. But to answer your question, the difference is that there can be no holding on to this . . . Who is holding on? Once there is a clutching, there is again the illusion of someone wanting something.

So where is Tony Parsons now? Is it that Tony Parsons still has thoughts and feelings but there's a distance now? Or is it that Tony Parsons has disintegrated?

Well, for me, and again this is just using words and others may describe things in a different way, for me the ego is the belief that there is a separate identity. In my way that's how I see the word 'ego' and that's consciousness creating the illusion of there being a separate individual. So, there's nothing wrong with ego – that's how it is at that time. And then a while after walking across the park, because there was still a residue afterwards that evaporated under the watching, there was no longer any form of ego that believed there was a separate being. And that can happen immediately or after a while with people. So, there is no longer any sense of separation, of there being a separate entity.

But there is a characteristic or preconditioned sense of Tony Parsons. There's a sort of shape and a way of personality, which expresses itself in the world. And that has no more flavour or quality than that flower in that bowl. It's just that it's part of the whole and isn't owned by anybody anymore. My voice at the moment is part of the play of consciousness manifesting itself. And so is your finger, and so is that man walking on the lawn. There is no valid difference. It is all the infinite expression. I am consciousness, the light, which allows that to be. I am the light of all. And so are you.

So, it's not about taking anything personally or attributing anything to oneself?

No, there is no one there that you can attribute it to anymore.

And thoughts, they arise?

Yes.

Do you get lost in thought?

Sometimes. If a thought arises – what I call an abstract thought – then the watching just chops it off as it arises. It's there for a moment but there isn't anybody who owns it. In the gaze, it just evaporates.

What is mind, then?

Mind is the tool which consciousness uses to create that tree over there. Consciousness is creating the tree. It's creating that tree so it uses the mind to say, 'There is a tree.'

Or 'I want a cup of tea'?

Well, that can be getting into complications – Tony Parsons wants a cup of tea. When you start getting into wanting, you're beginning to get into what I call abstract thought. Natural thought is, 'I am going to pick that up and put it down again.' It's what I am doing, like chopping logs. Abstract thought is, 'I wonder if I can pay the rent,' or 'Am I going to die of cancer next week?'

And the emotions, what are they?

They're just part of the colour of the manifestation. As far as I'm concerned, emotions and feelings are the red and the blue and the yellow of this manifestation. It's like they all just happen – anger or anything. But it's just all part of the infinite expression.

Umm, to get back to making love . . .

Right!

In all of us, there is this real desire to find happiness outside of ourselves rather than within, particularly in relationships. Why is there that need to find emotional, intellectual, even spiritual security in another person and why is it so seductive when it's happening? And yet it is so crippling in its outcome, it seems.

Is that your reality?

Yes, it's always like that! I can see that there could be support and strength in a loving relationship but it is very difficult to have love without an agenda. If consciousness is our true birthright, why do I want to find it in someone else?

All desire is only the longing to come home. There isn't anyone in the world who isn't a seeker. Everyone longs to come home but people seek it at the level of understanding that they have. That can be being successful in business or whatever – or being a victim. And yes, the deepest attraction is the relationship of being in love. It is very sweet. For me, it's very sweet because it is so near to walking across the park. Falling in love is like something so near to this surrender because, when you fall in love with someone, there is a surrender to something ineffable in them.

You give up your own will — you would do anything for the other person.

Yes, you do.

It's like you no longer exist as long as you love somebody.

Well, for as long as you're *in* love with somebody. After that there can be a rich relationship but, as far as I'm concerned, none of that bears any resemblance to awakening. It is the nearest you can get to that but it's only a reflection of that. But when that is there, everything just falls away and there is no longer a relationship with anything because relationship implies that I relate to you. But if there's no one, there's no relationship. There's no need for relationship with anything.

Well, people fall in love because of the colour of someone's eyes.

Yes! It's incredible. I was walking across Holborn one day — I was about 18 — and there was a woman getting on the bus and woom! Have you ever had it? I never saw her again but that moment was amazing. I think also in the act of making love when that energy is very rich, there's a possibility of no one being there. I think that happens a lot.

I actually think for the people walking down Camberley High Street, there are moments when there is no one there. It's just unrecognized. Certainly, making love, bungee-jumping, are definitely the same! In sport, people are talking about the 'zone', aren't they? In tennis, going into the zone — there ain't no one there! There's just tennis happening or running or whatever.

So, desire is the endless shopping basket, filling our lives with desire or thought but what there really is, is only one longing. And again, I have to reiterate that it is all the infinite expression.

I have been down the route where I thought that any form of so-called pleasure was not right because it was a form of attachment. I have had very few relationships because I have thought that's not where it's at. But it's not like that, is it? In fact, it's quite the opposite. I should really go for it!

Yes. I really loved that about Osho. He really did throw people right in the deep end. His whole way was get in there and get your hands muddy, you know. He was so lovely in that. He talked about sex in so many ways that were really quite powerful. And it didn't matter what sort of sex it was. It was with anything or anyone! And there was something beautiful about what he was saying – that, thrown totally into a situation, there can be a point where there is no one, there is just that. But then again, there is nothing you can do about it. That's just the way it is.

Could you speak about the time you were with Osho.

I was three years in a commune. Before that I was very well off. I had a yacht. I was married with four children. By the time they were about 18 or 19, I had a lot of money – but I needed to jump out of that. And in some way Osho was very big and I just leapt in. I went from a beautiful house in Surrey, with a swimming pool and all that luxury, and went to live in Medina with four other people in the same room.

I felt at the time that I would get into learning about therapy. I thought that I could use therapy as a vehicle to take people to somewhere beyond therapy. So, I went on a year's course. Then I was in the commune for a couple of years after that just helping run the building work. When I came out, I was well off enough to live in Wiltshire on my own for quite a time. I had left the family by then.

The therapy thing didn't happen though – I now see in some way that it wasn't for me because I was saying to people that there's therapy but there's also something beyond it – so that was a contradiction for me. And then I met Claire around about 1988 and we lived together and then we married, and it's wonderful because we see the same light and enjoy a deep togetherness.

The Open Secret was published in '95. But didn't you write a much longer book?

Yes. Just as when I was a kid I knew that I would find the secret, I also knew that I would be talking to a lot of people. Not huge numbers but a lot of people. So, I thought that I would write this book, a huge thing and very laboured and it just wasn't on. So, I gave up the whole idea of writing a book and totally gave up the idea of talking to people in any public sort of way. I just accepted that wasn't going to happen anymore. And then, one morning, the simplicity of the first bit of *The Open Secret* came through and the whole idea of writing something very minimalist and short and direct came and then bang! I wrote the book and then I went down to London and suddenly I was talking to about 30 people in Hampstead. It has really snowballed from that time.

What's extraordinary is the gap between your experience in the park and the fact that you have only recently started teaching.

Oh, it's a huge gap. I mean, I feel it's just like that. With some people what can happen is that they could be walking across a park or whatever and then within weeks or months or just a couple of years they could be talking to many people. Of course, I did talk to people on a one-to-one basis but obviously now it is appropriate for this to happen in the way it is.

Papaji said there can be understanding and then it's like a fine wine that becomes more and more mature.

Yes. The other thing is that not everyone has to be a teacher. There are guys out there driving buses, mothers mothering, who have this.

You don't have to give satsang then?

You don't have to do anything! You just drive a bus. It would be really boring if everyone was giving satsang!

You'd have a situation where there would be more teachers than disciples!

Yeah, and I'd be out of business!

It does seem that there has been a flourishing of teachers who are giving satsang at the moment. Wayne Liquorman said that's because the term 'enlightenment' has been redefined. Everyone is saying that they are enlightened now. It's almost a trend — first there was Tao, then Zen and now Advaita.

There are many teachers but there are very few who really understand the paradoxical nature of liberation. This whole idea, that there's something that you can do, is already a contradiction. The whole problem is the belief that there is a 'you'. I noticed that there are a few people who are teaching that very directly, straight off the shoulder. There are a lot of people who are ready to hear that and I just feel that this is the time when, as far as I'm concerned, a lot of people are going to leap. People resonate with this. People know that what they seek, what they long for, is totally and utterly simple and absolutely beyond the concepts of the mind.

It doesn't need 20 years on a meditation cushion or in some organization?

No, no, that's beginning to be recognized as being totally irrelevant, which it is. The whole concept that an individual can reach something that is not of the individual is just bullshit.

So why, paradoxically, has there been a mushrooming of every type of therapy imaginable — psychotherapy, aromatherapy, colour therapy?

Because there is always a balance both ways. Whilst there are more people seeking nothing, there are also more people seeking everything to do with 'me'. The whole trip is about 'me'. It is an inevitable part of the game in this age of understanding, and, although it involves looking in the opposite direction, it is still as valid as anything else.

Yes, you talk about this in your book. In one sense the growing interest in 'working on oneself' can give people a feeling of self-worth — forgive your mother and heal your inner child and all that stuff — which is a move away from the seemingly more guilt-ridden experience of Christianity, for example. But it also increases, paradoxically, the sense of the individual as a separate doer.

Yes. As far as I'm concerned the most intelligent thing that's happened in the last 50 years is therapy. If you want to make your life work, therapy is the most intelligent approach to that but there then comes a realization that actually you never *will* make your life work. Nobody's ever made their life work because that is a contradiction again. Whilst their lives are getting better, there is a longing. So how can that life work if there is still a longing? What people come to is the final realization that even in dealing with all of that stuff — material wealth, relationships — in the end, therapeutic work bringing you to a sort of self-improved person still isn't it. And so some move beyond that. But that's how consciousness wants to play it.

And it's all OK?

Oh, it's all still the infinite expression and absolutely OK. Really, really, really, all of that is part of the whole. It's absolutely appropriate. And if somebody feels that they should go to colour therapy in order to find enlightenment, that's what will happen and it's absolutely all right that they need to do that. The thing is, however you want it, it's OK. After awakening, it seems that there was no one who could have achieved anything. So, what's therapy?

But as a seeker, there is this pull to want to improve oneself.

That is as it is. Everything is it and that's appropriate. And you know, there are a number of teachers who I would say are totally misleading people — and that's absolutely fine also. That's just as valid as anything else.

But it can make a mockery of the whole spiritual thing.

Yes, but there isn't anything that is spiritual, except in the mind. Everything is appropriate. If someone needs to go to a teacher and be misled, that's totally appropriate.

But if it's OK to be disillusioned – that's consciousness's game plan – it makes you want to stick your fingers up at consciousness and say, 'Stop messing me about!'

Yes! Somebody in London said that they wanted to send a letter of complaint . . . but they couldn't find the address! Of course, it is their own!

You feel like you are constantly being duped. You know that you're being duped and yet somehow you're still going along with it.

Yes. But there's nothing you can do about that. This is what I really try and say to people, you know – 'Give up and accept that you are totally helpless. You are utterly helpless!' When that acceptance begins to happen, then another possibility can arise. A possibility that is both revolutionary and magnificent. This is the true beginning of the most wonderful adventure of all.

On the London Advaita circuit, Tony Parsons is one of the most popular teachers there is – his meetings seem to attract an ever growing collection of people in search of the ultimate truth.

Inasmuch as I can fully accept that, at an *absolute* level, all there is is consciousness and that 'I' am purely an expression of God's will, what I am still finding difficult to understand is however that there is nothing that 'I' can do at the *relative* perspective to taste my true Self. Indeed, though Tony agrees that practices such as therapy can help at the emotional and psychic levels, this teaching is about 'present awareness of simply what is' – in short, all there is just is. What I find even harder to come to terms with is the concept that the sense of a separate doer, as an act of consciousness and not through any individual effort, will simply fall away without any prior warning – like a bolt of lightning, in some random (or should I say 'predestined') fashion. It just seems to be so unfair.

So if everything is consciousness and consciousness is all there is, why is there still the implicit suggestion that to no longer believe in the sense of a separate doer is better than believing in it. Why do people like me revere those who have 'got it' (or should I say 'lost it') rather than those who haven't? And if there truly is no difference, why is there ultimately the need for teachers and satsang?

Q: All that I want to know is whether sat-sanga *is necessary and whether my coming here will help me or not.*

A: First you must decide what is sat-sanga. *It means association with* sat *or reality. One who knows or has realized* sat *is also regarded as* sat. *Such association with* sat *or with one who knows* sat *is absolutely necessary for all. Sankara has said that in all the three worlds there is no boat like* sat-sanga *to carry one safely across the ocean of births and deaths.*

Sat-sanga *means* sanga *[association] with* sat. Sat *is only the Self. Since the Self is not now understood to be* sat, *the company of the sage who has thus understood it is sought. That is* sat-sanga. *Introversion results. Then* sat *is revealed.*

Q: Why does not Bhagavan go about and preach the truth to the people at large?

A: How do you know I am not doing it? Does preaching consist in mounting a platform and haranguing the people around? Preaching is simple communication of knowledge; it can really be done in silence only. What do you think of a man who listens to a sermon for an hour and goes away without having been impressed by it so as to change his life? Compare him with another, who sits in a holy presence and goes away after some time with his outlook on life totally changed. Which is the better, to preach loudly without effect or to sit silently sending out inner force?

Again, how does speech arise? First there is abstract knowledge. Out of this arises the ego, which in turn gives rise to thought, and thought to the spoken word. So the word is the great-grandson of the original source. If the word can produce an effect, judge for yourself, how much more powerful must be the preaching through silence.

Be As You Are: The Teachings of Sri Ramana Maharshi

Francis Lucille

CHAPTER FIVE

COPERNICAN
SHIFT

I was sitting alone in silence, meditating in my living room with two friends of mine. It was too early to fix dinner, our next activity. Having nothing to do, expecting nothing, I was available. My mind was free of dynamism, my body relaxed and sensitive, although I could feel some discomfort in my back and in my neck.

After some time, one of my friends unexpectedly began to chant a traditional incantation in Sanskrit, the Gayatri. The sacred syllables entered mysteriously in resonance with my silent presence which seemed to become intensely alive. I felt a deep longing in me, but at the same time a resistance was preventing me from living the current situation to the fullest, from responding with all my being to this invitation from the now and from merging with it. As the attraction towards the beauty heralded by the chant increased, so did the resistance, revealing itself as a growing fear that transformed into an intense terror.

At this point, I felt that my death was imminent, and that this horrendous event would surely be triggered by any further letting go on my behalf, by any further welcoming of that beauty. I had reached a crucial point in my life. As a result of my spiritual search, the world and its objects had lost their attraction; I didn't really expect anything substantial from them; I was exclusively in love with the absolute, and this love gave me the boldness to jump into the great void of death, to die for the sake of that beauty, now so close, that beauty which was calling me beyond the Sanskrit words.

As a result of this abandon, the intense terror which had been holding me instantaneously released its grip and changed into a flow of bodily sensations and thoughts which rapidly converged towards a single thought, the 'I'-thought, just as the roots and the branches of a tree converge towards its single trunk. In an almost simultaneous apperception, the personal entity I was identifying with revealed itself in its totality. I saw its superstructure, the thoughts originating from the 'I'-concept and its infrastructure, the traces of my fears and desires at the physical level. Now the entire tree was contemplated by an impersonal eye and both the superstructure of thoughts and the infrastructure of bodily sensations rapidly vanished, leaving the 'I'-thought alone in the field of consciousness. For a few moments, the pure 'I'-thought seemed to vacillate, just as the flame of an oil lamp running out of fuel, then vanished.

At that precise moment, I awakened to my eternity.

Eternity Now: Dialogues on Awareness
Francis Lucille

Francis Lucille, like many contemporary Advaita teachers, can be something of an enigma. Before meeting him at Osho Leela, I am asked by his assistants to refrain from dwelling on his private details though Francis will, I am told, gladly answer any questions about the spiritual life. I suppose if the ego is no longer relevant, then they do have something of a point.

The first time I saw Francis was at The Study Society in Baron's Court, west London. I was impressed by his thoughtful and intelligent approach. There was nothing ethereal to his discourse — a seemingly brilliant mind fielded the complexities of philosophical debate being thrown at him from a lively audience. Nor did he make light of people's difficulties in trying to understand the subtleties of Advaita, which he explained with an elegant sophistication. Indeed, his diction is reminiscent of a Platonic philosopher, full of references to 'Beauty', 'Intelligence' and 'Truth', his French accent in some way completing the mystique.

Born in the South of France, Francis worked as a physicist, designing and developing sophisticated weapons for the French military. As his interest in the nature of the spiritual, rather than the physical, world increased, his career naturally conflicted with his beliefs. Through the reading of many of the main texts of Advaita Vedanta, Zen Buddhism, Sufism and most specifically, the writings of Krishnamurti, Francis was led to a living teacher, Jean Klein. This meeting precipitated the radical shift in his perception and the awakening to his true nature. Now in his forties, he currently lives in Middletown, California with his wife, Laura, frequently travelling the world holding meetings and retreats.

Francis greets me politely. He is dressed all in white, giving him an almost celestial glow. He asks me very genuinely about my trip but refrains from any other small talk, all the while observing me ironically through oval spectacles. We go and sit under some apple trees in the garden – it is the height of the English summer and the shade is welcome relief.

The immediate thing you notice about Francis is how incredibly still he is. Indeed he hardly moves during our short discussion, choosing only to gaze downward at the grass and then sporadically across the surrounding fields. I realize that when I am in the presence of someone who doesn't move all that much, it makes me feel incredibly nervous, serving only to emphasize my own sense of unrest.

Suddenly, I don't know what to ask him. All my questions seem ridiculous in the face of the shimmering beauty of the afternoon. I too start to look down at the ground. I ask myself what do I really want to know from Francis – not lots of sophisticated answers about the nature of reality but what or who I truly am. We sit in silence together for about 10 minutes before I have the courage to open my mouth.

Our conversation feels disjointed somehow. My failing confidence makes me tense. The long pauses between questions only make me feel awkward rather than relax my state of mind. I realize that my quest for understanding has turned from a joyous voyage of self-discovery into an angst-ridden trek into the unknown. I also know that I cannot give up this search – there is no turning back. I only hope and pray that Self-realization, rather than madness, takes a hold of me first.

Who am I? I keep coming up against concepts and phrases, which I don't really understand anymore.

Well, if concepts appear, they obviously don't appear in somebody else – they must be appearing in you. So, what you are is that – whatever that is – in which all concepts, perceptions and all sensations appear. That is what we all call 'I'. It's very easy.

So why do I feel frustrated that I am missing that understanding? And what compels me to seek and come to you and ask that question?

Perhaps because you have heard somewhere that, if you answer this question, the answer will solve your problems and make you happy. The answer is obvious – it's an open secret. That's why I told you that it's easy. The problem is that although it is obvious, we don't trust it. Instead of sticking to the answer, which is that we are whatever that is which *perceives*, we think, we believe, we feel, that we are something *perceived* – the body, a conceptual limited being, a human being, a woman. So, it is this belief – of being a separate entity and the accompanying feelings of being separate – that comes in and distorts the easy and clear answer. In other words, we tend to believe, to trust our belief, that we have inherited from our surroundings, education, parents and so on, rather than our direct experience of what we are. The experience of what we are is easy, simple, but we seem not to trust it.

Why is it set up that way? If I am all this and that which I am seeking is already within me, why do I deny it so? I don't understand the game. If awareness is so amazing and it is my nature, why don't I 'feel' that? Why do I create these barriers and then want to knock down the barriers? It's ridiculous!

Yes, I agree. It is ridiculous, so I am returning the questions to you! Why are you doing that? I guess because you are enjoying it.

But the whole world is in that state. Very few people . . .

Well, let's not worry about the whole world here but let's worry about the truth. What the whole world believes is totally irrelevant because truth is not a democracy. In 1905 Einstein was alone when he came up with his paper about the theory of relativity. Everybody, including the scientific community, thought he was nuts. It doesn't mean that he was wrong. He was alone. So, the fact that a large number of people believe one way is no proof at all that what they believe is true.

You ask me how is it that we feel that we are separate. That's a very good question. It's a question that you shouldn't ask me, you should ask yourself. By asking yourself this question, it will pave the way to the answer. How is it that I feel separate? Based on which experience do I feel that I am separate?

When I think about it, just sitting here, there isn't a feeling of separateness.

Exactly. But what is it that makes us feel that anything is separate from anything else? For instance, that an apple from this tree is separate from the tree. It's a concept. Even if the apple falls from the tree, does it mean that it is separate from the totality of nature? Does it mean that it's separate from the totality because at some point it has fallen from the tree? Now, when the apple has fallen down on the ground, it's just a concept that separates it. Nothing is separate from nature. It is the same air inside our lungs that is outside and the same water that is running in our blood as outside. So, at the physical level we are not separate. At the subtle level we are not separate either. We are exchanging thoughts, concepts – they are not yours or mine, they are just being exchanged. We don't know who owns what. It's always a concept that separates.

Is ego just a concept?

It depends what we call ego. I don't use this word much, you know. I certainly don't use it in the sense of a separate individual with individual characteristics and behavioural patterns and so on. When I use it, it is in the meaning of identifying that which we are – whatever that is – with a specific body-mind organism. So, it is the belief that I – whatever I am – is this body and this mind. That's what I would call ego – an identifying thought, an identifying feeling.

Peace comes with not identifying with these thoughts?

Yes, but the peace is there, no matter what. The peace of our true nature, of this reality, is already there, is already present, no matter whether there is agitation in the mind or not. Chaos in the mind, agitation, is triggered by this notion, this belief that I am separate. The moment I am separate, I am a fragment. The desire for completeness arises and also the fear that goes with the fragmentation. If I am a fragment, I may be threatened and that creates turmoil. The moment I understand everything is One there is no separation and the agitation of not being any longer, fed by the notion of being a separate entity, gradually wears out. It doesn't mean that the mind stops. It doesn't mean that there is no dynamism. It doesn't mean that there is no thinking that goes on. There might be thinking, there might be dynamism but it is harmonious without resistance.

This is a point that I have not really grasped – that all there is is consciousness and within that, chaos and agitation arise. And yet, there is some effort to move away from that chaos and agitation and the attachment to them. On the one hand, everything is all God, and on the other hand, there's some kind of movement to disassociate from those thoughts – which are still God. I don't understand.

We can, through an effort, try to disassociate an object from another object. But then instead of being left with one object, you are left with two! It would be enough to understand, to see, that that which we are is forever disassociated from any object that may appear within all of this. Just as the mirror is forever disassociated from any reflections that may appear within it. So, to try to disassociate the mirror from any reflection contained within it would be a childish effort.

But who makes that effort?

This effort is the product of ego or ignorance. Nobody makes it. It is the natural growth and subsequent decay of the seed of ignorance. It decays because we are meant to have an inkling of the thought that consciousness is already free from appearance, is already disassociated from it, which will sooner or later lead to peace, to harmony. So, these efforts, by a truthful seeker, to disassociate himself or herself from objects, no matter how childish and useless they might be, eventually will lead to the understanding that this disassociation has always been the case, that freedom has always been present.

There was something you mentioned in London recently that really struck me. It's like a process of seeing what you are not, which leads to a point of understanding of that which you are. But I am making an intellectual game out of all of it, to be honest.

Of course you are making an intellectual game. That's why you are writing a book about it. So, it's a way of being involved without being involved. It's a way of being serious without being serious. If you were being really serious about it you wouldn't try to write a book about it, you would try to live from there. It has to be of vital importance to you. It's like a matter of life and death. So, we can gather all the information we want, all the intellectual understanding, but that never replaces this strong desire for it, which is in fact the only prerequisite, you see – to desire it more than anything else.

And then it becomes clear?

It's because you see it as an intellectual clarity but intellectual clarity is only the tip of the iceberg. It has to become clear at the level of feelings and perceptions. It has to be clear in the way we feel our body, the way we feel our body no longer tells us I am separate. When the way we feel our body is a song to Oneness, then we don't have to worry too much about thoughts because the moment the feeling is of Oneness, it's not going to trigger thoughts that we are separate. But if the understanding is simply intellectual but our body is screaming that it's not true –

well, we have a problem. So, while our body is screaming that that's not true, there are all kinds of conflicting thoughts and doubts because we fear that existence or experience at the body level is contradictory with our theory of Oneness.

But I am not saying that to be intellectually interested in those matters is useless. You have to start somewhere. And that's as good a starting point as any other!

Freedom — it depends how much you really want it. Is that what you are saying? That's what it boils down to. I could ask you lots of questions about the mind and the emotions, about why am I not happy, but at the end of the day it depends on how much I want to be free.

Yes. You get what you desire, you see.

But I think I really want freedom. I really do! I have cried for many long hours. I have been on many retreats, done many things.

It's important to be free from all theories about freedom, to not become a 'freedom theories expert'. Some of these theories are quite good but they more or less boil down to the same thing, so it will be enough to take one in the end. But what truly matters is to have the courage and determination to live in accordance with the theory. The obstacles are fear and desire. A very strong desire for truth is however desirable in order to have the determination and the courage to put our money where our mouth is.

When we try to live in accordance with a non-personal or impersonal perspective, then we receive confirmation so that our love for freedom and our desire for it increase. It gives us more courage next time in more difficult situations to try again to make the impersonal choice and then again to miraculously receive a new confirmation. In this way, we are no longer stuck because we are implementing our theory. It is merging with our daily life from the book, from the library of the mind into the way we perceive, we feel, we relate to other human beings, to the world, the way we act, the way we decide and so on. And the confirmations we receive are very diverse, beautiful. They come from love, they come from intelligence, beauty, and they open new doors in all realms of our experience — the realm of feelings, understanding, of perceptions.

A lot of fear arises to make that leap. There's a knot of fear right inside me that prevents that final letting go. I flirt with the truth really.

It's neither easy nor uneasy. The facing of this fear is very important. You have to know it completely to be acquainted with it so that it stops making a slave out of you. Any time you act out of fear you are going to suffer. No matter what realm of your life your action refers to – making relationships, intimate feelings, your professional life, your financial life and so on – every time you act out of fear, it's a rule, a golden rule – there is a price to pay. There is a lesson to be taken so you have to know your fear quite well because it's made of bodily sensations, sense perceptions and feelings. It will be important not to entertain the desire to get rid of it – welcome it completely, be ready to live with your fear. The moment you are ready to live with it, without trying to do anything about it, it's already neutralized because you are already free from it.

It's like if you have to live in a room with a cobra. If you turn off the light you are in great danger, whereas if you turn on the light you can see at every moment where the cobra is. If you can move in accordance with the cobra's position, it is neutralized, you see. So, it's the same. Don't hesitate to turn on the light, to see your fear. There's no need to get rid of it because, if you try to come close to the cobra, it will kill you. So don't try to kill your fear, just watch your fear so that your fear can never catch you, can never kill you and can never feed on you. It's very important to face the fear.

Our interview together lasts for only about three quarters of an hour. Francis gets up to leave to give the afternoon's satsang, which is due to start in a few minutes' time. As I start to pack away all my equipment, he turns and approaches me once more, resting his hand gently on my arm and looking into my eyes. 'I can see that you are a sincere seeker of truth. I think it is good that you are putting together this book as part of your own spiritual journey.' A rush of adrenalin courses through my being. 'Thank you,' I reply, lost for words and now feeling completely choked. Francis then disappears into the white light of the garden.

A 'freedom theories expert' – that's me all over. Well, at least, that's what I'm trying to be. Over the past couple of months, my mind has been cataloguing and categorizing every teacher that I've met, comparing them with the great sages like Ramana and Nisargadatta, and then repackaging them to discuss them on paper or to pontificate about at great length with tolerant friends. Whatever happened to that pure impulse to go and sit with contemporary teachers of non-duality in order to taste the bliss of silence, the all-pervading consciousness, the very essence of my being? I am becoming lost in the theory of understanding, instead of dedicating myself to its practice; I am more than ever fixated with the plethora of interpretations rather than discovering my own inner truth. I start to feel nauseated by my intellectual vanity, my strutting about with armfuls of books and a sleek black camera bag hanging provocatively over one shoulder. Just who the hell am I kidding?

When I return home, I start to think about Krishnamurti and his famous quote about truth being a pathless land. I forage through my bookshelves to look for his works but without much success and so turn to the Internet for help. I hit the home page of Jiddu Krishnamurti, where there is an excerpt from one of his famous speeches:

> *Man cannot come to it through any organization, through any creed, through any dogma, priest or ritual, nor through any philosophic technique. He has to find it through the mirror of relationship, through the understanding of the contents of his own mind, through observation and not through intellectual analysis or introspective dissection. Man has built in himself images as a fence of security — religious, political, personal. These manifest as symbols, ideas, beliefs. The burden of these images dominates man's thinking, his relationships and his daily life. These images are the cause of our problems, for they divide man from man.*
>
> J Krishnamurti

Vijai Shankar

CHAPTER SIX

THE HOUSE OF
GOD

Pollen from the Casablanca lilies I hold as an offering to the guru dusts my jacket and cheek. I keep reminding myself to take off my shoes when I go in. Like so many homes of the Indian community in north-west London, Kalpna Dave's semi-detached, Harrow and Wealstone residence is outwardly non-descript but reveals itself within as a temple in praise of God.

Indian spices and frankincense stain the air, Vedic memorabilia bedeck every room. In the lounge, a majestic shrine to Sri Sathya Sai Baba dominates half of one wall — photographs and paintings of Sri Shirdi Sai Baba and his reincarnation, Sri Sathya Sai Baba, are peppered with *vibhuti* or holy ash. Mala beads hang over portraits of Krishna and Radha, Siva and Parvati, Hanuman and Ganesh; on the altar, an *Om* sign is written in rice.

I am particularly excited about coming to talk with Vijai. It seems a little ironic that he is the first non-Western teacher I will be speaking to — the Advaita teaching having always tended to be more the province of the Indian sage. I wonder if his interpretation will be different in any way. Somehow I imagine it will be embellished with superstition and mystery. Perhaps he will tell me about the stories of Krishna and Rama, the importance of Indian rituals and the magical powers of the Ganga.

Vijai's round and cheeky face — his left eyebrow soaring up towards heaven — greets me with loving respect. He is wearing the traditional *kurthapyjama*, giving him an exotic and dignified grace. He shows me through into the dining room at the back of the house, a very simple and modest room in contrast to the kaleidoscopic vision of the lounge. Kalpna, his devoted assistant, appears from the next-door kitchen, a living embodiment of an Indian goddess, the silk of her emerald-green sari swishing imperially as she enters. We greet each other with *namaste*; she smiles humbly, averting her gaze in an act of pious supplication.

Vijai was born in Bangalore in South India in the late forties. His initial interest in spirituality was inspired by his mother as well as his elder brother. Later, as he was growing up, Vijai was also influenced by the writings of Sri Ramana Maharshi and Sri Nisargadatta Maharaj, so much so that he was compelled to discover the ultimate meaning of existence. Embarking therefore on a search that would lead him to a meeting with Sri Sathya Sai Baba at the age of 16, he subsequently had the first glimpse of his true Self. In the early seventies, he was initiated into *tapas* by Sri Sivaramakrishna.

Vijai trained as a medical doctor, first working in India and then in Africa, specializing in cardiology and kidney diseases. In 1986, he came to London where he gained a Doctorate in Philosophy from the University of London. This led him to teaching at medical school as a research scientist in cellular and molecular biology. It was around this time that something occurred that was to completely shatter his ego – a fall from worldly favour but it is not an event that he will disclose. In 1997 Vijai moved to the United States, initially staying in a small garage apartment in Galveston. Now he lives in a new home built in Houston, Texas – the Kaivalya Shivalaya Ashram, the Abode of the Absolute.

Like many of his fellow Advaitins, Vijai has his own web site, giving details of his schedule of talks, directions to his ashram and interviews and comments from devotees. There is also a reminder of what I am:

> *A drop of water falling as rain into the sea dissolves into the ocean. It does not lose its dropness but it gains the whole ocean. It is the same with the personal 'I'. When it dissolves in the heart of awareness it gains the entire universe.*

It is difficult to conceive that I am in London, as I listen to Vijai and Kalpna jabbering away in Gujarati. Kalpna smiles at me and says that Vijai remembers me from a satsang he gave just a couple of months before in Kensington. As is the tradition at the end of darshan, everyone proceeded to line up in front of the teacher to receive *prasad*. In turn, each person knelt before Vijai, bowing graciously before him, whilst he dispensed a handful of white and red grapes into their outstretched palms. When my turn came, I too followed the ceremonial drill. 'May God bless you, my child,' said Vijai, pouring the sweetest affection into my eyes. 'And may God bless you too!' I impulsively replied. At these words Vijai looked up at the ceiling, bellowing with laughter. 'That's *so* sweet!' he chuckled, as I surmised that my words were possibly not quite the right thing to say.

As I start the tape recorder, Vijai waits meekly like a little boy, his fingers intertwined and resting on the table in front of us. As I ask my first question, he raises his eyes and rests them in mine. Suddenly his face contorts into a wry twist, he unlaces his hands and starts poking the air with his finger, his head bobbing in the familiar Indian fashion. His voice has an undulating quality, rising and falling, speeding up and slowing down, depending on the point he wants to make. At the end of an important philosophical point, he flicks his tongue against the upper palate, creating a popping sound, as if to give added emphasis, a full stop to the final proof.

Vijai loves to be provoked – the more you challenge him, the more excited he becomes, his arms gesticulating wildly, like the conductor of an orchestra. Throughout our conversation he continues to tease me, gently pushing me along to follow his line of thinking. You get the impression that talking about God is the only subject worth opening your mouth for – his personal life an irritating distraction, which he dismisses with a brush of his hand.

Kalpna makes the lunch. She waits at table for us, as is the custom, bringing in dish after dish of Indian delights. 'Won't you eat with us?' I ask. 'No, no!' she emphatically replies. 'It is a *pleasure* for me to serve you. In India, a guest is regarded as an embodiment of God. I am truly honoured that He should come to my home and bless us with His presence.'

I know that the truth can't be spoken about in words . . .

Why, Paula, can't the truth be conveyed by words? You should be very clear about why the truth cannot be conveyed by words. It cannot be. Why?

There are a couple of reasons for it. Now supposing there is an event that happened outside your house. Let's call that event an accident between two cars and let us assume that there were 10 people who saw that event. And you are well within your house and you have not witnessed it. So, you would like to know. You let these 10 people who saw this event come, one by one, to let you know. You let the first person in and he tells you what happened and he goes out. The second enters and he says what he saw and goes away. If you complete the list of 10, you will be surprised to find that all 10 are different versions. Therefore, an event can never be conveyed by words. All of them will succeed only to convey their opinion.

So, too, the words that they use will always belong to time and space. But they only belong to your mind. Every word has got two meanings – one internal, the other external. One verbal, the other non-verbal.

What does that mean?

I will tell you what it means! I will tell you one word and you describe that word, what you imagine it to be by your mind. Let me say only one word, OK! 'River'. Describe what that word conveys to you.

It is a stretch of water that flows from a high place to a low place.

No, don't give me a definition of the word. I said 'river' to you. Describe the word as it appeared to your mind when I said the word 'river'.

I saw blue water, a green bank on either side. I saw rippling waves on the surface.

Beautiful! The river that I meant was a small one, there was no greenery around, no mountains around, hardly a few fishes, grime is floating on the water. So, every word carries two meanings. One is the common, external meaning and the other is an internal, personal meaning. Everybody can only latch on to the external, common meaning and then thinks what he or she wants to think about it. But nobody can enter or penetrate or come in contact with this internal, personal meaning. If one word has got two meanings, a whole sentence has got so many words in it – that's the root cause of so many arguments and discussions everywhere.

The wife will say, 'Why did you say that to me?' The husband will say, 'I did not say that!' 'What do you mean you did not say it? I heard you, I heard you!' 'Yes, you heard me but that's not what I meant.' 'There you go again. You said it but you say you do not mean it!' And he will say the same thing to her and she will say the same thing to him and nobody is able to get to the internal meaning – that's the root cause of all divorces, all arguments, all fights, all discussions . . .

All religions!

Everything, everything! You can elaborate around those terms. If someone says, 'I'll speak about the truth', it means non-verbally, he has accepted the existence of false. The untruth is lingering somewhere behind, which means he has accepted something that is untrue.

Truth is a relative word?

Exactly. Nobody can speak about the truth because there is nothing called 'truth'. For every truth there is an untruth, you see. You follow what I am saying?

I follow exactly what you are saying.

So go ahead, my child. I shall not be speaking about the truth. I shall only tell you things as it is – illusion, the maya, which in reality appears as this unreality. It is a reality that appears as this unreality. Unreality is the appearance of the reality. But it's not the reality.

I'm confused.

It can seem very confusing, my child. But it shouldn't be confusing!

It's all such a paradox.

Life is a paradox!

I do not exist and yet here I am!

No, you exist as the pure Self. You appear as the non-Self. What is the colour of your cardigan?

It's blue.

You say it's blue. But I would say that's not at all the colour of the cardigan – it's everything else *but* blue. And that's the illusion. I'll explain why to you.

From a scientific definition, it absorbs all colours other than blue.

Exactly. The light absorbs all the colours of the rainbow and the one it cannot imbibe, it exhibits it. That's the maya, which is the illusion. You think something is real of something that is unreal.

What does 'real' mean?

'Real' means 'as it is'. 'Real' means that which is permanent – it does not appear or disappear. 'Real' is something that is permanently there. It is not something that is only there in the daytime – 6am to 9pm. It should be there even when you go to sleep.

OK, I get that. But I find this word 'illusion' troubles me. Take this table. I know it doesn't have reality in the sense that it won't necessarily be here in 2,000 years time, but it's real enough now!

It is unreal in the sense that it's not permanent. It's disintegrating even now. How can you call it permanent?

But it's not an illusion, is it?

It is an illusion in the sense that your conditioned mind is conditioned to believe that it's a table, so it creates the illusion that it's there. The conditioned mind has accepted it to be there. I tell you, my child, in your dream, don't you see a table?

Yes, but that's something else.

Why, my child? No, you got up from the dream and you said that this does not exist. You should get up from this dream and what is this dream? This daydream! What is it? Thinking!

But this table is here.

In your dream, too! You should wake up from *this* dream. Meaning? I will tell you what it means. It means the mind is active now, it is flowing, just like the way it was flowing in your dream. You saw the table, here and now; it is flowing like the river you described. The mind is not still.

Yes, I get that.

Good. You are conditioned to believe it is a table, table, table, table — that's the illusion. See, I'll tell you what. If you walk in a desert, wouldn't you see water, pineapples, fruits, in front of you?

Like a mirage?

Exactly. You call it a mirage but isn't it there? Don't people run after it? Have you been to a desert to experience it?

Well, no, but I have certainly seen faces in the patterns of curtains or fires but I know that they don't really exist.

Exactly. You will see what the mind longs to see. Do you follow?

But if I strike my head on this table, it will hurt! Is that still a dream?

Exactly! But it hurts you too in the dream, doesn't it? Doesn't your dream thirst get quenched by dream water?

Sometimes.

Oh no, my child. You are not deep enough in the dream. Of course dream thirst and dream hunger can be satisfied in a dream. Let me tell you exactly what's happening in a dream.

But this table has physicality, the dream world has mentality.

Oh no, this table too has mentality! You say there wasn't physicality in your dream. Weren't you driving your car? Weren't you walking your dog? Weren't you painting your house?

But I could prove that this table exists.

How do you prove it? How?

I . . .

You really think so. Is that true? Where's the proof of your proof?

I think this is just a semantic argument!

This isn't a semantic argument because you are not allowing me to proceed! If your mind remains still, absolutely still . . . OK, let me tell you another thing. Supposing you sit in front of a mirror, what do you see in it?

I see a person in the mirror whom I presume is myself.

Perfect! You will see your hair, your eyes, your eyebrows, your nose, your lips, your cheeks. Now try this, my child. Next time you sit in front of a mirror, you will see the same thing. How do you know that you see it? You see it merely because your mind informs you. Your mind says, 'Head, nose, eyebrows, forehead, cheeks, mouth.' Your mind tells you these things. There's nobody else telling you. Mind repeats it, repeats the previous information.

But you're asking me to deny everything that my experience tells me.

I'm not asking you to deny anything. I am asking you to *perceive*. You are not allowing me to finish this either!

I'm sorry!

When your mind informs you, don't pay attention to it. Just be yourself and watch your reflection. The mind will keep on repeating again and again information of your face in the mirror. Don't pay any attention to it. Not paying attention means not applying the thinking process to it. It will say 'hair' and then suddenly it will be thinking, 'Comb your hair, do this, do that!' See, that's the thinking process already started from the word 'hair'. Don't pay any attention. If it says 'cheek', it will see a small spot and you'll want to take it out, and again the thinking process has started.

As time goes by, as days go by, you will sit in front of the mirror. This is an exercise, an experimental exercise, not a pattern, not a technique, not a method. It will again tell you, inform you after many days, as long as your mind is not still. After a while, there will come a time when the mind will tell you 'hair', and then there will be a gap, and after some time 'cheek', and then after some more time 'chin'. A time will come when it will stop informing you because you are not giving any attention to your preconditioned mind. You are not paying any attention to the mind informing you that this is the face. Mind will not inform you. A time will come when the reflection will be there but it will not inform you. What has happened then, can you tell me?

There'll be nothing there.

Exactly. There won't be a reflection there, my child. The mirror will be there but the face won't be there. There will not be a reflection. That is what I say. You do not see objects, you see the thought of the object being there.

You would still see a mirror?

Yes, you would see a mirror as a thought but there won't be a face there, for there is no thought of the face.

But there will be colours and shapes in the mirror.

Nothing! There will just be a plain mirror. Your mind has become still. That's what I am trying to tell you. That's what the rishis have been saying – it's an illusion, the play of light and sound. You mean to say that there are men on the silver screen? You think Brad Pitt is there kissing somebody?

Oh, I do, I do!

Is he there really on the screen? Where is the movie? You should stand back and see the movie at the back and not at the front. On the screen is the play of light and sound, creating images, creating tables, the play of light and sound. Existence itself has created a movie, existence itself is a cinema director. This is what I am doing in life. This is a play of light and sound. *Nada* and *bindu* are the two Sanskrit words used for it. *Nada* is sound and *bindu* is light. The rishis have said this years, centuries ago, my child. This is not saying something new. If you decondition the mind to say 'table', if the mind is absolutely still, there is not a ripple. There wouldn't be even light there, water or anything else. Trust me! Your ego, 'I', is in the waking state. Once the 'I' goes right inside and gets sunk into your conscious- ness, you attain your sleeping state in the waking state.

Your sleeping state in the waking state?

That means that your 'I' is no longer operative. Your ego, you have pulled it down and you are there, in samadhi. And once you have reached it, you have opened your eyes, there will be light and nothing else besides that. And then you bring the ego out to function within the physical body and then everything appears. The problem is that people who talk about truth don't know what they are talking about.

[Vijai starts to draw some diagrams explaining the layers of the body.] You see, there is the physical body. Do you follow what I am saying, my child? It has got a corresponding physical mind, OK? This area – this is where people are, identified with their body and their mind. If you go deeper down, this is what you call *annamaya kosa* in Sanskrit. *Anna* means food, maya is illusion and *kosa* is a sheath. And then you go more inside and you have what is called *pranamaya kosa*, which can be translated into English as 'etheric body or astral body', OK? *Prana* means life.

And after the astral body, you have the intelligent body or what we call the *vijnanamaya kosa*. After that you have your soul or *atman*. And that's what they call the *anandamaya kosa*. *Ananda* means bliss. You follow what I'm saying? Up to the *anandamaya*, the mind extends – the etheric mind, the astral mind, the intelligent mind and 'I' operate from here, right through all these *kosa*. So strong is the illusion, the 'I' is there, the consistency of objects will be there, the name, the shape, the colour. Now bring the 'I' right from the *anandamaya* and immerse it in your *atman*, you follow me?

But why is it that way?

That is the illusion that the Lord has created. That is his magic, that is his creation. What is this? [Vijai points to a pen.]

I don't think I know anymore!

It is a pen, isn't it? Do you think anything such as 'a pen' exists? It is a bit of plastic, isn't it? Not a pen. Do you see the illusion? Do you follow what I am saying? People say they are wearing a ring. That is an illusion, isn't it?

It's just gold?

You got it, my child. You got it! Not even gold.

Just molecules?

You got it! Look at that building. You mean to suggest that anything such as 'building' exists? Can you give me building? Can you examine a building? What would you give me – rock! Look at the illusion, the maya. Green colour, red colour – it is the play of light! There isn't anything called 'colour'. It's just the play of light. Multiple colours are colours that are non-existent.

Plato said that all these forms and ideas are held in a subtle way somewhere in the universe – horses and buildings are held in the realm of forms. The world is a manifestation of these subtle forms.

As a thought form, yes. The whole world is a thought form.

Whose thought?

Consciousness. You call it whatever you want. Awareness. [Vijai draws another diagram.] This awareness in the East is known as Siva, OK? And then there is reflected awareness. When awareness reflects itself it becomes consciousness. Consciousness is kinetic, it's moving. Awareness is static. You follow? Awareness is called Siva and once it becomes kinetic it becomes Shakti. This entire consciousness is all vibrating. The initial vibration gave rise to the word *Om*, OK? So, *Om* creates space, water, earth, then fire, then air. It started vibrating.

Out of these five manifestations, the whole universe came into being as animate and inanimate. You follow me? And each 'animate' and 'inanimate' are points of consciousness. And each point of consciousness, each *atman* – which is the same as every body – has got a small mind. Mind is of the *atman*, a partial mind compared to the whole universe. Everything is appearing in this consciousness as a reflection. So each one has got a mind, reflected in one way. Can anyone see your mind, Paula?

No.

Exactly, Paula. Because that's *your* mind, *your* individual mind. So, all these individual minds are held by the super-mind here – that's consciousness. You see what I am saying? That's the thought form, the whole thing is a thought form.

Are even the elements of water and earth and fire just thoughts?

Yes.

They don't really have any existence?

No, not at all. Those were the first thoughts that appeared as air, water, fire and earth. And from that boom, the universe manifested!

So even this table is a thought?

Most certainly, my child. Do you know why I say it is thought? No?

Because . . .

Because? You must be sure that you know why.

Because it is a mental construct.

Why? Now listen to me. You must be sure.

Go on . . . tell me . . . I want to be free, Dr Shankar . . . and I want to know!

You have been with me for how long, my child?

Talking relatively, I have been here about half an hour.

And previously? When we met before?

I also listened to you for about three hours in the past giving a talk.

Exactly, so be patient. In three and a half hours, you want to know who you are! Be patient, I'll get you there! No matter how hard we try, the mind will say, 'I am seeing a pen'. You are right when you say that you are seeing a pen. I do not deny it. But pray, tell me. Do you think your eyes can see a pen? Supposing there is a 20-year-old healthy boy. He dies and, the very minute he dies, he still has his eyes there. Can his eyes see the pen? He's got a brain there. Can his eyes see this pen?

Not if he is dead.

But he's got eyes, hasn't he?

But there's no animated consciousness left within him.

Exactly. So, if eyes really see this pen, his eyes should still see the pen, isn't it, my child. Are you with me so far?

Yes. I understand what you are saying.

Now, second point. Is the pen moving towards your eyes? Do you think your eyes have got a capacity of receiving 'pen'? What are the eyes receiving, my child? What is the eyes' function? Is it not the eyes' function to receive light? What else? The function of the eyes is to receive light. Only light can enter the pupil – not pen, not trees . . .

It's just reflected light.

And it's reflected light! It is not light per se. Light the eyes cannot see. It only sees reflected light. Now, reflected light comes straight out of these atoms, quarks and super quarks and so on as energy and your eyes receive light, my child. And then it goes . . . Can I use your pen?

Of course, that's if it really is a pen!

[Vijai draws more diagrams with great enthusiasm.] Light waves go into the eye, OK? Light waves are transmitted by optic nerves and they go behind your brain. The light waves reach the back of the brain and there physiologists stop because they do not know what happens. Then the psychologists come into play and they say these light waves are converted by your mind and the mind says 'pen'. You follow me? Now what is your mind? Your mind is nothing but a bundle of thoughts, isn't it, my child? What is it? Your mind is nothing but a bundle of thoughts! So, what you see is a thought and not 'pen'.

I agree that the mind is just a bundle of thoughts but it must have certain properties and characteristics and . . .

Those too will be thoughts . . .

Yes, but I see that object as a pen and you would also agree that you too see a pen?

As long as you are in your physical mind, physical body, yes.

But a lot of other people would agree that is also a pen. So there must be a commonality of these thoughts.

Exactly.

So it must have a mental construct of some sort.

Exactly. There are conditioned constructs everywhere. You mean to say that when a five-year-old child comes, this is what happens. [Vijai draws another diagram.] This is your life from zero to 70. At five years, your self, your *atman*, sees a cat, OK? He will see a cat. You follow me? Now, the mummy will tell the child, 'See child, cat, cat, cat, see child, cat, cat, cat.' The child will just look. The mummy has just destroyed the child's existence because the child was simply enjoying the cat, not as a cat . . .

But as it is.

As it is! The child does not know where the cat begins and where the cat ends. The child was experiencing the Oneness of existence appearing as so many different forms. And he was thoroughly enjoying it not as a mental thought but as existence itself, just glorified. The colour of the cat was his own colour, he had no concepts of its colour. Then the mother keeps hammering into him 'cat, cat, cat' – the child doesn't know. Then the child says 'cat' and the mother is thrilled to bits. The mother thinks the child has become knowledgeable but mum doesn't know the child has become stung!

Conditioned?

You got it! Now, you've got a cat here. Then after some time, what happens? A dog comes along, OK? And the mummy says, 'What is this?' Do you know what the child will say?

Cat?!

You got it right! The mummy says, 'Oh, my child, it is a dog.' So she tries to teach the child, 'Dog, dog, dog, not cat, not cat, not cat.' One day that child will say, 'Dog, dog, dog,' and the parents will be proud. Like that, my child – pen, table, everything was conditioned to you, not in this lifetime, but how many generations has the conditioning been going on. Because it has been going on for so many generations, it appears real to you.

But there must have been a first person, whoever that was, who wasn't conditioned. Why did the conditioning start in the first place?

My child, it didn't start at all. The illusion is just created by the mind. As it is. It is an appearance to disappear. That is the drama, that's the *leela*, that is the illusion. How beautiful it is.

So it's OK that the child thinks cat or dog – there's nothing wrong in that?

Most certainly, there's nothing wrong in that. There's nothing wrong in conditioning. As long as you tell the child as it grows up to be aware that the mind is simply naming and labelling existence. You should be aware that the mind is simply naming and labelling existence. The mind is nothing but names and labels of existence. Give it a sticker, give it a sticker, give it a sticker! It is simply identified. There will come a point in time when you realize that, when you open your eyes, seeing stops, identification begins. When you close your eyes, identifications stops and seeing really begins. You understand what I am saying?

Got it!

Great! Now, I will tell you something, so listen very carefully. Everybody wants to find the meaning of life, yes? It only goes to show that they haven't found it up to now. It only means that the meaning of life is far ahead of them in the future – they have to find it. Somewhere, not here, but somewhere. You follow me? It's the end. It's not yet the middle or the beginning, it's somewhere at the end. That is the fallacy. That's why he is not able to find out the meaning because he thinks that the meaning of life is in the end.

Why do I say that? I say that because of this. Listen! If there's a seed that has become a rose, you know that in the packet you have got rose seeds. You know when you plant the seed in the ground that it will blossom into a rose, isn't it? You know the meaning of the rose is in the seed because you know they are rose seeds. Now you put a rose seed in the ground. Will you start panicking because it might become a lotus or a daffodil or a sunflower. Will you panic? What's the meaning of this? You will not panic because you know the meaning, you know the source of it. You follow what I am saying?

I follow what you are saying. But if that source is within me, why do I not know that intrinsically, right from the start?

It's not that you are lost in your reality, you are simply lost in your dreams. That is why.

But why? If I am God and I am amazing, why does a little speck of dust, which is my dreams, obscure my true nature?

Because your mind is attentive on that which is not. Your mind is busy in the morning – table, pen. You're continuously naming, you're continuously running away. I told you the definition of thinking – thinking is nothing but dreaming in the waking state.

But God put that thinking there.

For you to realize that you are dreaming!

It's like God has created a trap.

Well, get out of it! The drama is over. There's a director who makes a drama, the drama is going on, the spectators are watching. You need to become the director. If you become the director you will be able to watch this drama and then you will become happy.

This is the bit I never understand. If I am God, why don't I realize it!

It is because, my child, your mind is not still. Your thinking process – you're giving attention to it. The thinking process hasn't been completed as yet. You are still thinking and thinking and thinking. You have to become a master of your mind. The body is a wheel and the centre is the axle. You have to become an axle in the centre of the wheel. The whole wheel of life turns and turns and, when you are not bothered, everything disappears.

When will my thinking mind be still?

The moment you say 'when', my child, the mind has jumped into the future. 'When' indicates future. Future is non-existent. You will never be there.

At what point will my mind be still?

I'll tell you, if you proceed with this, it will be still. [Vijai draws more diagrams.] This is the present, OK? This is the past and this is the future – past, present, future. Where is the past? Is there any place where the past is stored?

No.

Are you very sure? Maybe the past is somewhere behind Iceland somewhere?

The past is back here in my mind.

Exactly. What I mean to say is that there is no space where the past is stored. Nobody can bring the past in my hand for me to objectively analyze. It's all a thought, isn't it? Now, what about future? Do you think there is a space where there is future you can go, find out what's happening and come back to the present? So what's the future?

Just a thought.

And what is the future if not a strengthened past which is projected into a non-existent time scale? And the future is nowhere else but in your mind. You got it now?

I got it now!

Good, so there's no future too. There's only the present. Present means there must be something called time if you want to call it present.

It seems that time doesn't exist in the present.

Exactly. Past indicates time, isn't it? Present indicates time, isn't it? Future . . .

Yes, present is relative to past and future.

Exactly, exactly! Now what's the fundamental characteristic of time? When you say time, what has penetrated that word 'time'?

Movement?

Movement. Time is measured by movement. Time has also got something called duration. If there is no duration, there is nothing that can be called time. Time always has to do with five minutes, one hour, three hours, six, seven, it has a duration. When you talk about time, you say how long. That is duration, isn't it? Duration has a beginning, it has a middle, and it has an end. That's the duration. Tick, tick, tick . . . So, time has got a beginning, it has a middle, it has got an end. You follow what I am saying?

Now, let us come to the present. The moment I say 'present', the 'pr' has gone in the past, the 'es' has gone into the past, 's' and 'en' have gone into the past and the 't' has gone into the past. Do you follow? You cannot even say 'present' in the present, my child. You can only respond to the now where there's no time! There is no present.

We are in the constant flow of the *now*. You are always in the now! That is why nobody can speak about the truth because, the moment you say something, one word has already gone in the past. You have to link up, you are living a dead life. You are not fresh, you are not alive. If you are suspended now, then you are alive. Then your mind becomes still. What can you think in the now? What can you judge in the now? What can you criticize in the now? What can you interpret in the now? What can you say about anything in the now? You have become the now. You have become existence. You are flowing. You have come home. Do you follow?

It's beautiful, my child. You've got to melt in the now. The only way to melt in the now is to watch your thoughts as they come and don't apply your thinking process to them. Let them come, watch them, witness them, don't interpret them, whether good or bad or right or wrong. What authority do we have to judge them being right or wrong?

I think you have made everything very clear and precise. I spent about 10 years studying Advaita theory . . .

Advaita is not a theory. Advaita was seen by the rishis – they had to use that word because Advaita is a beautiful word, which means 'not two'. They included duality in Advaita.

You recently spoke about the reason why we use the word Advaita, which means 'not two', and not the word ekant, *which means 'one'.*

The rishis were so clever. When you say 'one', there is only one. One has got a meaning in relation to two, isn't it? That means when you say 'one', you admit there are two already. You see? You say there is only one but in the back of your mind, there are two. One has got a meaning in reference to two, my child.

Truth and untruth?

You got it! So they say Advaita, which means not two. Not two! Even *dvaita* is included in Advaita because *dvaita* is Advaita. Advaita is here and *dvaita* is there – duality, an appearance. *Dvaita* enhances Advaita. Appearance enhances reality. Existence sees itself dressed up. You see? It is simply an appearance. It is not the reality.

The appearance exists within the reality.

You got it!

This is the thing – appearance or illusion is OK and this is the way that reality plays itself.

You got it! So you enjoy the illusion!

I shouldn't deny it?

No! You should not!

I don't have to be detached?

How can you be detached? If you got it, enjoy it! If you've got yourself a Mercedes, enjoy it. You did not get it, it was *given* to you. That is the stand you take. It happened to come by. The Lord gave you something. I mustn't say, 'I got it, it's mine'. That is the illusion – to say that's mine. That's what gives you bondage.

There's a lovely sentence that you sometimes use – 'I'm not a human being having a spiritual experience. I'm a spiritual being having a human experience.'

Most certainly, you are a spiritual being having a *humane* experience. If you consider yourself to be a human being, wanting a spiritual experience, you're on a dead end because all experiences are in the presence of your mind, isn't it? It's all within time and space. All experiences are separate and bounded and chained within the concept of time and space. That is why it is called an experience, isn't it? A divine being bound by time and space? When you are in the now, you are experiencing the experiencing.

And there's no experiencer?

Exactly! If you are in the now, you will be experiencing the experiencing. You will not be experiencing the experienced. If you are experiencing the experienced, you are living a dead life. You follow me? You become the mystery now when you are experiencing the experiencing. You become the flow. The existence has become one with us. Do you mean to say that the bird knows where it is flying? No, consciousness says, 'Look, I can do what I want in that form. I'll do what I want in this form, too!' Don't think that you are doing it. You follow?

Yes!

Beautiful!

One last question, then.

One last question and that's it?! What is your last question, my child? You must remember that it is not the function of the mind to receive an answer. Put it down in black and white. The function of the mind is always to question and not to receive an answer. But it keeps propagating, 'I want an answer, I want an answer!' Why? The moment any answer reaches any mind, the same answer turns into 100 questions. That is the food for its existence. That is why life is not a matter of questions and answers. There is nothing to be solved. Life is not a pattern. You can't dictate life, you can't predict life. If you can, you are better than God! You will have solved his creation. But it is a limitless and manifold manifestation, of endless variety. Endless and beginningless. He is nameless and formless. Now, do you understand why they say he's nameless, do you?

I do.

What is your reasoning, to say he is nameless and formless?

Because, when I try and think about it, I can't attribute any name or form to him.

No, my child. Vishnu gives us a very good clue. There are 1,008 names to God. What do you mean 'that he is nameless'? Listen to me very carefully. People have got it totally wrong, I tell you. You are the God in you, isn't it? God is there in you?

I think so.

You should not be thinking about it. Do you *think* you are alive?

Yes.

Do you need proof that you are alive?

No.

Exactly! There is something alive in you. Do you follow? Consciousness is alive in you. In everybody, isn't it? If everywhere is God, if only God is, which name is his then? He's nameless in the sense that no particular name belongs to him – all names are his! That's why he is nameless. You can put any name for him – Paula, Kalpna, Vijai . . . Everything is his name! And if you say God is Paula, then he is named. He is nameless because you can take any name. That's why there are 1,008 names of Vishnu. Every name is his. The rishis were very clever. They could have given 10,008 names to him!

And that's just the Hindu tradition!

Exactly! Every name is his. That's why he is formless. How can you say he is this form? That means you have only given him that form. This form is his too, that form too is his. Every form is his. That's why he is formless. Because every form belongs to his form, he is formless, he is nameless. You understand? You're different. He's different. The room is different. The cockroach is different. The butterfly is different. The beetle is different. The bug is different. The fly is different. Everything is different – the daffodil, the nightingale. You follow what I am saying?

I tell you a nice story, a nice parable. There was this man, a birdwatcher. He went to watch birds. He took along with him his binoculars and his book of birds. On top of a tree were two woodpeckers. So the birdwatcher was reading about them. One of the woodpeckers flew from the tree and sat on his right shoulder in order to see what he was reading. He read it and then he flew back to the other woodpecker and he said, 'Hey, guess what, we're woodpeckers!'

You should stop, then you will know your true nature. You have forgotten because you have remembered that which you should not remember. You will remember your true nature if you forget all what you have remembered. You follow, Paula? You should be the *sakshi* – that is Sanskrit for the 'witness'.

The realized one is the one who has unlearnt, he is unidentified with all that which he has learnt. What has he learnt – this is mine, this belongs to me, you are my wife . . . Everything belongs to existence. You came with empty hands, you will go with empty hands. These things came by you, this body is using it and it will go. When you melt into life, by becoming mysterious, unpredictable, you'll come home because life is mysterious. Once you become life, you become mysterious too. Nothing will touch you. You will transcend all opposites. All opposites will look like complementary for you. Positive will exist because of negative. For me, everything is nice as it is. It's beautiful. It's perfect. It's imperfectly perfect. Every moment is fresh, Paula. It can never be repeated again.

As I sit here and look at you and I hear what you say, there is no doubt. And I have been in this space before but the buts keep coming back. When will the buts stop?

The moment you stop asking when. That is your barrier. You keep asking me when. When the mind is in the future, my child, I cannot penetrate and bring it back into the now. Recognize your mind saying 'when'. Don't believe anything about it, don't make an effort to stop it. That itself is another effort by the mind. When is it – tomorrow, next week, 2002, 2040? You expect some answers from me. So, I go, 'OK, Paula, 2002.' So what? Do you think your mind will be quiet? You'll be longing for 2002. You'll be restless until that time. It will never happen.

Recognize the mind as saying when. When the mind does not say when, you're home. Nobody is lost in reality. You're only lost in your dreams. That is your thinking. You can never be lost in reality because you are always in reality. It's a falsity to say that you are lost in reality. Find reality! Are you sure you have lost it? Thinking is the dreaming in the waking state and dreaming is the thinking in the sleeping state.

Conquer death before death conquers you.

A couple of weeks later after our interview, I receive a postcard from Washington, depicting the Jefferson Memorial. It is from Kalpna – she is on a world tour with Vijai who is currently giving satsang in America. Headed with the Sanskrit symbol *Om*, it reads, 'This is Dr Vijai and Kalpna saying hello and *namaste* to you. Dr Vijai sends his blessings and lots of love from me too.'

Questioner: Then what am I?

Maharaj: It is enough to know what you are not. You need not know what you are. For, as long as knowledge means description in terms of what is already known, perceptual, or conceptual, there can be no such thing as Self Knowledge, for what you cannot be described, except as total negation. All you can say is: 'I am not this, I am not that.' You cannot meaningfully say, 'this is what I am.' It just makes no sense. What you can point out as 'this' or 'that' cannot be yourself. Surely, you cannot be 'something' else. You are nothing perceivable or imaginable. Yet, without you there can be neither perception nor imagination. You observe the heart feeling, the mind thinking, the body acting; the very act of perceiving shows that you are not what you perceive. Can there be perception, experience, without you? An experience must 'belong'. Somebody must come and declare it as his own. Without an experiencer the experience is not real. It is the experiencer that imparts reality to experience. An experience which you cannot have, of what value is it to you?

Q: The sense of being an experiencer, the sense of 'I am', is it not also an experience?

M: Obviously, every thing experienced is an experience. And in every experience there arises the experiencer of it. Memory creates the illusion of continuity. In reality each experience has its own experiencer and the sense of identity is due to the common factor at the root of all experiencer-experience relation. Identity and continuity are not the same. Just as each flower has its own colour, but all colours are caused by the same light, so do many experiencers appear in the undivided and indivisible awareness, each separate in memory, identical in essence. This essence is the root, the foundation, the timeless and spaceless 'possibility' of all experience.

Q: How do I get at it?

M: You need not get at it, for you are it. It will get at you, if you give it a chance. Let go your attachments to the unreal and the real will swiftly and smoothly step into its own. Stop imagining yourself being and doing this or that and the realization that you are the source and heart of all will dawn upon you. With this will come great love which is not choice or predilection, nor attachment, but a power which makes all things love-worthy and loveable.

I Am That, Talks with Sri Nisargadatta Maharaj

Mira

CHAPTER SEVEN

A COURSE IN
MIRACLES

I have come to meet Papaji's bride. I arrive at the home of the Ramana Maharshi Foundation, situated in a back street just off the Finchley Road, Hampstead in London. An outwardly modest abode, its deceptively large rooms are collaged with portraits and lined with bookshelves weighted down with the words of the wise.

Mira enters the room. I turn to greet her. Her face bursts into a smile as she fixes me intently with her grey-flecked eyes – like the gaze of a lover, their slightly contracted, penetrating shape makes my heart race. Her long, sun-bleached blonde hair is draped around her tanned face. She looks more like a sixties model than the widow of one of India's most revered gurus. She kisses me on both cheeks and says, 'Allo, Pola,' in a high-pitched, exotic Belgian accent. We go up a steep blue-painted staircase and into a small back room, overlooking a railway, from where we can hear the sound of trains, ringing and rumbling in the distance.

The first thing that hits you about Mira Pagal is that she is so outrageously herself. By being utterly spontaneous, unashamedly outspoken almost, she manages to defy any notion about how a so-called spiritual teacher should be. A couple of Mira's friends come in and sit behind us as we begin to talk, careful not to disturb the intimacy of the moment. I am surprised that I do not feel threatened by the sudden arrival of an audience. There is just something about Mira that puts everyone at their ease – her laughter, her caricatures of sadness and joy.

Mira was born in Belgium in 1947 but, at the age of only three months, she went to live in Africa – the Belgian Congo – until she was 13. 'I knew I was in paradise,' she reflects. 'My childhood was wild and happy and sunny.' Nevertheless, following the independence of the colony, she had to return to Belgium, knowing that her idyllic childhood days were over. 'When you fall from what you know, when you lose paradise, you just ask what happened. What's reality? All those metaphysical questions arose, which I was totally unable to answer. So I started searching in the arts, thinking that I could find something else and something more true.'

Her initial efforts went unrewarded nonetheless. At 18, she decided to go to university to study archeology and the history of art but it was still a very dark period of her life. 'Then one day I read the famous phrase of Socrates – 'Know thyself' – and this jumped like a tiger on my heart. It spoke directly to me and I knew that it was what I had been searching for. Immediately I made a decision to find a living Socrates or living Buddha and three days later, I was on the road with onions, bread and a bottle of wine, hitch-hiking to India!'

With only a little money, she first travelled to what was then Yugoslavia, staying in a small village where she met some local gypsies and danced and sang with them all through the night. 'The next day I was totally blank, and I said, "Oh God, I will never make it!" From that moment I didn't touch a drop of wine and I started really seriously to find my guide.' Crossing over to Istanbul, she picked up the hippie trail, taking her in the direction of India.

After travelling around for many months, meeting different sadhus and swamis, she reached the point where she yearned to be completely on her own in order to contemplate 'cosmic consciousness'. With only one dress and a towel, Mira retired to a cave close to the river Ganga. When she was finally down to her last rupee, she decided to make the most of it by spending it in a local café. She was absorbed in a book of poems by Kabir, when an Indian man entered the café and approached her, asking whether she needed any help with her study. Defiantly, she turned down his offer but the Indian man persisted in saying that, if she were to change her mind, he could always be found at five o'clock in the morning on the banks of the Ganga. The following evening, Mira was to see the Indian man again – this time in her dreams. It was then that she knew she had met her living Socrates. The next morning, Mira set off very early to wait for Poonjaji at the river's edge.

Inasmuch as I have enjoyed the mental rhetoric of the male teachers I have interviewed so far, there is a completely different energy experienced in the presence of a female teacher. Perhaps it takes a woman to know a woman. But it seems that the integrity of a woman is subtler somehow; more a question of intuition, almost. In the Hindu tradition, the creative aspect of Brahman, the divine, is perceived as being feminine. Shakti is the energy through which the entire universe arises:

> The quality of being divine appears in that in which there is most energy. It is only when the qualityless, shapeless, motionless substratum becomes 'spotted through' by the great energy, centre of limitless energies, that the universe can be created, maintained, and destroyed. Without energy, Siva, the lord of sleep, is unable to create or destroy, is as powerless as a corpse. The divinity of divinity rests upon energy.

She is the power of the Self; she it is who creates appearances.

'*Sri Bhagavati tattva*', Siddhanta V
Karapatri

We go outside to take Mira's photograph. Everyone else joins us and after the shoot we go for a stroll around the back streets of Hampstead. The afternoon sun beats relentlessly down on the pavements. Mira's china-blue *salwar kameez* quivers in the light stirring breeze.

As we walk, Mira admires the trees and flowers that greet us on our route – overwhelming beauty is everywhere. Why have I not noticed it before? As we walk, Mira chats impulsively, laughing and smiling with all of us, our hearts full of joy, our souls perfectly at peace. And as we walk, people passing by turn to see who Mira is. Is she famous, a celebrity? What's all the commotion about? And I think, it's just life.

When did you arrive in India?

It must have been early September '68. I stopped for three months in Afghanistan, in Kabul. In the countryside there was a Sufi master and for me it was the first time I had met a saint. Of course he didn't speak English but his presence just gave me a taste. But somehow there were still a lot of intellectual questions, so that was not enough. So I went to Delhi and I didn't know where to go because I didn't want to have any addresses of known gurus. I really had the conviction that I would just meet the one I needed. I went to the Himalayas and then to Ganga where I started to meditate for three months.

You met a guru called Chandra Swami?

Yes. I was in Sapt Sarovar, which is upstream from Hardwar. I was wandering around one afternoon trying to find a good place to meditate. I crossed a little arm of the Ganga to go to an island and there I saw a wonderful being of light. He was beautiful – the picture of a yogi. He was quite naked and had a long black beard. So I came to Chandra Swami and sat and then he spoke to me in English! I was amazed – it was very good English. He was very learned. I asked him if I could visit him every afternoon and at some point I asked him if he could initiate me. But after a month or so I felt that I still needed more answers to my questions – and they were burning questions.

What were the questions?

My first worry when I started to meditate was that many people give different ways of meditation and I wanted the short cut. And some say it's through devotion, some say it's through *jnana* or knowledge. Although I was at the beginning of the search, I wanted the top, you know. So, what to do? I thought at that time that cosmic consciousness was the reality so I was searching for that. At some point, I left everyone because I wanted to be by myself and really see. So, I went to live in a nearby cave.

And then you were down to your last rupee . . .

Yes, I went to a café and this man came and he said, 'Do you need some help, my dear child?' And I said, 'No thank you!' I was really determined not to listen to anybody. So he said, 'Well, if you need any help, I am there in the morning at five o'clock at the bank of the Ganga.' I thanked him and I didn't look much at his face. I wanted that everybody just leave me alone. He left and the next day I did my usual thing of washing my robe and myself and meditating on the bank of the Ganga.

But in the night, his face came and said, 'Maybe it's me that you search,' and that was enough to bring me there at five, of course! It was the same face. So, when I came, he laughed very loudly and I felt it was a very warm welcome. I sat in front of him and the Ganga was flowing by. He asked me simply, 'What do you want?' It was just direct like this and I said, 'Cosmic consciousness and if you know more, the 'more' as well!' I realized that if I could know more, I wanted that 'more' because I knew that the mind with its limits thinks *it* is always the top. He said, 'What do you do for that?' and I said, 'I meditate.' 'Show me!' So I showed him how I did it and after a while, I just opened my eyes and I looked at the Ganga, at the sky, and very slowly I remember – it's still alive – and I uttered, 'It's so simple.' I just fell down and simultaneously I recognized my master. Then he said, 'Now you go!' *'Mais non!'* I was totally in love! I said, 'I sought you for so long and now I have to stay.' And he said, 'No, no, you go and when you need me I will come.' So I had to leave.

I went but I was not in my so-called normal state. I was in total ecstasy. I left for the forest from the cave. And I remember there was a smell I could not define, which was such an extraordinary smell. I was kissing the trees. The next day, I didn't see him and I didn't know his name. He didn't know my name and I realized that the only known thing between us was that place. There was a little tree with shade and I was absolutely determined to wait for him till I died if it was necessary. So I just stayed there at that spot.

And it looks like eight months passed and one evening, meditating in front of Ganga, I looked behind me and saw this man coming again. He came to me for 10 days, every day at four o'clock in the afternoon. He gave me food, answered my questions. I was living outside and then, one morning, he woke me up at five and said, 'Today you can walk with me all day.' And we went, we chatted and from that day I could be with him all day. So that was just stopping everything. It was perfect.

Would you explain what it was like to be in the presence of Papaji.

You know, it's like when you meet something totally beyond imagination — total fulfilment of whatever craving you may have, total fulfilment of life — you feel a stop, you live in eternity. This is called a presence, real presence. You see, that's the meeting with the master. It stops everything and still a life is pouring out.

And then you never left him.

Yes. We stayed one or two months there and at some point he said that he was going travelling in India. And I said, 'Can I come?' And he said, 'No, I never travel with anybody.' And again I had that devastating feeling — it was very strange because everything was fulfilled. There were no more questions and I don't know why I needed to be with this being. He was very serious and strong and I was quite desperate. In the morning I again asked him. He said, 'When I tell you to go, you go!' And I had to sign a piece of paper! Then we never left each other for years!

Do you still have the piece of paper?!

No, I don't have it anymore. He may have kept it because he knew I was quite careless with things! And so we went to Brindavan. I didn't know this place we were going to. It's the place of Krishna — a divine mad place. In Brindavan, I recognized everything. I knew the lanes, I knew the place, but in a flash, you know, and then all was over. So, some magic started, a total magic. We were thrown into this archetypal place of Radha and Krishna! I was Radha, he was Krishna and we just lived that. And it's true, from that time, it looked like we were divine lovers.

So when did you and Papaji marry?

We were not very traditional. It was when we came back to the Ganga. What does it mean, those celebrations? Every moment was a celebration of this divine marriage. The soul marries and then eventually all the rest does. My first marriage was in the Ganga. But I never took any event as ordinary happenings. There was an extra beauty in them because, on top of everything, I never forgot that he was my master. It is only now that I hear, 'Oh you were husband and wife!' But it was like a total, unknown language because I never related to him like that at the time.

A lot of people speak about the need for a master. Some people say it's not important.

I think there is no law. It looks like in general cases it's such a help and blessing to meet a free soul. But we should not make laws because we are born free and some people do not need a master in this form. In my case, I needed a living master and I needed him many times. I really was determined to finish totally this time this unique journey. Many times we have been together — free and then together again because of some desires or thought.

To meet the living master, the one who points to what is, directly from heart to heart, it is so important in general cases for seekers. It's nothing to do with words, nothing to do with understanding in the end, though understanding is of utmost importance to clarify the search at some point of the journey. A living presence of that silence, of that beingness, helps. It is unique.

I do not feel that I am bringing anything new, yet what is expressed is totally spontaneous. It does not come from memory. I believe any free being also in the past said the same. But we have the arrogance in our time to think that we bring something new! And no doubt, there's a new time coming, which demands quite new ways to say these are big waves, you know. In reality nothing happens for the ocean. The reality, just now, is ever the same.

Why do I create all these problems, all this illusion, and then crave my natural state, which ironically I have all along?

Consciousness can do anything — even that. This is freedom.

Even the veil of ignorance?

Oh yes. Everything. It doesn't exclude anything. So, even that. And also, you see, no one can understand the mystery. This is my understanding. At the same time, personally, I do not pretend that I have a mind subtle enough to always give interesting and intelligent answers!

I recently to spoke to a teacher who said to me, 'You come here with all your fancy intelligent questions. Why don't you just be yourself!'

It is true, yes, but it's good to be inspired this way otherwise you never speak. I do not feel to talk so much. To say the obvious? It's not so easy. So I like these questions — it's very nice. And you know, sometimes you bring something up. I consider it and it gives inspiration. That's why I accept interviews.

When will I find peace? Often, I find in interviews the questions fade away and then there's this silence. I get to the point where I feel I am on the edge of something. There is a knot in my heart and half of me wants to just let go and the other half of me wants to hold on. There is this constant battle within.

You say the questions just fade away. So, this is a fantastic moment. This is satsang in fact. The questions fade away! But then you translate it another way and that's why you get this knot. If you know you are just in satsang, your nature speaks and you *know*. Then you open. But you translate, 'Oh, I feel this and it reminds me of that in the past.' All this comes afterwards and this is wrong interpretation. Just focus on staying here – it all fades away. And this is it, it's your own Self. You see the habit of mind? It wants always to know what's going on and then it's too late. It's lost instead of surrendering. Knowledge is really arrogance. Surrender!

But the mind still wants to make a concept or grab hold of those moments of surrender.

You know, you get a glimpse like that and for some reason it quickly goes. The trouble is that you want to repeat the same glimpse because that glimpse was real. The trick is that reality is ever renewing itself. It will never appear twice in the same way. So, we should not remember even glimpses to be able to live it now. Otherwise we would not recognize it because we would have an idea how reality is, you see. This is the beauty of now. Ever fresh now.

I know that it's here. But something takes me away again.

What took you away? What is here?

There's nothing here now!

OK! Then don't go away! Don't go to memory, otherwise you never give yourself the chance that forever it can stop, all this. You have to give you a chance.

So, what's the next question? Finished?!

Well, I had a whole list of them – all mind questions.

I don't mind!

I keep coming back to the question about why life is set up this way. Why?

But *you* see that. I don't see that. You see, once you lose control of life, once you lose this so-called owner of the personal life, the same life will then not be struggling, it will only be this and that. That's why it is so mysterious. Once you lose the sense of 'I', the same life is totally differently lived. Being blended with the Self is just like consciousness, just like magic. It's unexpected each time. And what you see as troubles before, you will not see them as troubles anymore. So, why this mirage?

I don't understand the difference between the 'I' that thinks that it has its own separate identity and the thing that's within me which makes a decision to surrender.

When this comes — 'Oh, I want to be free!' — this doesn't come from the 'I'. This is grace. This is grace coming through the 'I' to show this soul to be embraced by reality. The 'I' is absolutely unable to decipher its disappearance. So, we can call it grace, we can call it a blessed moment of life, we can call it reality speaking directly.

Is that an act of God's will?

To say that 'I' am fully determined to know truth — this is owing to God's will that the 'I' gets this decision. At the same time, you can say that this 'I' obscures space to God's will, so it is not His will. You know, it depends how you prefer it. I am a bit of a fighter so somehow I have seen too many kinds of situations where people say, 'Oh, it is God's will and this will happen,' and they are just like vegetables, you know! No, I want to kill them in the heart and say, 'You have to fight, you have to desire!' Like that. I feel that this fire is not your own. When it invades, to honour it is just to go with the fire and the 'I' gets burned. It is the fire that goes to the 'I' and tells it, 'Yes, I want freedom!'

In the Indian tradition of yoga (meaning 'union') there are four main paths to the divine. These are *raja* yoga, which focuses on mental concentration and meditation; *karma* yoga, which is concerned with selfless service; *jnana* yoga, which is the path of Self Enquiry and negation of attachment; and *bhakti* yoga, which is the way of devotion.

The *bhakti* movement, one of the most popular paths to union with the Absolute in India today, recognizes the importance and function of the emotional realm. It is also believed that the heart falls in love with that which it knows to be beautiful and true. Harnessing this emotional energy and directing it towards a beautiful teacher in human form can lead to a falling in love and union with that which is beyond the name and the form, a falling in love with Brahman itself.

And with Mira, I experience that I am falling in love. Falling in love with her sensuality, her beauty, her divinity. It is not a mental decision – the mind appears to be temporarily satisfied. It is as if I am being pulled by something beyond my own will. Somehow, I can sense my heart cleaving open and I am truly beginning to feel free.

> *Anyone who wants to pursue this goal correctly must begin by turning to physical beauty, and then if he gets the right guidance fall in love with a particular individual and with him produce thoughts of beauty. He must then perceive that the beauty in one individual is similar to that in another, and that if beauty of form is what he is pursuing it is stupid not to recognize that the beauty exhibited by all individuals is the same. With that recognition he becomes the lover of all physical beauty, and his passion for a single individual slackens as something of small account.*

> *The next stage is for him to reckon beauty of mind more valuable than beauty of body, and if he meets someone who has an attractive mind but little bodily charm, to be content to love and care for him and produce thoughts which improve the young; this again will compel him to look for beauty in habits of life and customs and to recognize that here again all beauty is akin, and that bodily beauty is a poor thing in comparison. From ways of life he must proceed to forms of knowledge and see their beauty too, and look to the fullness of beauty as a whole, giving up the slavish and small-minded devotion to individual examples, whether a boy or man or way of life, and turning instead to the great sea of beauty now before his eyes.*

> *He can then in his generous philosophic love beget great and beautiful words and thoughts, and be strengthened to glimpse the one supreme form of knowledge, whose object is the beauty of which I will now speak . . . For anyone who has been guided so far in his pursuit of love, and surveyed these beauties in right and due order, will at this final stage of love suddenly have revealed to him a beauty whose nature is marvellous indeed, which is the culmination of all his efforts.*

> *The Symposium* Plato

Bharat

CHAPTER EIGHT

MAGICAL MYSTERY
TOUR

you are just there
no future
no past
a table is a table
a chair a chair
just being

all is being

Split Seconds
Bharat

'Woodstock was a wake-up call for me; 500,000 people all full of peace and love,' says Bharat with the look of someone who has seen a thing or two. 'I met the Merry Pranksters of Ken Kesey fame and thought these people were from outer space – turning everyone on with LSD. But that kind of started everything off for me.' Bharat is your veteran hippie, his deeply sun-tanned face almost a testament to his many years journeying around the globe. Although his interest in the science of drugs started out as purely academic – he was taking a university research course in pharmacology – it soon led him to turn that interest into a lifestyle: 'I started experimenting with psychedelics and mushrooms. Then I became a hippie, dropped out of university and got involved in the student demonstrations. I decided I just couldn't be a part of this society any longer.' This is the philosophy by which he has lived ever since.

Bharat and I are sitting opposite each other, cross-legged, on some puffed up multi-coloured meditation cushions. This is one thing you notice about people who have embarked on a process of self-awareness – that there is a notable lack of need for personal body-space. In the beginning, I found this phenomenon disconcerting to say the least; now it comes as almost second nature to sit right up close to someone, so that you can practically smell their breath. His accent is the melody of his many years on the road – a Jewish New-York drawl, overlaid with the incantations of India.

Melvin Rochlin was born in 1948 in New York City to Jewish parents. Although it was a comfortable middle-class life, it wasn't necessarily easy, as his mother was mentally ill. In 1974 Bharat decided to travel to Europe, first stopping off in Paris where he lived for a year, making money by busking with his guitar together with a friend who was a singer. He then travelled south to Greece where he was to meet a man called Magical Mike: 'He was really tall, wearing make-up and earrings and he had spent most of his life in prison.' Magical Mike, tripping on LSD and mustering forth all that narcotic wisdom, told Bharat that, if he was looking for an alternative society, he should make his way to Goa. Bharat took his advice. 'Goa was where for the first time in my life I could be really mad and crazy, but there was also something very real and alive about it. The chemist who was making up the LSD for Ken Kesey was coming over to Goa and giving out acid – there would be thousands of people tripping amidst the palm trees.'

But it was an experience with a pregnant neighbour, a hatha yoga practitioner, which was to push Bharat on the path to find God. She asked Bharat to attend the birth. 'She said, "I'm having this baby in my hut without a doctor. We're going to trust in existence." When the baby was born it was like a hurricane coming through the hut. It was so clear that God was there. I knew I had to find out what this yoga meditation thing was.'

His next spiritual experience happened in Benares, where he went to buy a sitar from a Spaniard called Fernando. One night at Fernando's house, Bharat stepped out onto the verandah. 'All I can say is that God was there again, totally surrounding me – everything disappearing and there being this timelessness. It's hard to describe. Then my mind said, "If God is here, it means I'm going to die." I was totally freaked out.'

However this was to be the first of many out-of-body experiences, the most profound being an encounter with two sadhus in New Delhi. Hanging around outside a store, the first sadhu espied Bharat, beckoning him over with his eyes. 'I thought he was a beggar so I went over to give him some rupees but then he grabbed my arm. His clothes were really immaculate and then I realized, "Oh shit, this isn't a beggar, it's a holy man!"' They went for a stroll in a nearby park where another sadhu joined them. 'The second guy had a hooked nose like the size I had never seen before. He stood in front of me and started making these weird sounds. He then went criss-cross with his hands from the top of my brain to my first chakra. He took my right hand and put it onto my forehead. Then I felt this energy at the base of my spine travel up and explode at the base of my third eye. I left my body – I shot out into the cosmos.' When he recounted the story to Papaji, whom he was to meet some years later, he asked Bharat when the sadhus were talking to him, where *exactly* did they look? 'They weren't looking at my eyes, they were talking to something up there, about a foot or so above my head. It felt like they were talking to a higher Self. I had total ego disillusion and I became One with existence. All the blocks, the fears, the depressions, the suffering – all gone in a split second.' Bharat was to remain in this state for two months but his ego, he says, was soon to return. He was to meet again, albeit briefly, one of the sadhus in an alleyway. He beckoned Bharat to go with him, but he refused – a voice in a recent dream had been calling him to Poona where he knew he must go. 'Then right in front of my eyes the sadhu disappeared – like in Carlos Castaneda when Don Juan opens up a world and steps in.'

Poona was to be Bharat's final stop. Arriving at the station, he hired a rickshaw to take him to any local ashram – he was dropped off at 17 Koregaon Park, the commune of Sri Bhagavan Rajneesh. 'At the desk there was this blonde lady and I said, "What the hell is going on here?" She looked at me with an incredible big smile and said, "Why don't you stay and find out?"' So he did, for the next five years. 'It was like fantasy island – relationships and sex and drugs. Plus there was this great Osho – hearing his discourses was like hearing the Sermon on the Mount. He encouraged us to be like "Zorba the Buddha" – living life to the fullest as a Zorba and being detached as a holy man.' Bharat thus became a sannyasin, hoping to regain the experience with the sadhus in New Delhi.

Even though Bharat found moments of freedom, he became deeply resentful towards Osho when all the scandals broke out. 'We all felt betrayed because we had put our trust in him. The ecstasy of living in Poona had turned into an agony.' And the elusive prize of egolessness was still unclaimed. But that was soon to change.

When did you meet Papaji?

In 1991, I was in Poona and I heard about Papaji via a fax from a friend. It mentioned a guy who had been to visit Papaji and had said that he got enlightened in two weeks. At first I thought this was nonsense. I knew the guy and I just thought he must have got freaked out. I left Poona and went back to Europe. I was in Amsterdam and the subject came up again about this guy meeting Papaji. I was with some friends and we decided to call the guy up who was living in California. We spoke to him and, I don't know, something started to smell. The way he was talking on the phone – it was like something was clicking inside me.

Later that day I went to an esoteric bookstore and I saw a book by Andrew Cohen, *My Master is Myself*, and I read it and I thought, 'This is really nice'.

So I got a ticket for Lucknow. I didn't even know where Lucknow was. But it was like meeting the sadhus in Delhi. It was the same exact feeling – I was going into the unknown, I had no idea what was going to happen, you know. It was scary.

I met Papaji's son and he said that I could come the next day. So I went to Papaji's house the following morning. I walked in and there were about eight Western people there – satsang had already started. Papaji was sitting on a dais – his eyes were already closed. So I just sat down and closed my eyes and instantly there was like this avalanche of energy. It just continued and continued and continued . . . and by the end of the satsang I was beginning to recognize what had happened to me with those sadhu men 15 years ago.

It was like, ah, oh, ha ha, yeah! I went back the next day but I didn't make any contact with Papaji. We didn't talk or anything. And I went back the day after that and the exact same thing happened again. This time it was deeper. I felt the peace in my heart more than I had ever felt before. I asked Papaji a question about effort. He said, 'Don't make any effort, drop all your concepts, knowledge and all your experience and just be quiet.' I thought, 'I don't know about this', but the energy of his *shakti* was so strong that I didn't care about 'being quiet' or 'not making any effort' or not. Effort can arise from the Self but it's something different than that coming from your own decision, the ego or the body, to make an effort.

Anyhow, the third day I went there and I opened my eyes and Papaji opened his eyes at the same time and we looked at each other and it was so strong. It was like I had to hold on not to look away, you know – I forced myself to look at him. During the break time, one of the assistants came over and said that Papaji wanted to see me. I walked into his bedroom and he was sitting on the bed and he looked up at me and smiled. I tell you, there was so much love and so much energy and so much happiness coming out of him that I almost ran out of the room. I sat down next to him and he said, 'When you walked in that door, I knew you came here for a purpose. What was the purpose, why did you come here?' At first I wanted to say, all kind of wishy-washy, 'Oh Papaji, I came for enlightenment,' but then the lion in me roared, 'Papaji! I'm here for enlightenment!' And he just started laughing and we started hugging and kissing and rolling around on his bed, you know. And then he got up and he was like a rooster and said, 'I always get them at the end and I work really fast. Don't worry, in just seven days you'll be enlightened!' And I said, 'Yeah, right!'

Firstly, he asked me if I had anything to say, so I told him the story of what happened with the sadhus. In fact for 10 years I didn't even tell Osho – I told nobody about what happened to me. I could not talk about it, it was so sacred. I told him the story and he confirmed it and said that these men were very special. And then he totally dropped it and I couldn't talk about it with him again, which I see was because I was hanging onto that experience.

But I still couldn't believe that I could be enlightened. I was still thinking that I wasn't good enough. Me, Bharat — enlightened? So this was what Papaji was doing in the beginning. He was getting rid of this belief that you can't be enlightened. What he did first of all was bring it out in me again but 1,000 times beyond it. In the next two years, what I experienced with Papaji and where he took me was like what happened with those men in the beginning. Papaji kept me in experience for at least two years. Whenever my mind would start to come back he would do something again. And I would remain in presence or beingness for those two years. I went through every esoteric spiritual experience you can think of. He gave me that gift — he let me finish that. So the first thing he did was show me truth again and then he gave me the confidence to live it.

Papaji said to me, 'In seven days you'll be enlightened!' So there I was, waiting. Day one, day two — yeah, this is good but I'm not enlightened. Day three, day four, five, six, day seven . . . There I was in the first half of satsang and nothing was happening. When we went off in the break I started to get really frustrated, even a little bit angry with Papaji. I said, 'Papaji, it's seven days now and I'm not enlightened.' And he just looked at me and laughed and he said, 'You know, if you go to the other shore, we're not going to have you anymore and we love you so much.' But then when he looked at me and I at him, all separation disappeared. There was no me, there was no him, there was nothing — just absolute beingness. Absolute beingness. Again, I just collapsed.

All I could do during this time was go to satsang and go back to my room and sit on a chair and look out of the window. It was so overwhelming. Just beingness, being in being. Every day would just get deeper and deeper and deeper. Levels of peace would get deeper and deeper and deeper. And then what also became apparent was the illusoriness of the mind, you know. I would walk into Papaji's house lost in some incredible, heavy mind-trip and within one second it would be gone in his presence. And this would happen over and over. All this mind is maya — it is illusion. It's not real and it can disappear in a split second. It's just a matter of being quiet.

One day in satsang, I was standing at the back and I was in this really depressive state but by the end of the satsang I was really feeling great. Papaji got up and walked out of the room and as he passed by me he said, 'Feeling better?' I realized what he was — not a little old man but this true *sadguru*. I began to see the immensity of who he was or what he was and what he was doing. He invited me to stay with him and live in Lucknow. This continued and continued and continued from '91 until '97 when he died.

I kept going higher and higher with him. What can I say? Papaji's main thing is that nothing exists. One day, I was sitting in my room and then the idea of my body disappeared, time disappeared, and I was in this place or no place where nothing existed and nothing ever existed. It was so absolutely clear that there has never been a creation and never was a creation. One is never born and one will never die. Absolutely that's the truth. But it's a very paradoxical thing because then the idea of the body would return and then I would be back here like this. Everything seemed really real again. That was confusing me for some time but Papaji would always tell me that there was no difference. But to me it felt different. So this went on for at least two years.

At one point I thought, 'God, I am enlightened.' But I had to keep checking. Am I enlightened? Am I enlightened? Then there was a point where I would think, 'I can't say yes, I can't say no. I can't say I'm enlightened, I can't say I'm unenlightened.' So that went back and forth. At one point, when I was leaving Lucknow, Papaji said that I should go out and give satsang. He gave me the name of Bharat – Bharat was the name of the brother of Ram and means 'India'. So I gave satsang wherever I was but I always came back and, within minutes of being with him, I realized that I was still accumulating things. I always chose to be with Papaji – that was more important than any kind of satsang or ever being special. There would be plenty of time after Papaji died.

Papaji said enlightenment for me happened with the sadhu men. But I didn't have the right understanding about what was going on. There was no wisdom – I had no consciousness knowledge of what was happening to me, I had no confirmation. I found out these things are very important, even as important as the actual breakthrough. Dis-identification with the mind – that's only the beginning. It's not like you become enlightened and you're now in this bubble and you're not touched by anything and you've got full knowledge, you know. It's not like that. Everything that you read in a book about enlightenment is not true and you only know it when you meet it face to face, either with your own face or a *jnani* or a *sadguru*, like at the level of Papaji's. Then you see what it's really about.

You know we read these spiritual books and get ideas about how a master is or what it means to be enlightened or what it means to be with a master. Living with Papaji, I got to see how he ate and pissed and did everything and it wasn't always easy to be around him. It's like when you're close to the sun, you get burned. You get totally burned up and, if you have resistance, it's going to hurt, just like when people walk on those burning coals – if they start looking at the coals, their feet start burning. So, it's the same kind of thing.

I have hundreds of ideas of what it is like to be in this space – 'space' seems to be the most apt word that I have met so far. Many people describe it as bliss but it would seem that these euphoric and ethereal descriptions could delude people into believing it is something that it's not.

When you first have this breakthrough from identification with the ego into truth or whatever you want to call it – this is what can delude people. The experience of it is fantastic – the experience of the bliss, the Oneness, the feeling of enlightenment. But what they are is experience. So this, at some point, goes because everything you can experience comes and goes. Even all these feelings of enlightenment – they come and go. That's why everybody freaks out. They confuse enlightenment with the experience of enlightenment. There's a difference because at some point you realize you have to look for what is real. And anything that comes and goes is not real. So you find that within yourself, which never changes. And there's only one thing that never changes – and that's consciousness. At some point you get more understanding about it and so you're not so bothered about these great experiences.

I mean, now I really know that. In fact, that's what it's like now with the 10 years of being with Papaji since 1991 – that it doesn't matter. It used to be that when I was feeling angry, bad or something like that, it meant that I wasn't enlightened. And now, it has absolutely nothing to do with my emotional state, you know. I am that, no matter what, no matter what I'm feeling. But one needs certain things to happen to oneself before one can make that statement. One needs to have that breakthrough. Like Mira says – one needs realization first. You need to have made this commitment where emptiness is your home, where this is your being. You need to make this kind of switch. And then everything goes around you and nothing matters.

Someone like Papaji who was living 100 per cent in higher consciousness – everything that he did was enlightened. There's no such thing as enlightened behaviour or unenlightened behaviour – it cannot be. I would walk into Papaji's house and he would be glued to the TV watching cricket, which a lot of people would think is very unenlightened behaviour. Or he would be chewing pan all day, which is an addictive substance, a drug. But I tell you, with Papaji, he'd be doing all this – he'd be reading the newspaper, watching the cricket, chewing his pan and people would be sitting next to him and getting enlightened, having total satsang, total darshan with Papaji. That's when I saw that there's no such thing as enlightened or unenlightened behaviour. It's consciousness and it's not dented by any behaviour.

In the *Bhagavad Gita*, when Arjuna has to go and kill his uncles, it's the same thing. Even if you have to kill, if what you are doing is being directed from something beyond, from God, then it's OK. There are a lot of people that go on about this — you have to live this enlightened life, they say, you must live your enlightenment in a certain way. That's a big thing for people but it's just not the case — at least that is what I have found.

So the concept of being at peace in oneself doesn't mean a still mind, a still heart, no anger arising. It's nothing to do with that.

Absolutely nothing to do with that.

So all those things are going on but the reference point is peace?

Not peace. Peace is not the right word. If you have peace, you have war — it's something else because you are in Brahman. It's like the centre of your being is no longer in your body. I'm only talking about my own experience now but it's like the centre of my being is no longer in my body — I am centred somewhere beyond that, which has an intrinsic bliss to it. This Brahman is *satchitananda*, which is existence, consciousness, bliss. They are the three attributes of us. This is what we are — existence, consciousness, bliss. But the thing is this bliss is something that only happens when you come to accept consciousness and existence as real and everything else as being unreal. But not intellectually — it happens in an existential way. So then there is this oozy kind of undercurrent or inner matrix of bliss but it's not bliss, it's something else. It's not the bliss one generally thinks of that comes and goes. It's something else but this only happens when you are centred in that, when you have done your enquiry, when you have done *vichara*, when you've gone back to the point of total emptiness. And it's not even something you can do but somehow it happens.

OK, so what's confusing you now?!

This is the thing I keep coming up against and I don't want to get too intellectual about it. But people say that when there is some kind of awakening, it's nothing that they have done — it was an act of grace. Then I think that sounds like there's some predestination in all of this. Because I still believe that I am the doer, I think that there is something that I can do to help precipitate awakening.

But there's the other side, that nothing is set. It's not that now there is nothing you can do — it's also there's nothing you can do and there's nothing that you *cannot* do.

Ah, right.

You know, freedom is freedom. That's the problem — everyone tries to make a model of it, tries to make a concept of it. And there are no concepts. Like there's effort, no effort — but sometimes you make effort. There's no choice — you cannot decide not to be Paula, not to wake up in the morning. So there's no choice. On the other hand, existence sometimes gives you choice, gives you the grace that comes and gives you the power to make choice. And then you're making choice. Your personal 'I' is making the choice – it's all included. And that's such a relief. When that light bulb finally goes off – right, it's all included – then I can be angry, I can be this, I am still that, I am still God and I am still in deep communion with beingness.

Advaita sometimes seems to be a rather detached interpretation of life.

People come to my satsang and when they say that they are not the body and it's all a dream, I ask whether that really is their experience. I can get very down on somebody when it's an intellectual thing because you can make anything a dogma. The whole Buddhist thing I think is nonsense – even though it's true that all suffering is from desire, when you hear it as dogma, it's not true. That's why right association is very important – who you are with – and the association with a *sadguru*, with a true master.

So association with a true master is necessary?

As far as I'm concerned in my life, I think it's very necessary. First of all, you need confirmation. You need somebody who is living in higher consciousness – well, this is my opinion, I don't know. But this is my experience and I know for sure that Papaji felt the same way because we talked about it. You need confirmation and it's very mysterious. You need somebody who is a *sadguru* or a master to say, 'Yes, that's it'. There's something about lineage but I don't understand it – it's something beyond me. But I know that there's truth in that, that one has to get confirmed.

Someone explained it being like a tuning fork. You start to resonate at the same frequency as the master.

That's very Gurdjieffian – his wavelengths of beingness, different notes. He had the law of seven and each one representing a different vibration. That's why you need a master first of all for the transmission, to get on that highway, so to speak. So that's why I am always asking what a person's lineage is, where they are coming from.

It seems in this age it's horses for courses. There's a whole array of different teachers saying different things – but there's so much opportunity to meet somebody who is right for you.

Exactly. What we are going through is such an incredible age right now. We are still in what we call the *Kali Yuga* – the Dark Ages according to the Hindu scriptures. But still, in this *Kali Yuga* a lot of people can become enlightened. And that's exactly what's happening on the planet right now. It's a very opportune, very auspicious time. If you are into Gurdjieffian types of thing, his thinking is that there are 56 forces that are preventing us from being enlightened.

The fact is that if someone has true intention and the karmic thing is correct and they meet the right master or whatever it is, then this is a time for many, many people to wake up. It's not the time to lie back and watch the river go by. It's time to jump in and swim with everybody else because who knows how long this is going to last. But right now, and you can see it around the world, there are so many teachers. Advaita teachings have just exploded in the last 10 years. And there's a reason for it — everyone is waking up. Everyone and their uncle are giving satsang!

There's certainly a weariness of arduous meditation practice, karma yoga or sheer hard labour to bring you into the present moment.

Yeah, that's like Gurdjieffian-type work. He showed absolutely that effort doesn't work because nobody became enlightened through it. Nobody made more effort than Gurdjieff to get people to have this experience of consciousness or to go beyond the mind through effort — and look what happened!

Where do you live now?

I lived with Papaji until he died when the whole thing in Lucknow finished. In the last two years, I haven't found a place where I can say this is my home. I have been kind of running around looking for a home. I have been indulging in my *vasanas* in the last two years — going into relationships, having all sorts of situations. I also wasn't feeling like giving satsang but Mira had cancelled her July satsang in Gent in Belgium and asked me to give satsang again. This time when she said it, something in me knew that I just couldn't say no. In that moment that I agreed, something changed inside me. I don't know what it was but something changed again, something switched again. Nothing's different — I am still sitting in this same silence as I was when I was going through my *vasanas* but I'm not indulging in them so much. I'm much more focused on giving satsang because when I went and gave satsang in Gent, it was so incredible. Never before have I given a satsang where I was absolutely not there — it was not me giving it. There was something so strong coming through. And the 60 or 70 people that were there, there was so much love and so many people coming up to the couch and getting it and falling into it, it was just so clear that I had to continue doing it. So right now, I'm back doing satsang but it could also end. Meanwhile, I can't say that I live anywhere. When Lucknow ended, all the bridges were burned. There was no turning back anywhere.

Papaji's death marked the end of an era, you could say.

It was the end of Lucknow as a place to live but Papaji didn't end at all. If anything has happened, my connection with Ramana Maharshi also became much more direct. That was when I would go to the Himalayas and go to certain places and hook into things very directly. That I could really thank Papaji for – I was able to go to these places, holy places, and experience the primal source. So that's been very, very good. In the last two winters I have been in Tiruvannamalai, living at the foot of Arunachala and that is the first time in my life that I experienced a rock being a *sadguru* – the rock is a *sadguru*! It's even beyond Ramana, it's Siva himself. Siva manifests and this is absolutely the truth. So it's very good to go there even though it's super intense, you know.

All I can say is that it's worth anything to have – making the emptiness your home. It's the way out of suffering. Even if the suffering is going on around you, even if you are lost in it, it doesn't matter because you're always coming back to the Self. At some point it just happens automatically and nothing changes. You don't have to change, you don't have to be a better person. That's the whole thing with these teachings. You can be as fucked up as you want. The subtitle of my book is *How To Be Enlightened While Remaining Neurotic* because it absolutely doesn't matter. It's a dream. This Bharat, this Paula sitting here having this conversation is a dream. We're dreaming. It doesn't matter. But to get to that point where you know that – it's not just an intellectual understanding – I don't know how that happens for somebody. It is a mystery for each person. So, something with determination is there, somewhere, somehow. And it is grace, grace coming to you.

For me, Mira has really been a wake-up call. When I met her last year in San Francisco for the first time after Papaji's death, we just stood and stared at each other and there was such incredible unconditional love between us – it was really amazing. We were both really surprised. And somehow since that time, this kind of love has started to come through her to me. I felt so loved by her and it was absolutely needed in the moment. Also my energy levels started to rise and I began to feel younger and younger. What I noticed was that a lot of people around Mira also become younger. When I sat up with her in satsang on the couch, it was very clear to me that same thing was there – the same thing I met when I used to meet with Papaji. And that's when I recognized that Mira is carrying the lineage. Papaji has given her the begging bowl and stick. So that was a totally big relief because I thought I was totally on my own again.

Something happens when she is around which could mean that even your life could fall apart. She has such an expressive personality. But still there is the combination of that personality with the silence in which she lives and the understanding which she has and the strength she has. You know, in 1968 I was still wanting to be at my mother's breast and she was already going to India and looking for a master by herself. Then she went and met Papaji and sat under a tree for eight months — this is incredible strength. She also has a very strong and serious intent.

How did your book Split Seconds *come about?*

Papaji used to love to hear expressions of emptiness and as soon as someone would kind of get it, he would ask them whether they could say something about it. He would try to get people to describe it and he loved expressions. So I was thinking how can I express the inexpressible. Then I came up with this idea of having several moments in my life where truth happened. And maybe if I try to describe each one of those moments it would be like something would come through in a whole way, in an organic way. So I wrote about seven moments which I called *Split Seconds* — these moments when time disappears and a transformation happens and you are never the same afterwards. Peak experience-type situations. I wrote about them in either prose or poetry with an introduction explaining it. Chapter three is the miracle of Delhi, which describes that whole thing about the meeting with the two holy men. It's a small book and you can read it in one or two sittings. Mira has done some drawings, which were a total split second and which are in the book.

The truth of these teachings is that there is no need to do anything. One needs simply to relax and watch the whole show go on and just be with Oneself, you know. But the thing is that if one does get to Oneself, that's absolute salvation, that's the peace, that's where it's at, that's the direction to go. I have no doubts about that and I see my life as living in that clearly. But even though I am that all the time, when I am actually living in that, that's when I am not suffering. When I am not living in that, that's when I am suffering. The thing is if you engage in looking for happiness outside yourself, you will get burned, no matter how enlightened or what state of realization you are. If you engage in desire — you might not even care if you're getting hurt — you will suffer. Papaji said to me one day that he had to be really careful about what he desired since anything he desired instantly manifested. I would sit with Papaji and see that — for example, a tape recorder was needed and then all of a sudden somebody from Germany would come with a tape recorder. He said anything you desire has to be fulfilled, no matter if it takes you three lives. He said you have to be careful about what you hook into because you are going to get burned. And you have to go through the whole thing once it starts.

Somebody said to me that it's OK to fulfil your desires, just be prepared to accept the consequences. Desire brings with it a whole train of cause and effect.

Right. And then what happens is that very often someone forgets what they desired. I don't mean a piece of cake or a tape recorder but the true desires, the pull that keeps us incarnating, which is totally different from what people think of as desire.

Nisargadatta said that if you have really strong desires for certain things you should actually go out there and do them so as to get them over with.

Yes, Papaji encouraged people who had a desire to go do it, very much. He would say do it, live it, get rid of it. He would also say that if you can't live it out physically, you can live it out in your dreams.

Let's say in your last life you had this strong desire to have this perfect woman or perfect relationship, for example. So you have to come through each life until you get into the relationship and you forget that you desired it a life ago. Then you are in the midst of the suffering and you want to get out of the suffering. But anything you do you can't get out of it. People forget first of all that the desire is causing the suffering and that they got what they desired. So there they are – they got what they desired but then they want to get out of it 100 per cent because they want to be free. But you can't because you have to complete. I've seen that in a lot of my own life. Once you hook in, it has to run its course unless you're strong and intelligent enough to withstand the suffering.

Are you saying that there are previous lives – you talk about reincarnation?

I'm not actually sure if we live these different lives or are just picking up something in the collective unconscious or what actually it is. It might be something more. We are so small that we don't see the whole picture. It's all very multi-dimensional. We only live in three dimensions so we can't really see what that means in terms of past lives but I think there is a lot of truth in it. I mean, I have a lot of conscious memories of past lives.

Papaji did as well.

Papaji as well. He's gone back to where he'd been buried, back to the temples and ashrams where he used to be in the grave. So this for me is not a belief, it's my experience. If you read Ouspensky, he talks about the multi-dimensionality of the world that we are living in. We think of it as three dimensions but actually it's 10 dimensions or infinite dimensions. We never see the whole picture, like the meaning of existence, the whole meaning of this life, why we are here. Actually, it's meaningless to even try to answer because we can't even answer it. And nobody on the planet actually knows, you know. If you go to somebody and they say they know all the answers, run away because it's not possible. The most that we can know is only part of it. All I can say from my years with Papaji, and all those years of having every kind of spiritual thing happen to me, is that I don't know anything. How does that happen to me, why does this happen to me, what's the meaning of existence, all of that. The only thing that I do know is that it is possible to be truth. It is possible to conquer the mind. I also feel that if *I* could do it, anybody can do it. But still that's also a statement — I can't even make that statement.

So if someone is desperate to find their true Self, what's to be done?

It will happen. It will absolutely happen. I mean there's no getting around it, you are it already. It's just the hallucination, the dream that you are not it, that you are not bliss, you are not contentment. It is absolutely a dream. So I mean anybody in any moment in any split second can experience that — that is what is meant by this instant enlightenment. But we also have many layers of mind so it doesn't just happen like that all the time — so there are both sides.

Papaji talks about this burning desire for freedom. It's like the candle is there but the candle has to be lit. You need another burning candle so that your candle gets lit but then, once your candle is lit, it's independent. But you need your candle to be lit. You need someone to show you the meaning of maya, the illusion, but not in an intellectual way — in a way that you can truly experience it. And it's up to you and how you can do it but it all goes back to that burning, burning desire for freedom.

I have always been a space case — the only earth I have in my chart is my moon in Virgo. I've never had a job for more than six months in my life — I'm 51 years old! But there's this burning desire for freedom and what happens is that, at some point, it's a matter of life and death. The early days with Papaji with me were like that. It was absolutely life and death — I can't describe it. It's like either I have it or I want to die. At one point, I was in satsang with Papaji and I told him that when I went deep into meditation I got really spaced out and I couldn't relate to people — it hurt me. And he just looked at me and he said that I should forget about people. It didn't go right in straight away but, a few days later, I was sitting in my room and then the light bulb went off. It was like, yeah, I want this enlightenment so much that if I never walk out of this room and never see another person in my entire life, I am ready to do it. And in that moment that I said that to myself the whole mind thing, that I needed to share with people and be with people, disappeared. It's just mind, it's just illusion. We are all constantly trying to relate and be together and feel at one with everybody but, actually, it's just a mind thing.

In that moment, I went so much into truth that I fell into samadhi. So those were the kinds of things that were happening to me. Papaji says at one time in your life, you go to the beach, you take off all your clothes – which are all your concepts, your knowledge, your ideas, your personality – you take them off and you are nude. Then you even take off the nudity and jump into that ocean of consciousness and have a swim and come back and put them all back on again and go on. And that's what he would say is enough and it's true, though it might apparently take some time. You may have to go through some things but it goes on and on and on, you know. In fact, what happens is that grace itself comes and gets you basically. And how that happens and why she chooses this person or seemingly doesn't choose that person, I don't know.

So why not me now?

Well, no one knows why that is so. But when you have been chosen, you could wish you hadn't been because there are all these dark nights of the soul coming out even more intensely. This is the blackboard effect. If you've been living in the satsang of Papaji or you've experienced purity and you know what beingness is – that's the blackboard. Then the white chalk of tendencies and *vasanas* comes up. You're really noticing them now, as before you were only living in the mind. It's like you didn't know if you were really depressed because everybody's depressed and it never seemed that much different. But if you're in this actual beingness, then you get your depression or anger or whatever even worse. And that can happen for years.

I'd be around Papaji. Every time he would come to me I would just react like this little five-year-old. People run away from those things because when you go to the sun, the wax melts. Only a certain type can take that and so you have to be very strong. It's not for the weak-willed. Satsang is not a child's game and many people who are on the edge freak out. So that's the other thing about the importance of having a master because it is at some point a tightrope that you are walking. Papaji would always say you need a healthy body and a healthy mind to come to satsang. We would have people freak out and very often Papaji would send me to take these people to the mental hospital in Lucknow! But there was not much you could do about it. Papaji could cure them but if somebody is mentally ill, it's better that they go have therapy even if they have the intelligence to realize themselves in the moment.

So realization is possible even if the mind has a tendency to madness?

Yeah, but this is a very high state of realization, when you realize that there is no difference between satsang and *vasanas*, you know, that there's no difference between *samsara* and truth. If you're truly realizing that truth is *samsara*, you're doing really well — you're at the level of Ramana. That's very, very, good because it's not so simple. The way Ramana lived was the archetypal example of what it means to abide in the Self. Ramana was living without any movement towards the tendencies — that is such a purity of soul. Most of us don't have that purity. But in fact, I don't even know how much purity of soul is needed once you have a full understanding of what's going on. I think people get confused about that too. If you have that realization and you are still engaging in desires or you are still believing in the dream, you know it's hard not to. There's a difference between a Papaji, even though we are all the same, and one of these messengers, for example — it's like diamonds. A diamond is a diamond but it still can have an impurity. In fact it might be even a bit more brilliant when there's a little bit of impurity in it.

Someone made this expression about the wine in the bottle — the same wine in different bottles. It's totally wrong that expression. The bottle is in the wine, not the wine in the bottle. It's not a good analogy at all because it's the other way around. It's a major point — to say that the wine is in the bottle is really wrong, you know. It shows to me not a clear understanding whatsoever. Consciousness is not limited to the body — the body is within consciousness. That's the way it is.

I found Bharat's history riveting — I could have listened to him for hours talking about his adventures along the spiritual path. I realize that I feel envious of all the things he has done, people he has met, not to mention all his experiences of God.

Then I start to reflect on what he had to say about the bottle being in the wine, whereas others have said that the wine is in the bottle. More contradictions, I think, and yet at the time each one seemed to make perfect sense. Maybe that's the key — everything included, nothing excluded. All interpretations equally valid and applicable to everyone. And just like with so-called enlightenment — realization of God is not like an alchemist's potion, known only to the mystical elect. Paradoxes and intellectual inconsistencies aside, the truth is freely available to everyone, right here and now, if it is really and truly desired. As Christ indeed once said:

> *Ask, and you will receive; seek, and you will find; knock, and the door will be opened. For everyone who asks receives, he who seeks finds, and to him who knocks, the door will be opened.*
> Matthew, viii, 7–8

Q: It is said that the Self is beyond the mind and yet the realization is with the mind. 'The mind cannot think it. It cannot be thought of by the mind and the mind alone can realize it.' How are these contradictions to be reconciled?

A: Atman is realized with mruta manas *[dead mind], that is, mind devoid of thoughts and turned inward. Then the mind sees its own source and becomes that [the Self]. It is not as the subject perceiving an object. When the room is dark a lamp is necessary to illumine and eyes to cognize objects. But when the sun has risen there is no need of a lamp to see objects. To see the sun no lamp is necessary, it is enough that you turn your eyes towards the self-luminous sun. Similarly with the mind. To see objects the reflected light of the mind is necessary. To see the Heart it is enough that the mind is turned towards it. Then mind loses itself and Heart shines forth. The essence of mind is only awareness or consciousness. When the ego, however, dominates it, it functions as the reasoning, thinking or sensing faculty. The cosmic mind, being not limited by the ego, has nothing separate from itself and is therefore only aware. This is what the Bible means by 'I am that I am'.*

When the mind perishes in the supreme consciousness of one's own Self, know that all the various powers beginning with the power of liking [and including the power of doing and the power of knowing] will entirely disappear, being found to be an unreal imagination appearing in one's own form of consciousness. The impure mind which functions as thinking and forgetting, alone is samsara, *which is the cycle of birth and death. The real 'I' in which the activity of thinking and forgetting has perished, alone is the pure liberation. It is devoid of* pramada *[forgetfulness of Self] which is the cause of birth and death.*

Q: How is the ego to be destroyed?

A: Hold the ego first and then ask how it is to be destroyed. Who asks the question? It is the ego. This question is a sure way to cherish the ego and not to kill it. If you seek the ego you will find that it does not exist. That is the way to destroy it.

Be As You Are: The Teachings of Sri Ramana Maharshi

Catherine Ingram

CHAPTER NINE

ALL YOU NEED IS
LOVE

That we are at all is the great mystery. The unknown force animating us, present in all that is blooming and fading, is our deepest felt sense, and strangely, the feeling we most often overlook. Like breathing, this aliveness — this passionate presence — is taken for granted, and we pay attention instead to an endless stream of thoughts. Yet, as our attention comes to rest more in pure presence, a natural intelligence emerges. This intelligence bypasses our genetic gifts, IQ, age, cultural conditioning and education. We might call it an intelligence of the heart.

Free of dogma, ideology, and religious beliefs, Dharma Dialogues point to and celebrate that silent luminous presence which awakens natural intelligence and suffuses our lives with love.

Catherine Ingram

Born in 1952 and raised in Virginia, USA, Catherine Ingram became interested in Eastern philosophy and meditation in her late teens. Inspired by Ram Dass's spiritual classic, *Be Here Now*, she visited the Naropa Institute, founded by Chogyam Trungpa Rinpoche in 1974, where she met Ram Dass and other teachers from a variety of philosophical and mystical traditions. Fascinated with Buddhist practice, and in particular *vipassana* meditation, she went on to help set up the Insight Meditation Society in Barre, Massachusetts. After settling in neighbouring

Cambridge, she took up journalism as a way to continue to meet other people working in the pursuit of truth. Travelling the world writing about social activist and spiritual issues, she has interviewed, amongst others, Thich Nhat Hanh, Jiddu Krishnamurti and His Holiness the Dalai Lama. Her book, *In the Footsteps of Gandhi: Conversations with Spiritual Social Activists*, is the culmination of that quest.

Still haunted by the elusive goal of 'enlightenment', a commission by *Yoga Journal* to interview Poonjaji took her to Lucknow in India in 1991 — a meeting that was to change her perspective forever. The realization for Catherine came in the understanding that all that is needed is to choose freedom, here and now; that clear seeing is always available if it is truly desired. Currently living in Portland, Oregon, she regularly travels abroad to give Dharma Dialogues and retreats in Europe and the United States, sharing this insight, the most simple of truths.

I have come to Gaunt's House, only a mile or so from Osho Leela, in the Dorset countryside. This will be a week's silent retreat — a real opportunity to be, quite literally, quiet. I am more than excited about coming to spend time here as it was the previous year, on a similar retreat again with Catherine, that I glimpsed for the first time the infinite potential of life. (I refrain from using the phrase 'spiritual experience' as it is now beginning to sound utterly pretentious.) Each day has a gentle and optional schedule — in the morning, yoga, breakfast and then satsang, followed by a walk in the countryside before a long and relaxing lunch; in the afternoon, a guided meditation and more strolls in the country before supper, followed by satsang and then early retirement to bed. And, although dialogue is permitted in satsang, the silence is to be maintained throughout the rest of the day's activities. During our time on retreat I have been assigned the duty of ringing the eight o'clock breakfast bell — walking around the house and its outbuildings delicately striking a large copper-coloured gong. A simple enough task you might think but, again, it's something else to add to my list of worries.

For the first couple of days, my mind goes completely berserk. I start to hold conversations with myself. How am I doing? How do I compare in blissfulness to the others? Hey, I think I just got it! Wait till I tell everyone else in satsang. I also feel incredibly tired — I sleep deeply at night for the first time in what seems like years, as well as taking a regular afternoon nap. And because there is no need for my social persona, I start to become aware of the amount of effort that is involved in creating my public identity and how tense and weary it makes me feel at a very deep level of my being.

I decide to go for a walk along a lane that stretches away from the east side of the house, through fields of cows and tall trees — the same lane where I tasted 'awareness' the previous year. Would it be possible to repeat the experience, I hope — after all here I am, back in the silence, the same surroundings, psychologically prepared . . . The autumn weather is mild, a little chilly almost. I tuck my scarf more tightly around my neck. The faint smell of incense impregnated in its fibres evokes a nostalgia for something, like a spiritual comfort blanket representing something I know and feel I can trust.

It is said somewhere that when the holy man sits, he just sits, and when he walks, he just walks. It is strange that here is something that I have been practising for the past 30 or so years that still proves to be a bit of a challenge. Would it be possible, I think, to walk the length of this lane without thought? Or more realistically, to walk simply observing what is happening and, if and when thought arises, just to witness it pass through my mind? (By this time, I have walked about 100 yards whilst debating with myself whether I am capable of walking without thought or not.) Suddenly, I stop abruptly in the middle of the path. This is just insane, I think. This is utterly ridiculous – either I am simply incapable of achieving this task or it really is asking of me the impossible. Sometimes I wish to God I hadn't heard of the words 'bliss', 'Self-realization', 'God consciousness'. After all, only a handful of human beings at any one time 'attain' unity with the universe, so the chances of 'me' arriving at a place, at any place for that matter, which is better than this mental hell, are zero. Then I think, my God, my entire life is all about me. It is almost as if spiritual practice is a form of collusion in the obsession in how to handle, to analyze and to discuss the subject of 'me' . . .

We reach the middle of the week. I meet with Catherine in her room on the top floor of the house. 'You can see why they call this the pink room,' Catherine smiles, motioning for me sit on the bed, which is covered by a pink duvet, in a room papered with an intricate rose motif. I put my list of questions on the bed beside me, to glance at if I lose my train of thinking. 'I used to do exactly the same!' Catherine reminisces on her own days as a journalist, her face breaking into a smile, her brown eyes almost empathizing with the task in hand. Indeed, she looks at me with such compassion, I start to feel foolish about my literary aspirations. Even though I am following in Catherine's footsteps by writing about the spiritual search, whether it will come to any kind of permanent understanding, I am beginning to doubt the fact that it ever will.

I've been going about talking to teachers – my own spiritual odyssey, I suppose. Sometimes there has been understanding, sometimes confusion. Even in Advaita, there appear to be two schools of thought. On the one hand, there's 'pure Advaita' where there is absolutely nothing you can do, life just unfolds as it does. On the other, there's 'practical Advaita', so to speak, and there is something you can do, like relax or give your attention to something. I get stuck between these different interpretations.

As I have been saying this past week on retreat, there's a perspective whereby being and doing are one continuum. In other words, there's a sense that there's a movement or flow out of beingness that doesn't necessarily feel personal but is, nevertheless, creative.

So, you make plans to come to 'do' a so-called retreat and that can seem like someone with a mission, hoping to gain understanding. But the paradox or the irony is that you find yourself in beingness here and you realize that there is no doing and there's no doer. It's a flick in perspective. It goes from thinking there's a personal agenda to finally seeing that all you assumed as a personal agenda was all along being breathed through you, like an instrument being played by some mysterious musician.

And all of your running around, your attempts to gain insight or to get spiritual or to get enlightened is just the pageantry of consciousness. It's just that consciousness has manifested as this creation that you think of as yourself. It has this interest, this particular interest, in looking at itself.

When people say that there's no doing, it's because there's not a 'you' there to do it. It's like watching these trees blowing here outside the window in the wind. The wind is moving for some conditioned causes, the leaves are blowing for the conditioned cause of the wind passing through them. There's nothing personal about it. And yet, it happens!

I can see that in the external world, particularly in nature. I can even see that with events in my life — you can never know what's round the corner. But with the mental plane, because it's so close to you, it's right inside . . .

Right. You take it much more personally. But it's as impersonal as, well, I often say, 'You're not growing your hair. You're not growing your bones.' And in the same way, you are not thinking your thoughts. For the simple reason that the one, the 'you' who's the controller, the boss, the manifester, is just an idea — just another idea. So, there's this flow of phenomena, this flow of thoughts. Digestion is going on, hair is growing, wind is blowing through the trees, thoughts are flowing. And there's an interest arising in something called the spiritual life. It's very impersonal and at some point even the idea of the spiritual life falls away and there is only *this*.

And everything, as I've been saying this week, just becomes normalized in its own extraordinary ordinariness.

I can see that here.

Yes, it's very obvious in silence.

I can also see I have a spiritual project — this book in particular.

Right. Well, with this sense of the doership, there is a sense of someone to be improved. Another great paradox is that there is no one there who needs to be improved. So, you're no longer fighting the conditioning whatsoever. There's no aspect of the awareness that is now trying to change the conditioning. There's only a relaxation in the face of the conditioning.

And the thoughts don't need to be cleansed or purified?

No, no.

In a way, bad thoughts are quite easy to dis-identify with. It's the pleasant and spiritual thoughts about meditation and one's image that are much more subtle and difficult to detach oneself from. I can see bad thoughts as not being me and yet I can't see good thoughts as not being me. But actually, all those thoughts are just thoughts.

Right! It's true. They are all equally impersonal. You just get used to really being relaxed in the face of whatever is arising. There's no one there who cares what is arising. There's not an idea that someone has to fix it. That's what has happened in my own case. For so many years, my spiritual practice had to do with trying to purify the contents of the mind and, as I've often said, that became a more and more depressing project! The goal was constantly receding.

The great freedom is in the total acceptance of and relaxation with the conditioning, the non-involvement with the conditioning, the non-reaction to the conditioning and the non-identification with the conditioning. That's what freedom is, that's all that it is. I often say, it's no big deal. People have so many projections and misconceptions about some big bang that's going to happen called enlightenment, you know. That it's going to mean that you have this big explosion and you live in bliss and everything goes your way and you only have lovely, insightful, altruistic thoughts . . .

Or no thought?!

Or no thought, even better! But the truth is much more simple and ordinary and like I say, very much 'no big deal' — it's very accessible, very peaceful. A kind of 'nothing special' — that's what's special about it. You're no longer looking for some sort of peak experience, you're no longer like a junkie, out looking for highs. You're just at ease in being and it's glorious enough. It's amazing. As one of my Buddhist teachers used to say, 'It's empty phenomena rolling on.' You just let it roll on. You just hang out and watch the show.

My own tendency in the past had been a kind of interpretation that was blue, you know, kind of slightly depressive . . .

Yes, it's the same for me!

So, that would always be the way that things would be coloured. My experience of reality would be coloured by this blue haze! And those tendencies can continue to arise — they do arise. Little moments of certain kinds of blue interpretations. I've come to really enjoy those. It's kind of got a little romantic hue, a little poignant, poetic moment. And there's no aspect, at least that I can see, of the awareness that has any resistance to it or thinks that it should be different, wishes that it should go away — nothing. It's just a kind of an enjoyment of the arising.

For myself, I spent about 10 years in a spiritual organization. I had many peak experiences, spiritual experiences. We used to go on retreat, we'd be up at five, in the kitchen all morning making meals for between 200 and 300 people. Then we'd meditate and study. The whole day was work! And being a very traditional school of Advaita, there was the belief that women had to serve men so, in between all of those activities, I would have to iron shirts, get cups of tea for the man I was assigned to look after — I was a complete physical wreck! Then I would get these moments of euphoria when I was meditating or learning Sanskrit . . .

Probably just as a relief from being in the kitchen!

I mean, I shudder now at the thought of it! When I came here last year to the retreat with you, I remember walking down the lane and it just struck me that — it sounds ridiculous — but this is IT! There's nothing that I can do to 'do' that or to 'be' that — just here it is!

Nothing to enhance it or to diminish it, yes!

And then I chucked in the organization and there was a real shift in perception and lots of things fell away. But that conditioning still arises.

The thought you have to work hard . . .

Yes.

Well, that conditioning is strong in our cultures here in the West. We are in these so-called 'type A' cultures whereby there's a belief system that anything worthwhile requires hard work. And that may be true for many aspects of existence but it cannot be true for being itself. Because, here we are, already being! So, all that's required for the enjoyment of that is relaxation into it, a surrender into just that, without the presentation of being somebody – being a woman, being a teacher, being successful, being in relationship, whatever it is, whatever the fixation of the presentation of how one defines oneself as somebody. That is stressful. But when you just drop into the pure presence, it's very, very relaxed. You just let the awareness rest at ease in naturalness.

The conditioning is very deep and very subtle, I find. Without speech, there's been incredible space and relaxation but the conditioning has kind of gone underground – you know, shall I wear this, shall I do that? It seems like there's no bottom to it, this 'Paula project'.

That's the whole point I am making – it doesn't matter. None of that matters, even if to your last breath, the 'Paula conditioning' is arising, welcome it. It doesn't mar or diminish or stain present awareness. It doesn't touch the presence. Presence remains ever fresh. Alive. This, the unconditioned, remains completely fresh and unstainable. Nothing sticks, nothing adheres to it. So, it doesn't matter about the conditioning, it doesn't matter if it's a bottomless pit of conditioning, you know. I say, assume that it is. Let's just welcome it. Let's not bother with any kind of hope that it's going to stop, that madness and neurosis will stop. It doesn't matter. It would be a very paltry kind of freedom that couldn't handle a little arising of neurosis or even of profound grief. It would be a pathetic kind of freedom that couldn't welcome grief. It wouldn't be freedom.

So, this is yet another spiritual concept – people think that in real freedom, there's this neutrality whereby you don't really feel suffering and I disagree. I say that in true freedom, awareness enables you to feel vast suffering and to always know that what you are is ultimately untouched by it. Both exist simultaneously.

There was something you said in London which was really profound – about the concept that I am not the body and I am not the mind. You said, 'I am not "merely" the body and I am not "merely" the mind.' But I have been living in a state of detachment, I've created a cage and to embrace suffering or relationship or grief – I find the prospect terrifying. And yet, I'm denying life itself.

Yes. It's not very juicy that way, is it?! From my perspective, that kind of denial is erroneous on all counts. This is consciousness itself at play or in manifestation. Here it is! Here are these beings, these creatures, these mind-body organisms – it cannot be denied. Now, we can speak on molecular and space levels and deconstruct and find that it's mainly space or mostly some sort of energy within the space. But it's just one of many displays emanating from the One, so why would we be separate from it? Why would we say, 'I am not this organism. I'm the rest of totality except for this very mind-body organism!'?

So, that's why I say we are not 'merely' this mind and body, that we *are* included in the totality – we are not reduced to our small manifestation of it. Our knowing of the fundamental nature doesn't need to be reduced to just this mind and body. That's where we get into this profound sense of love that we have been speaking about whereby you realize that, as Poonjaji used to say, 'You walk in the world as an emperor because everything is your own. Just as an emperor walks out into his kingdom without a penny in his pocket, you can walk in this world without a penny in your pocket and it is all your own!'.

What I would like to point out is that when he said that it's all your own, he didn't mean it as ownership – it's your own because you *are* all of it. So, for myself sitting here, looking through this window, wherever my eyes happen to go, wherever the awareness lands, there's a sense that everything is in this consciousness. Not inside my body but that my body and everything else is composed of consciousness itself. And that's why, you could say, that the purest form of love is inter beingness. It's knowing yourself as so-called other or as the totality and therefore having the natural feelings of care and tenderness.

Not just for other people but oneself.

For oneself and for other beings, not just humans. Everything. Forgetting to make distinctions between animate and inanimate, sentient and insentient, you know. One time when my niece was six, her mother sent her out to water the garden and as she had already watered the garden, she started watering the rocks. She explained to her mother that the rocks also looked hot. So, like that, just a certain sense of the aliveness of all of this and a care for it, a genuine celebration of this whole manifestation.

I do get a sense of that particularly in satsang when people speak. When you really listen to people – if there is fear arising or some kind of personality in their voice, there is no judgement there.

Right, you just see the richness and the diversity of the One and it is so beautiful to see. I am absolutely awed by the creativity of whatever it is that is blasting this into form. It's really, endlessly creative. So, each of these expressions we celebrate for its own unique flavour.

We were talking earlier about spiritual smugness – I've really created an ivory tower of beingness.

Yes, but a lot of that stuff just falls away, you know. In true surrender into beingness, there's just no place for spiritual pride and arrogance – you really are able to meet and realize that everyone is a perfect manifestation of source, that you have no special domain of the source of being. You are not more consciousness than anything else, no matter your own recognition of it.

Could you speak about your own spiritual project. You said that up to about the age of 17, you had quite a miserable childhood, for whatever reason. It seems with so many people, there is an initial suffering and anxiety in early years that pushes people on the path.

Yes, it is mostly the case that over the nearly 30 years of dharma being a passion in my life, my observation has been that most people who are so-called spiritual seekers have been motivated by a lot of suffering. This is true in my own case. It's like Trungpa Rimpoche said, 'Suffering is the manure for the field of wisdom.' Often it is the suffering that is driving us. There's no resting in any vulnerable kind of happiness when you've suffered a lot. You're ill at ease in any kind of half way happiness or happiness that is conditioned or happiness that depends on something that you might lose – you already know what it is to lose or be wounded by clutching to the transient.

In my own case, there was a kind of relentless push that would not let me rest with any of the more conventional forms of happiness that I had found along the way. I would try them all – money, sex, power, romance I've tried everything! But there was never a sense of peace. I also tried, of course, spiritual practice, spiritual attainments and spiritual progress, which I was never very good at!

What was it that attracted you to Buddhism?

Its logic. I love logic. I eventually came to feel with Buddhism that, although I loved its system of the study of the mind, I don't really have much relationship with the beliefs that are rife in Buddhism anymore. I would say that what attracted me most, initially, was the logical approach to working with mind. It seemed hopeful that if you could just understand the arising of mind and the working of mind, you might have some influence over it. It seemed that the techniques of sitting and watching the mind, watching it in a microscopic way, would give you a kind of knowledge or the map of how it works. And it certainly is very insightful in that regard – you do get to see very deeply the nature of how it's conditioned and the endless stream of conditioning.

So, that's what attracted me to Buddhism and it was a wonderful study for a long time. It was very enriching and I was in a worldwide community of fantastic people who are still my dear friends – many of whom are now famous Buddhist teachers. But for myself, all of the 'isms', as Abbie Hoffman once said, are 'wasms'.

I should say while we are on the subject, I don't really consider myself as an Advaita teacher either. It's a term and it is now bandied about to the point where it no longer has meaning, as far as I can tell. My love affair is with beingness and love itself and that's all I've really ever cared about. It doesn't need labels and it's not about a religion or a philosophy and it doesn't need to be part of any club or any tradition or any particular teaching or teacher.

I recently read the Dalai Lama's new book, Ethics for the New Millennium, *in which he says something really extraordinary. When he moved to India he initially thought that being a Buddhist was the only way to live – it was the most perfect religion there could be. Then, in his meetings with many people who came to him, he realized you could be a member of any religious tradition. And then, after a while, he realized that, actually, you didn't even need to believe in God – it was just about compassion and loving kindness.*

He actually often says that his true religion is kindness. For myself, also, I don't really have much use for the concept of religion. I would say that my true passion is the sharing of this love which comes and emanates naturally from the recognition of beingness and of the One – or not even One but we have to speak in these concepts – of the One manifesting itself. The source is just pouring itself out in all these myriad ways. In the recognition of that, love arises. It's not a subject-object love, it's just an appreciation, a gratitude and a celebration. The rest of it is just philosophy and mind games.

I suppose there is a danger that we can become obsessed with all the technical, Sanskrit terms for every aspect of human experience.

Ah! Yes, but it gets all so much more simple. And we can use our own language, which is quite rich, to say it. Why have any veils of separation, why have any philosophy that we need to present. In the true seeing, as I said this morning in Dharma Dialogues, instead of walking in this world as an alien, you walk in the world and it's all home. You're just at home, you're at peace in beingness itself. And it doesn't matter where you are or who you're with, you know. You just experience presence with everyone whether they have ever heard the word 'dharma' or have the slightest interest in any of this or not.

I am reminded of your story of the Dalai Lama and the Dog Boy. His Holiness met a young boy raised by dogs who subsequently started to show dog-like characteristics. Whereas everyone around him recoiled in dismay, His Holiness patted and stroked the Dog Boy as if he really were a dog, thereby befriending him.

Yes, exactly, that's the perfect example. Just being able to go right to where someone's consciousness is hanging out. When you know yourself as consciousness, there's a very fluid adaptability that can just meet aspects of itself very easily.

I can taste that here. We were speaking earlier of a natural intelligence.

Yes, it's what I call the natural intelligence of clear awareness that is almost like a universal intelligence, which bypasses IQ and education and cultural conditioning and spiritual training and all of that. When we relax and surrender in this pure presence, that kind of intelligence just starts flowing through, unimpeded.

So how do I carry what I have tasted here on retreat into my daily life?

Well, the one and only thing that I can say in response to that is the more drenched you are in this, here and now, the deeper it will haunt you. And the more you taste this, here and now, the more familiar the terrain is. It's like you have a reference, so that at any second, one can notice that presence is just here, hanging around, always here.

What I find, what I see as the real beauty of retreats, is that it just normalizes this view. It's not that you retreat and escape from the dreariness of the world for some period – that's not really the point. It's that we come here and dive into reality and it becomes more normal all the time. You realize how ordinary it is to just be in quiet presence. It's about noticing that all thoughts are just flickers, just little electric impulses going on and off.

The trouble is I find that I have a model that I should be on retreat as much as possible. Working in the world can distort that awareness so I think that I'm only going to be truly 'aware' if I spend most of my waking moments on retreat in silence.

Let the mechanism be drawn to where it wants to be, what it's naturally drawn to. For some people, living a quiet life, living a retreat-like existence, is their destiny – I don't mean a pre-destiny but their unfolding destiny. That's what their highest, most beautiful expression is. For other people, they have business in the world, the so-called workaday world, or need to support themselves or their family somehow. In that case, this quiet can still be available, is available.

But it's so easy to get lost. There isn't a habit of awareness. There is just a habit of being lost.

Until that habit of being lost dissolves and the habit of awareness takes over or it takes over gradually, you just relax all along, even if you are forgetting at times.

There's a knowing that nothing is stained, no matter how much you have forgotten or how much nonsense you've indulged in. You just find yourself at ease. You know, I often quote the *Ashtavakra Gita*: 'The awakened one is not distracted even in distraction.' So even in so-called forgetting, the awakened is not forgetful, though there may be some drama being played out that the attention is fixed on.

It's very gentle, isn't it?

It is. It's very gentle. My way of living this and experiencing it has really been that of surrender – it's really been a falling into it. Like finding yourself floating in water, you know.

On this retreat, no one's saying a word, no one's even looking at each other and yet I know exactly who's standing by me just by the sound of their footsteps.

Yes, or you get a glance of the way they walk out of the corner of your eye – you don't even see their face. We know so much about each other, there's such intimacy happening here and we don't even know everyone's name. So, like that, you know your own sense of presence deeply, you know that presence pervades everything. So-called tree and grass and plastic – you have a sense of this shimmering presence just flooding everything and that's all you really need to know. It's very intimate.

There is a quote from George Herbert that Andrew Harvey uses in Hidden Journey: *'Love bade me welcome; yet my soul drew back guilty of dust and sin'. I suppose that I really don't think that I deserve to be immersed in this shimmering presence, to be in the face of love.*

It's understandable because love obliterates us. It destroys the one who wants to be at two with it – it's a kind of obliteration that happens in the face of it.

There's a wonderful story about some students who are asked to write the final essay of the term about the miracle of Jesus changing the water to wine. The headmaster is walking around and notices that there's one student in the room who is not writing. Now it turns out that this student is Lord Byron. So, just as the bell is about to ring, Lord Byron picks up his pen and he writes one line. The master comes over, picks up his paper, kind of sternly, and reads, 'The water met its master and it blushed'. I love this story.

There is something beautiful about humility in the face of love.

The sense of existing in shimmering presence, of being limitless and free, stays with me for many weeks after the retreat. But as the world takes its toll, I feel that my perspective is becoming clouded once more. In fact, I start to become incredibly depressed. I realize that for most of the time, I am still entrenched in this idea of 'me' — I cannot seem to disengage from a psychical hologram of perceptions and dreams with Paula as its central protagonist.

But the memory of freedom still remains. I no longer perceive it as an elusive prize, only ever to be really tasted on retreat in silence. Mind-body programming or not, I know that one day it will, finally, be mine.

Wonderful am I, my salutations to my Self! I am beyond the range of decay. When the whole world from Brahma to a blade of grass is destroyed, I still remain.

Wonderful am I! In spite of the body and its properties, I am One. I go nowhere, I come from nowhere, I abide in my Self, pervading the whole Universe.

All praise be to me, I am most skilful, I, without a form, uphold the Universe through all eternity.

I am wonderful, adoration to my Self. I own nothing, and yet all that is thought or spoken of is mine.

In reality, Knowledge, the Knowable and the Knower do not exist in me. That faultless Self am I, by whose want of Knowledge the three appear to exist.

The conception of duality is the root of all suffering; its only cure is the perception of the unreality of all objects and the realization of myself as One, pure Intelligence and Bliss.

I am pure Intelligence; through ignorance I have imagined the illusory conditions in myself; meditating thus, all the time, I am the Absolute.

The Ashtavakra Gita

John de Ruiter

CHAPTER TEN

LOVE ME
TENDER

Waking up is not necessarily pleasant:
You get to see
Why all this time,
You chose to sleep.

Unveiling Reality
John de Ruiter

Of all the people I planned to interview for this project, I sensed that my meeting with John de Ruiter would probably be one of the most profound. First, because John, having grown up in a more traditional Christian community, is not of the Advaita background I am more familiar with. Second, and more importantly, I am excited and intrigued by the phenomenon of John de Ruiter — the Aryan looks, the invading gaze, the messianic presence . . .

I am sitting in the Council House, College Green, in Bristol. Some 300 to 400 people have come to pay homage. John sits up at the front on a raised platform — confident, relaxed. Various helpers sit in attendance to one side, next to a tower of recording equipment and an array of promotional material. An anticipatory thrill hovers in the room. Seemingly oblivious and unmoved, John gazes at someone in the congregation. Indeed, throughout the three-hour session, he barely moves at all. There are only two positions he assumes — either leaning back with his arms resting on the arms of his chair; or leaning forward, arms resting on his legs, his hands clasped together as if in a position of prayer. Such a paradox, I think — a man so devoid of physicality and yet so seemingly full of physical presence.

John is tastefully dressed – he wears a woollen jacket and trousers with a dusty purple shirt. He has a brown beard, moustache and hooded eyebrows and his shoulder-length hair is swept backward, cascading into yellow coils behind his ears. When John is asked a question he swivels around in his chair to meet the person square-on. His face betrays no criticism, no judgement. There is a childlike innocence in his innocuous manner – a shyness, almost, in the curl of his lip and the gentleness of his Canadian accent.

Born in 1961 and raised in Stettler, Alberta, in Canada, John remained indifferent to any form of religious instruction during his youth. At the age of 17, nonetheless, he experienced, without preparation or warning, a state of awakening which, he claims, was to last for a year but which was to leave him at the speed at which it had come. John was then to embark upon a gruelling journey through the investigation of many mystical and philosophical traditions, in an attempt to regain that place of peace. 'I allowed honesty to look at each doctrine, each teacher and each technique I encountered, only to discover that they were all less than absolutely true. I became completely devastated. Each time I discovered yet another untruth, I let myself drop even deeper within. As consciousness, I was at the bottom of my own well, a well I had carved out through letting myself be continuously cracked open, deeper and deeper . . . and there was no water. At last, through simplicity of heart, through pure and absolute honesty, I just let go. I surrendered . . . unconditionally . . . to just simply being at the bottom of that well of darkness and never again trying to get out; warmly never again hoping for water. And it was at that moment that I became re-immersed in the benevolent reality of pure being . . . I am no longer my own. I belong to truth.'

The interview is scheduled for the two-hour interval between the first and second sessions. When it comes to the break, John is so completely surrounded by devotees, clamouring for attention and the opportunity to get physically close, I wonder if we will ever have the chance to speak one-to-one. An assistant approaches, informing me that the interview is to be postponed to the following morning, giving us greater privacy and as much time as I need. I am then asked to sign a consent and release form, a standard procedure I am told for anyone wishing to do an interview, and am given a sketchy map outlining the journey to the place where we will meet.

The following day, I drive to a secluded village called Barrow Gurney, half an hour or so from Bristol. I have been invited for breakfast with John and his hosts. The sky is angry and overcast – the leaves whirl and turn like Sufi dancers, heralding my arrival into a long straight drive leading to an Elizabethan manor house. I drive onto the forecourt and park next to the chapel. I ring the bell and wait. My heart is beating so fast it is now one thudding vibration. I am disturbed by the weather, lost in anxious thought. A sense of desolation overwhelms me — can I really go through with this?

The door is opened by a man restraining a histrionic German shepherd dog. 'Come in, come in! She's very friendly, really.' I slalom through the doorway, past the yelping animal and climb an oak-panelled staircase leading to a bright room. A munificent feast awaits my arrival. I greet John's hosts warmly and yet realize that I can barely look at John. I am not quite ready for his penetrating attention and yet I am offered a seat right next to him. The dog suddenly reappears seemingly from nowhere and crash-lands at my feet. I caress her smooth-rough coat, glad of the distraction and the momentary shift of attention away from me.

I notice a familiar book, *Answers* by Mother Meera, lying on top of a side-cabinet. 'Apparently, Mother Meera recommends that people go and see John,' our hostess smiles. 'John is reading her book at the moment and Mother Meera says all the same things that John does.' I wonder if John is on the same spiritual level as Mother Meera or indeed, whether Mother Meera is on the same spiritual level as John. Can there be a hierarchy of teachers, I wonder? Levels of enlightenment? A league table of beings?

Advaita for me was the most democratic of beliefs. Realization of one's true nature did not ultimately need attendance at some organization, the proximity of a teacher or guru; all that was required was the surrender to truth. And yet here was a man, hailed by many as the new Messiah, attracting followers in their thousands and leading people to the promised land — or more specifically meetings in Edmonton — to discover their innermost.

I try to chat casually with John about this and that, about different teachers, the spiritual path. 'If I read another spiritual book, I'll be sick!' My God, what am I saying? But it's OK, everyone laughs, the tension breaks. I finish my meal and the breakfast things are cleared away. I set up my recording machine. People fade back into other rooms. The door closes. Silence.

You say that in order to let in truth, you have to forsake the lie. What does that actually mean?

The lie that has to be forsaken is that you are worth something, that you belong to yourself, that your life is yours. Your preferences, those things that you have made to be important — all of that is not true.

And yet, the way that life is set up, I have all my experience forming this lie. I am just baffled why something as profound as truth, which is something that is inside of me, is just beyond my reach.

It's not beyond your reach — it's amazingly close. It touches you all the time, all throughout the day, every day. If truth were to be extracted out of your experience, then you would feel absolutely dead. There is a constant input of truth all the time. What makes it seem far away is that, when in your heart, you go up into your mind and through your thoughts, you ask, 'What is it that I am looking for?' Then you call it truth, you call it something. And because you are looking through the mind, you are looking for something that the mind can identify with, that the mind can take apart like a Rubik's cube, like a puzzle where you can take all the different pieces and figure it out and work with it.

Truth is something that is just as accessible to a little child or someone who has Downs syndrome or is mentally retarded or insane. So, it does not require intelligence, you do not need a good mind. A good mind does not even help. It also does not make it worse — there is nothing that makes it worse or better because the mind has nothing to do with it.

I have been engaged in a process of Self Enquiry — constantly deconstructing what I am not. But it is still a mental process and it doesn't tell me who I ultimately am. So what is the point of the mind?

The mind is there to express what we love. It is a vehicle of expression and we use it as a tool to acquire what we experience to be missing inside. We tend to use the mind to get something, instead of using the mind to express what is already there.

Through Self Enquiry, instead of discovering who I am, I've created an incessant commentary on myself. I can't visualize a moment without mind.

The mind is not a problem. The more you are not OK with the mind, just the way it is, the greater the problem will be. When there is 'not-OKness' in the heart, then whatever is presently filling your heart will express itself through the mind because the mind is for the expression of what is in the heart. So if your heart is in any amount in 'not-OKness', that 'not-OKness' manifests itself in the mind. Then you have all these thoughts of disappointment, confusion, trying, heaviness of mind, because that is what is in the heart. So the mind is just doing its job. When the heart in any way comes to rest and it is being quieted and there is a tenderness that is flowing through, then that comes through the mind and the expression of that is one of tenderness manifesting on the outside.

So mind reflects this inner state.

Yes.

So what's the heart then?

The heart is your conscious capacity to either close up or open up, to either harden and tighten or to open and soften. The heart has the capacity to exist as a holding energy that will then manifest want, need, insistence, demand, ownership, mine, 'for me'. Or the heart can be a capacity to be completely other than that holding energy, to be an energy of openness where it can see past itself, where it can enjoy something outside of itself, without having to pull that inside and make it about oneself.

The heart has a capacity to enjoy something on the outside without having to control it and pull it all in. The more the openness to enjoy anything without having to make it about oneself, then the more truth there is. So truth is not something that can initially be appreciated by the mind – truth is something that touches the heart. Truth then is like tenderness, like softness, it's like openness. Truth is the absence of needing anything. It is the absence of want.

When a little puppy comes running up to you and your whole heart opens up, that little puppy is 'doing truth' to you. When you hold a little baby, it is communicating to you – what is happening is that you are being touched by truth. Just look and see what happens inside of you when you hold a baby – that is truth. So that is how easy it is, that is how close it is. When you see a nest of little baby birds, then you see what that does to you inside – that is truth happening. And this is happening all day long. Every time you see a tree or you smell something nice, the fragrance of something, immediately it does something within – it opens you up.

You are enveloped by it all the time. It is just letting yourself enjoy what you honestly enjoy, without you having to seize it. In order to enjoy it, you let it in. You are not taking it in but letting it in and continually enjoying everything without trying to fill yourself up or store it all up inside, so that you have this storage container with all the things you enjoy. Just letting in and letting it through. So then there will be a simplicity of heart instead of having a complex heart.

Yes, I have certainly experienced that — there is a pure loving flow. But then, so often, a fear comes in — I think I am going to lose the love, which provokes a grasping. As soon as that mechanism is put into action, then the love is lost. I don't understand why I have to do that or why fear arises, when I know from experience I will never lose that flow of love.

It is because consciousness exists, which is different from the consciousness of a tree or an animal or a plant or a stone — the consciousness of the human. There is a full spectrum of consciousness. The human being has the capacity to share in the consciousness of every kind of consciousness in existence. Because we have a full spectrum of consciousness, then what we also have is power — the ultimate kind of power. We have the power to be something that we are not, whereas a tree does not have that kind of power — a tree can be itself but it cannot be something else. It cannot be in non-acceptance of itself because it can only be itself.

The larger the spectrum of consciousness of anything, the more there is an increased capacity to have movement, to have internal movement. An animal has emotions, an animal can take in more, express more, than a tree. A human being has the most. There is a full spectrum of consciousness so that we have more power to self-reflect and experience things — tenderness or the enjoyment of love. We experience that and we have the power to say, 'This is truly what I am in love with, so any time it touches me I want to make it mine.' We have the power to grab that and claim ownership and we then have the power to push out anything that does not feel good.

Then we become this holding, pushing consciousness instead of a consciousness that is open and letting in and enjoying. The awakening of such a consciousness is to realize the truth — that the very thing we love most tells us how to be. What we love most is love.

When we begin to realize what love does to us, then instead of closing, we can let go of basically what we are not and let in what we know we are. What we are is that tenderness, that softness, that love. And when closure seems to happen, which is normal because we want to have that love, we see that all we need is to be gentle with ourselves.

You often speak about a liquid OKness. Everything just being OK as it is, even in those contractions.

It is letting that be OK, so that the contractions within you are no longer an issue. It feels like a problem but you do not have to make it a problem.

Sometimes when a contraction comes I think, Oh God, here I go again. And then I'm just off, missing what is.

It does not matter if you miss. It does not even matter if you experience love and then you grab hold of it and say, 'It's mine, it's only for me, I don't want to share it.' It does not matter if that happens, just so long as, as soon as you see it, be gentle and not hard on yourself, do not judge yourself. Give yourself as much space inside as you see outside. When you see yourself contracting and being angry or hating or whatever, don't lock yourself up in a small space inside. Be gracious with yourself. Give yourself a lot of space.

When I have been compassionate with myself, gracious with myself, the contractions naturally lose their sting – they just fall away by themselves. But there is such a habit of self-deprecation and seeing everybody better than myself. Like with teachers of truth – the idea that they've got it and I haven't or there's some club and I'm not a member or whatever.

In terms of teachers, it is not worth believing what any of them say. It does not make any difference what teachers say. The only real authority, your only real authority is not some teacher outside of you. Your only authority is what touches your heart, what nourishes you inside of you. And you may be impressed by a teacher because he or she can speak of great things and speak of things that perhaps you cannot argue with. But when you are being impressed by something that does not nourish you, that does not touch your heart, that impresses your mind and your mind goes wow! – that does not mean anything. If the mind is wowed, that does not touch your heart.

If there is something, anything, that you are hearing from a teacher or reading in a book that does not directly touch your heart and nourish you and leave you quieted and gentled, it is not worth believing. And it does not matter how great it sounds.

At your meeting yesterday in Bristol, I was impressed by what you said. I've only met you a few times and to be here with you now, I feel very rested. But I don't want to start thinking that I have to be in your presence to be at rest – I don't want to have to need you. I don't want to get into that stuff.

But what is wrong with experiencing an inner pull or an inward needing? That is only an assault on your own sense of personal ownership or your own sense of identified personal space. As soon as you experience yourself being needy, then that is an affront to that personal space because that personal space wants to be able to be totally self-contained, because if it is not self-contained, it is not in control.

But what I am trying to say is that I want to stand on my own two feet, to have the truth within me. Krishnamurti says that truth is a pathless land – you don't need to be a member of anything or follow anybody.

But if you are enjoying the rest that exists in someone's presence – that is worth being with because that is being with truth. Then as soon as you experience that there is a desire to be with that – there is a pull. That desire is fine, that desire is clean. As soon as you take that desire and turn it into a want – 'I must have that' – then immediately there is a closure. But the inner desire itself, as long as there is no closure, as long as there is no insistence that I must have that, if there is just a gentleness within, then there is a constant openness and a softness. You can call it neediness because there is a pull but that kind of inner neediness is totally fine.

The only kind of neediness that is not fine is the neediness that says, 'I must have it my way.' When a little child gravitates toward you in a way that is really, really open – there is something that melts you. If an adult is the same way toward you, then others would judge that adult as being needy but if it is a small child, then all of a sudden it is OK. When you see a small child being like that, it moves your heart because you see the openness of heart in the way that that little child just crawls into an adult's lap and is totally at home there. And it would rather be there than be by itself. We are not judging that as being needy, whereas when an adult is like that, we say, 'Why aren't you just being yourself, why do you need that person?'

So, there are two different kinds of neediness. The one that is OK is wonderfully open and very soft and very nourishing and that is an awesome neediness. And within that there is an attraction of being.

How can one find a true teacher? If one is at rest with a particular person – great, go and see that person. Is that the only real litmus test?

People gravitate toward the kind of teacher who confirms most of what the individual wants to have. So if there is a teacher who has an agenda in teaching, then that will attract an individual who will want that kind of agenda and want to be able to hide and justify it in a way that that particular teacher does. A teacher who has no agenda will attract those who would love to live agenda-free and who do not want to cater to their own agenda anymore. Those who still want to have an agenda and are on a spiritual path – they are looking for a teacher, in some way, to help them have what they want to have. When an individual like that encounters a teacher who has no agenda, then for that individual it is almost like stepping into the room and quickly backing off before it destroys everything, before that individual's own wants and agendas are exposed.

Most people feel much more secure when they can detect some kind of agenda in a teacher. And even though they truly do not appreciate it, that agenda still makes them feel safe because they can say, 'I don't have to really deal with my agenda yet, this buys me some time, this gives me some space for my dishonesty.' Most people are like that. Most people would be more comfortable, mentally more comfortable, with a teacher who has an agenda.

Whereas if you were to encounter a teacher without an agenda, it could pull your whole heart in because there would be a love of something there that you could taste that is utterly true. And there is a fear in that – 'Wow, this is the real thing and this generates such a powerful response within me that I feel myself just like a moth that just wants to fly into the fire. Wow, I don't want to get all burned up, I love the heat but it's just the real thing that is dangerous.'

Yes, I don't always find that teachers today are teaching without an agenda. I find that worrying because I can't understand what the truth is anymore.

There is a huge misunderstanding with awakening. Awakening does not mean very much but there are a lot of people out there focusing on it – some of them teaching, many of them not teaching. What awakening is, is that you can see, whereas before you could not see. When you are given internal sight as to what it is that you already know is true, then you are awakened. But so what if you can see? Just because you can see, that does not mean that you will completely surrender, be in absolute surrender to what it is that you do see.

Awakening is not of such great value. All the value is mistakenly placed on awakening, so much so that when you hear of someone speaking of great and wonderful things, your mind is impressed. But that is not what you are in love with. What you are in love with is anything that touches your heart, that causes your whole heart to open.

You are not in love with your mind being impressed. When someone is awakened, he or she can speak of things that impress your mind. But that does not necessarily mean that it touches your heart. The only way that it will touch your heart is if that individual's heart is completely open and soft. If he or she has surrendered to what he or she knows is true, then you will be in love with that kind of heart. You will know it. Whether that individual is awakened or not does not make any difference.

You meet some little grandmother somewhere. You spend time with her and everything about her is just so incredibly tender inside but she is not actually doing anything right. But your immediate response is, 'I'd love it if you were my grandmother, I'd love to come over here every day and drink tea, just drop by for five minutes and then go – it sets my whole day straight because in my whole heart this is what I know it's all about.' That individual, that little grandmother, did not have to explain a thing – it was her presence that taught you. It is the presence that tells you what is true.

Just because someone is awakened, so what? Just because you know what is true, that does not mean that you have become what you know. You can see into reality but that does not mean that you are at one with it. You can speak the right things but that does not mean that you are one with it. You can have all the right information, so what?

I've never heard it explained that way before.

With someone who is awakened – it does not matter how massive the awakening was. That is not impressive. What is impressive is when that whole heart just totally bows down to what it sees and knows is true, regardless of how tiny that seeing or that knowing is, and merges with it. If with the tiniest little touch of seeing that whole heart bows down to what is true and responds to that, that is impressive.

When someone's heart is open – like a grandmother as you say – you're just suffused in love. You don't need to put it into words, there's just a knowing. You can feel it. I always thought awakening was this great bang, the dissolution of ego and attachment and all of that.

No, that does not mean a thing. The only thing that has any value at all is purity of heart. Awakening does not mean anything at all. So what if you can see? So what if you can see into all of reality? So what if I can see into the great ocean of reality and explain all of its wonders, so what? Seeing does not mean very much. All that seeing means is you are awake, you can see.

And that's just a mind thing?

The mind cannot see unless the heart has been opened, cracked open to see. Once the heart has been cracked open to see, now it sees. But if it does not surrender to what it sees, then there is an impurity of heart. But once the heart has cracked open to see and once the mind also sees, then the mind always sees. The seeing stays. The honesty allowed the heart to crack open to be able to see – that may close but the seeing itself will remain open. So you can be awakened and have an uncleanness of heart or an impurity of heart or have an agenda.

There are people who profess to see and do indeed appear to see and who say amazing things and understand the workings of the mind. But, in certain cases, there can be something that's not quite right — there can be a kind of unease in their presence.

That is right. It is only purity of heart that has any value at all. And purity of heart is a heart that will allow itself to be completely aligned with whatever it honestly knows is true, with whatever it does really see. It does not have to be much. If you have a heart that is not awakened, it knows almost nothing but that whole heart is giving into a little bit of what it knows to be true — that heart is absolutely beautiful.

If you have a heart that allows itself to go through a massive cracking open and then the mind opens up and there is a full seeing by heart and mind and a surrender into reality, then that is someone who is home. But if there is not an absolute surrender to what it sees, if the heart does not just let itself completely fall in and turn into that, if it is retaining some sort of identity in the midst of being able to see so much, then there is the opposite of beauty there — there is more of a pungency of self-ownership. It is like dropping a fly into a perfume bottle. Just a little bit of a holding back and putting that holding into something beautiful changes the whole thing. It really stands out and we can experience the difference. When you are with someone like that, you might at first be impressed but it is not like being with that little old lady who, when she looks in your eyes, causes you to just melt. That is what the true value is. You are presently impressed with the awakened knowledge but that is not worth anything.

Why does fear arise? Why can't I let go?

Fear is an interesting thing. There are different kinds of fear — some kinds of fear are extremely dense and have a tremendous edge to them. That is the kind of fear that hits and wounds. There is also a fear that is the kind that would show up in the context of innocence — like a tiny little child who experiences something so much larger than itself. It is not anything substantial but it is like a little baby when you take it into the wind or you blow into its face — it is like there is more there that is happening than it can presently take in comfortably. So you blow into a baby's face and it reacts — there is fear in that but it is a kind of fear that is touching to see because it is happening to an innocence, and that innocence is not losing anything with that fear being there.

It's almost instinctive.

Yes. When inwardly you encounter something that your whole heart responds to and experiences, then there can be a fear because it is a fearful thing that your whole heart is moved to jump into. And the mind says, 'Wow, what's happening, I've lost control of that.' The mind has lost control of the heart because the heart is just in love and is diving in. There is not a oneness between the mind and the heart. The heart is gone, it is diving, it is in love with what it sees. Until the mind and the heart become One, fear will always touch. When the heart stays with what it knows, then the mind has to come along and as it is taken along, then the mind ends up being dissolved in the very thing that the heart is diving into. So in that, the mind joins the heart and the mind becomes one with the heart – there is no other way.

The mind is to be the follower of the heart. Normally, we always have it the other way round, where the heart is the follower of the mind. Respond to what touches your heart. Be in love with what you find your heart to be in love with, regardless of what the mind thinks. When you have existed following your mind instead of letting your mind follow the heart, then when the heart does encounter what it is most in love with and dives in, the mind is going to do a lot of squirming. It will be saying everything that it was taught to say by the heart because the heart would always go to the mind and consult the mind and say, 'What do think of this? Should I do this? Should I not do this?' Always consulting the mind, asking its permission – 'What do you think I should do?' And then the mind just creates a whole story – it makes a great thing of it and after all of the consulting, the heart does not seem to know either.

When your heart stays with what touches it, then that touch moves your whole heart and that is simple. When you stay with that touch, it does not matter what the mind's input is. It does not make any difference. The mind has nothing to do with this. The mind was not involved in your heart being touched. The mind followed after the heart and then, because of how you used to feed it, the mind will keep being the way that you have taught it to be. The mind will come in and say, 'Well, you have not consulted me on this but I think such and such.' And if you are used to following the mind, then you will stop and think, 'That's a really good point and I heard that lots before and read that in books, there's a lot of back up to that and yes, I'll have to really consider that.' And now your heart is not touched anymore. You are not moved and the simplicity of heart is gone. So you are taken away from it.

Instead of trusting your own opinions, instead of trusting what you think, trust only what touches your heart. If it touches your heart, believe it. If it touches your heart, you already know something because your heart can only genuinely respond to something that is just like itself. So when your whole heart is moved then your heart is already convinced. It already knows. And the mind may come in with all these objections . . .

And evidence to prove otherwise . . .

Yes. But that does not mean anything because the heart is already convinced. As soon as it is touched and moved, it is convinced. It is already merging with something that is just like itself. The mind has nothing to do with this, so it can be left out. It might be uncomfortable because the mind will come and bring all of its objections and doubts. But doubt will never tell you what is true. Doubt will only tell you what might not be true. Doubt will present you with all of the maybes. That is the most that it can ever do, so doubt cannot give you anything. Doubt can only take away. So instead of listening to what you doubt, listen to what you know. What you doubt does not matter, it is what you know that matters. So then you just remain with what you know. Stay with what touches your heart. With anything that causes doubt, then instead of consulting the doubt, go to what you know, go to what touches your heart and let whatever touches your heart tell you about those things that touch your heart. And then your heart will be even more moved and more filled.

I can see that there is that knowing in the heart but the mind keeps interfering with things because of past conditioning or wanting to behave in a certain way.

Then simply allow that to be, as is. And even objections such as, 'I don't want to be needy' — since when does what you want or not want have anything to do with anything? In terms of what moves your heart, all you will find is your heart responding. When a little puppy comes running over to you, even before it gets to you, it has already won your heart. So when your heart starts to respond to this little puppy that is bounding toward you, your mind can say, 'Aren't you being a little needy here? Your heart is going out of yourself here. Just stay within yourself, you don't need anything. Why are you going out to that puppy?'
    But the mind just screws up everything that is happening, if you trust it. Stay with what you are in love with. If your whole heart responds to that little puppy, if your whole heart jumps right out of itself to that little puppy, let it. Your heart knows what is true. It knows what it loves.

It does, doesn't it.

So then believe it — your mental opinions have nothing to do with the wonderfulness of what is happening between you and this little puppy that is bounding toward you. The opinions are all based on information that has an element of truth but which is all screwed up and turned around. They end up being used against people, instead of allowing people to respond to what they know is true. So in that way, there is this control that is placed on people.

Information is powerful but information does not touch your heart. So there is nothing impressive, truly impressive, with someone who is just merely awakened. Or even massively awakened — so what? Unless what is there within that awakened being truly and genuinely wins your whole heart. If it does, then believe it because your heart already knows it. But if your heart is not moved, completely moved, then so what? The only authority that exists is the movement of your own heart — that tells you what is true.

I seem to need an authority to say that my own response is valid. It's been crushed by so many years of being controlled by the mind and what other people have been telling me about the nature of mind. When I meet certain teachers there can be conflict within me between my mind and heart about how I respond to them.

It is because when you are getting together with these teachers they cannot give you something they do not have. They can only give you what they think they have. Teaching like that — as much as you might be amazed or impressed in your mind — if it does not move your whole heart, if it does not just take your whole heart and set it free, is not true. Then that teacher is using you — he or she needs followers to be the teacher. A teacher of truth will take a heart and just show it how to be. And that heart will just be totally in love with it. There are a lot of teachers out there who are awakened and can really see but inwardly they have not died. A teacher who has not allowed the inward death of self-created agendas is a danger.

What needs to die?

Self-importance, the 'somebody'. What has to die is the importance of the mind within that individual to that individual's heart. The death of the authority of the mind. If the mind has any authority within that heart, then it does not matter how awakened that individual is — he or she has not died. It is not the heart that has to die, it is the authority of the mind within that heart that has to die because the mind is not an authority — we give it authority.

Something that confuses me is the concept of individuality and 'I'. People speak of ego, being attached to the ego, how one should transcend the ego. But there is a sense of individuality within me that I am unable to deny.

There is teaching out there that says that there is no 'I' and asks who is the 'I' that speaks.

Yes, who's asking the question?!

That is just someone having information, which, when it is presented to you, entices your mind to say, 'Wow yeah, who am I?' And it is made to be huge and complicated and the grand prize of awakening is made to seem just like a universe away – 'If I could just get to that star out there, then I know that I'll be just like that star. When do I get there?'

And yet the reality, not of awakening but of living in truth, is something that a little child's heart understands. It knows a whole lot – it does not understand. A teacher understands but a teacher does not necessarily have what the heart of a little child has. So when a teacher does not have it, then the teacher is not the star out there that he or she is pretending to be.

And there are teachers who say that none of this exists . . .

That it's all an illusion.

Yes, they say it is all an illusion but that is not true. It all exists. It is all exactly what it is. The only thing that is an illusion is your relationship with all of this. If this chair becomes something to you, such that you cannot be happy unless this chair is always clean, and then someone makes it dirty and you are not happy any more – that is an illusion because the well-being of your heart, the nourishment of your heart, is not in reality dependent on whether this chair is clean or not. That is the only part that is the illusion.

The chair itself is fine. The chair is real. This whole existence is all real. The only thing that is a dream or an illusion is the untrue relationship that we have with everything in existence, within our own consciousness.

And does 'I' exist? Does Paula exist?

Well, not Paula because then you are giving a name to it, but yes, 'I' does exist.

When mummy says, 'Who wants ice-cream?' and this little two-year-old says, 'Me!' and it just brightens up – that one that brightens up exists. To ask that little child, 'Who is that "me"?' and then start doing this playing with the mind, would destroy the sunshine that speaks through that body.

I've heard some people say that the concept of individuality is just a bunch of thoughts, that when one looks for a personal self, one can't hold onto it. But something exists within me — I am here.

There is a personal self but you cannot take that personally. As soon as you take it personally – the personal self – then you turn it into something that it is not. But if you enjoy the personal self, then all that happens within is that the sunshine comes through.

The personality is a reality within consciousness. There is nothing that is untrue or wrong with the personality. The personality is a manifestation of consciousness itself. When consciousness takes the personality, assesses the personality and gives the personality a value other than its actual value, then consciousness is being something within that personality that is not true. When consciousness itself that is within that personality says, 'I have the best personality of any personality that I know and nobody had better dare touch it because if they try to hurt it, I'll hurt them back,' there is all this illusion surrounding the value of that personality. Let all of that illusion wash away and what there will be is this innocence of personality. An innocent personality is just utterly loveable.

It's just someone being themselves quite naturally.

A little puppy that comes bounding up to you – there is an 'I' in that little puppy, a personality that sees you and totally responds. The innocence in that personality is absolutely pure. There is nothing untrue about it.

But some people interpret Advaita as saying that even 'I' as a personality does not exist — that all I am is consciousness.

That is true but personality is consciousness too. Consciousness has two different flows. There is consciousness that comes out of its innermost, that comes out of the source. Coming out of the source, it begins to move into form. Then personality starts to come into being, the mind comes into being, the emotions come into being. The capacity to be in relationship with this whole existence comes into being – all of that comes out of truth, all of that comes out of the Absolute. When consciousness comes out of the Absolute and it comes into form, there is unending movement that never, ever, ever, ever stops coming farther and farther out into form. That is why we have a whole universe that has a physical reality to it.

And there is another flow that is taking place and that is a flow of dying but it is the sweetness of dying, it is a sweetness of returning to the source. The returning of consciousness to its own source is a yin energy or a dissolving energy or a letting-go energy or an energy of something solid returning to its form.

So there is this expression outward into the personality and the receding of personality as it is being drawn back into formlessness. The 'I' exists – the 'I' is what is manifesting itself in the personality, through that outward flow of consciousness.

And there have to be both. With the different traditions in the East, there is a gravitation toward the Absolute and there is an imbalance in that. Where there is gravitation toward the Absolute, there is no existence – all of this is just an illusion, all that exists is just the Absolute, all there is is the source. People end up in caves living with half a garment wrapped around themselves and they cannot in a complex way be part of this existence. So what they do is reduce their whole existence to eating a little bit of rice and wearing almost nothing. They can speak of wonderful things and there may be an incredible measure of purity in that but there is still not a balance. So you can have a purity of heart, have an absolutely wonderful heart, but it will be out of balance. To be with that heart is still totally incredible – that is different than being with a teacher who has an impurity of heart.

The natural balance to consciousness coming out into form is the ever deepening knowledge of the Absolute or the source that it is continually returning to. It is simultaneously letting itself be free to integrate everything within this whole existence. That kind of heart can exist within the Absolute at the same time as, for example, running a corporation and being involved in the complexities of this existence, without getting attached. That kind of heart is going so far out into existence, handling thousands and thousands of details, and yet still soaking in the Absolute. What an incredible balancing combination! And that is what you find lacking in the East because all that it is focused on is the Absolute, the source. The source is the most awesome of what there is because that is what we have all come out of. But then the source expresses itself into form, into all of this, so then to make this something less than it really is, that undermines the source because this is all its expression.

It is only our inner tightness, it is only our insistence on our relationship with wanting to be in the source or our insistence on our relationship with everything within existence that is the problem. We say, 'This is mine, don't touch it – if you touch that, I'll hurt you.' Any kind of insistence regarding going out into existence or going back into the source – that is the only illusion that exists. Outside of that, there is no illusion.

I have found Eastern traditions quite gruelling actually – all that self-denial. I have been driven crazy with it. I don't know who I am any more but in Advaitic terms, that means, wow, great! But I don't feel fulfilled by that knowledge, I just feel very lost.

You have only been screwed up within the mind – that is all that has happened. This impressive information got hold of your mind and said, 'Wow, what a thought!' Then there was an ache inside because you were impressed by this thought. So what about that thought? When you see a mother bird feeding its young and experience what that does to you, that is telling you what is true. You were not impressed by that in your mind but your whole heart was filled as soon as you saw it.

What happens in the meetings when you look at people? I've not come across it before, being so looked at.

I'm not doing anything different from what a little baby does. When you hold a little baby that looks into your eyes – a one-year-old – that look just goes all the way in, it goes right inside of you. But you do not feel fear with that because there is nothing you perceive within that little baby that can have control over you. Whereas an adult can hurt you, an adult can say things about you, an adult can say things to you that can mess you up inside. A one-year-old is not a threat to you. What is that baby going to do to you? It cannot do anything to you. So you are not threatened by it.

   If anything, it quietens everything within you because it is looking past your issues, it is looking past your stuff, it is not seeing those things – all it sees is you. So then you love it, there is no threat. But when an adult looks at you or looks into you exactly the same way as a one-year-old, then all of a sudden it touches fear because you do not let anybody in – 'What are you doing inside of me? I don't want you inside of me because you can talk about me, you can talk about what you see, perhaps you can do spooky things inside of me.' When anyone has the capacity to look right inside of you and be inside of you and you perceive they have an agenda – you perceive you are in trouble. So then fear touches.

There are two responses simultaneously occurring when you gaze at me. On the one hand, I think that I'm not going to look away, like it's some sort of competition almost. On the other, it's very restful. I feel incredible peace now, though there have also been flashes of intense terror.

The terror is there because with encountering what I am your mind does not have a chance. And any part of your heart that is up in the mind does not have a chance. The only thing that has a chance within you is that part of your heart that just comes to rest. And then that part loves what it sees, loves what it hears. It is not threatened – it is nourished. It is brought to rest, so there is no issue. But any part of your heart that is up in the mind, consulting with the mind, saying, 'Wow, what do you think of this, wow, what's happening here?' – that part of the mind cannot handle this. It has no answer. So it just sort of seizes. It does not know what to do.

You say that you are a living embodiment of truth. What does that really mean? Your mind no longer has authority over the heart?

When the mind no longer has authority over the heart, that heart is home. But that is still not an embodiment of truth. For there to be an embodiment of truth, then there needs to be a heart that is no longer ruled by the mind and a heart that is awakened to the whole ocean of reality. When that heart merges with the whole ocean of reality, without the mind having any authority over it, then that heart embodies reality. So then there is an embodiment of truth.

Can I be a living embodiment of truth?

Right now you can be a living embodiment of the tiniest little bit that you know is true. So in that tiny little bit, yes. It does not have to be more. It is you letting your whole heart live being totally in love with the little bit that you are genuinely in love with. It is you no longer being pulled away by what impresses your mind about truth. Truth is no longer something that you wrestle with in the mind – truth is only something that you are totally in love with in the heart. Then you will embody the little bit that you do know is true.

Our hosts, and the dog, have re-entered the room and have been listening attentively for the past hour or so. We then all go outside and I ask John to stand by a doorway for the purposes of his photograph. As I take the shots he asks me about the progress of the book. 'I have felt like throwing in the towel,' I shrug. 'Sometimes I have felt incredible moments of clear seeing. But more recently, I have often been confused, disillusioned, depressed.' 'Press on and finish the book.' John looks into the middle distance, analyzing my predicament. 'It's very important to write about what you truly see. You are in a unique position, having such close contact with all these people. Just be completely honest about all the things you observe.'

Do I have a valid voice? Should I include my own opinions in a book of spiritual journalism? I was trying to be objective, to just simply let each teacher speak for themselves. What I didn't want was to give a verdict as to whether they had 'got it' or not; in short, I didn't want to commit myself to things I don't ultimately understand, things about which my interpretation was changing on a daily basis.

John and I embrace. 'If you need to know about anything else, please ask.' He gently smiles and disappears. As I drive away I feel that, for the first time, all my questions have been answered, that what John said actually made complete sense. There are no philosophical conundrums left for me to agonize over, no intellectual puzzles to screw my mind. Everything is clear.

The journey home is a five-hour car ride. For the first hour or so, my driving is effortless, my mind very calm and my heart wide open. I feel charged with power but not of a competitive kind; rather a centred self-confidence, an invincibility, almost – I am the still point in a moving world.

It is difficult to isolate the time exactly when my mind re-materializes, like a mirage in the heat, tantalizing my attention. I begin to reflect on my need for verification from others to reaffirm what I know deep inside. Aren't I equipped with all the tools I need to discern the ultimate truth? After all, if truth is within, why do I need all these teachers to tell me so? Then I think why isn't my mind an issue here – isn't discrimination the most important gift to mankind? Isn't it vital to question all the things that John said? I just cannot get my head around his claims of being 'a living embodiment of truth'. Indeed, why should I even believe him? Doubt, anxiety, frustration – once again, the familiar characters reappear. Exhausted and upset, I ask myself what I know to be absolutely true. I fall still. To think about John, there is perplexity; to be with John, there was perfect peace.

Q: 'Brahman is real. The world [jagat] is illusion' is the stock phrase of Sri Sankaracharya. Yet others say, 'The world is reality.' Which is true?

A: Both statements are true. They refer to different stages of development and are spoken from different points of view. The aspirant [abhyasi] starts with the definition, that *which is real exists always. Then he eliminates the world as unreal because it is changing. The seeker ultimately reaches the Self and there finds unity as the prevailing note. Then, that which was originally rejected as being unreal is found to be a part of the unity. Being absorbed in the reality, the world also is real. There is only being in Self-realization, and nothing but being.*

Be As You Are: The Teachings of Sri Ramana Maharshi

Pamela Wilson

CHAPTER ELEVEN

AMAZING
GRACE

A few months have now passed since my last interview. Meeting John de Ruiter seemed to have such a profound effect on me that, for all the grey and bleak wintery months afterwards, the mental anguish and depression that I often experience has momentarily passed.

It is now the end of April. It is interesting how the coming of spring inspires poets and musicians to praise the rebirth of the plants and flowers. But not for all – T S Eliot found April to be the cruellest month, a time when memory and desire are mixed by the spring rain. For a long time, I had not really known what Eliot actually meant – his work seemed abstract, erudite, aloof; quoted ubiquitously but with a meaning that so often eluded me. Why should the advent of emerging beauty and freshness be so cruel? Watching nature from my window rejuvenate herself, paint herself into life, is like observing a Renaissance artist, equipped with the knowledge of divine proportion and harmony, administering God's design through vermilion and ochre and cyan. Oh, how I envy her! The ability to have another chance, to start again on a fresh canvas, unblemished by memory and decay. Is this what Eliot meant? Was he jealous of something he felt he could not have or of something that he had once had but now had lost?

I had not heard of Pamela Wilson until only a few weeks before her arrival in London. But people were speaking so highly of her I just had to come and find out for myself. The Advaita community in London is only a small collection of seekers, so-called refugees from various spiritual institutions or just those simply hanging out for the ride. Naturally everyone loves to discuss the latest teacher in town and Pamela was no exception. What I was beginning to appreciate was, like everything else in life, teachers are a matter of taste – for every devotee there will be a denouncer, with of course all the supplementary evidence and facts. And yet, with Pamela, not one single person suggested anything other than praise – for her warmth, intelligence and even good looks. This was sounding just a little too good to be true . . .

I have come to a large Victorian semi-detached house situated on The Avenue in the back streets of Kilburn in north London. Having assumed that the satsang was taking place elsewhere and then discovering my error, I arrive about half an hour into an afternoon session. The house is deathly quiet. I creep into the kitchen to catch my breath and to sort out as noiselessly as I can the change for the satsang money bowl – its presence always evoking a sense of guilt that I really should be giving a bit more, to be followed by an equally fervent sense of justification why I don't. There are about 10 people in the lounge – some sitting on chairs, others on cushions, propped up against a wall. Pamela is sitting in an armchair at the front. She acknowledges my arrival with a faint smile and a raising of her eyebrows as I sit on a cushion at the back of the room. I always hate entering a room when things have already started, particularly when I am greeted by the welcome of silence. I almost feel like an intruder and painstakingly try to make myself comfortable on my wafer-thin seat without making too much of a performance.

Pamela is a very striking-looking woman, with long honey-coloured hair rippled with blonde highlights. She is wearing a stone-coloured jacket and neutral straight skirt. She has tucked her legs under her and is looking into her lap. I immediately like her apparent lack of airs and graces. There is none of the more familiar paraphernalia of satsang – eye-gazing, portraits of great teachers, burning candles. As I look around the room, this more casual approach is reflected in people's postures – everyone looks a little less self-consciousness than at more formal gatherings, their backs not quite so stiff, their necks not quite so erect. I even think someone has momentarily drifted into a peaceful sleep, his head bobbing quietly . . .

Currently living in Sedona, Arizona, Pamela Wilson was born in San Francisco in 1954. 'My mother was very kind and loving and accepting. She was very soothing in her energy. But my father was a little jarring – he was very energetic and loud and booming. A little daunting in fact.' One of her earliest memories as a very young child is of going to Episcopal Church: 'I used to fixate on the Jesus – it was ooh. I don't know where it came from but I would look at his statue with such feelings of love and awe.' Despite such divine connection, her parents' marriage was breaking down and, when Pamela was six, they divorced: 'Then there was a closing down, of course, and a sense of losing love and a decision that I was not going to love again. I couldn't relate to others anymore or relax and just enjoy.'

It was during her teens that she was to have the first of a number of significant experiences. 'When I was 15, there was an overwhelming and a not understanding of human behaviour and the world. I called out one night and I said, "If there is anyone out there who knows anything, please come here." And there was a visitation of an Indian man and there was beautiful light around him. It was alarming and I got scared and I threw a pillow at him and he disappeared.' This is reminiscent of the story of Robert Adams who reputedly saw Sri Ramana Maharshi at the end of his bed, although Pamela at the time did not know about the sage of Arunachala.

It would be many years later, studying at college, that Pamela would see the Indian man again. 'The same thing happened – fear arose, the throwing of the pillow and then he disappeared.' But despite being blessed with dreams of holy men, at the age of only 21, she received the most devastating news: 'My mother died and that was the big blow – she was only 46. It was a wake-up call and the start of spiritual enquiry or practice.' Not wanting to die young like her mother, she took to studying health and nutrition. 'I started reading all the books and from there I discovered yoga and meditation. There was this recognition that stress equalled 'dis-ease' – within me there was tension and discomfort and a not feeling relaxed with people.'

Transcendental Meditation offered partial relief. 'But there wasn't a teacher around to explain that the persona can never be this absolutely exquisite resting presence because it's an imposition on the resting presence. I was always trying to fix the persona like a seamstress, taking out the loose bits and adding something nicer. I was basically trying to do God's work.' It was now time for someone else to show the way.

So could we focus on the way things were when 'realization' occurred?

What came with my practice was an arrogance that built up because I thought, 'OK, I can handle life because I have all these tools. If the going gets tough, I can release my way out of it or meditate my way out of it or enquire my way out of it'. There was a kind of artificial bubble of peace that really had to be maintained through effort. Life was very much a trickster and would say, 'Oh yes, you think that you're so peaceful.' And then whack!

Finally the life just started to fall apart. All of a sudden there was a maturity, seeing that I have absolutely no control. There was also a seeing that I couldn't even manage the thoughts and feelings and I certainly was not in charge. And luckily, at the same time a friend took me to see Robert Adams – this was about 1994. Just walking into the room, there was an instant recognition of this immense peace. And since all I had done was to walk into a room, that was a big clue. It was like, 'Ah ha, maybe you don't have to do anything.' Robert then confirmed that and he said, 'Just let satsang dissolve everything, let grace dissolve everything and just enquire into who you are.' Now I didn't have an affinity for formal enquiry and yet somehow awareness was always enquiring into what was true without realizing it. So I guess a kind of natural enquiry would be going on.

I knew something was going on because the body would deeply relax in satsang, in a way it never had with all these other tools. And there was a trusting in that, which was undeniable. The brain couldn't discount or reject it. Robert was very welcoming – he didn't see you as a mess that needed to be fixed or that you needed to do anything. He knew that there was full realization and just because it was obscured, that meant nothing. So there was such a sense of 'aah'. I felt for the first time, other than in the presence of my mother, unconditionally loved and welcomed and in that there was such a melting. I felt safe. I felt that I was taking refuge in this immense mountain of love. There was a maturity in that recognition of how rare it was to sit with somebody like Robert but there was also this immature naivety that would follow any whim.

Where was this happening?

In Los Angeles, there was this one house at the top of a hill where he gave satsang. After that I moved up north. I started to go to satsang a lot in Marin County and it was one of the benefits that you could go and sit with Gangaji or Catherine Ingram or Francis Lucille. There was a seeing that it was the grace at satsang that was the ultimate guru, not really the body or whoever was there. And yet when I heard that Robert was going to leave the body, I went to see him in Sedona and it was very beautiful to have his final blessing. It was quite intense.

Didn't he ask you to come and stay with him before?

On one of the visits to Sedona, I asked him whether I should move there to be with him and he hesitated and then he said yes – and those sorts of things are not to be taken lightly. But of course I took it lightly and I said, 'Robert, I don't like Sedona!' It was me being the me I thought I was, which was actually being true to itself, which was immature.

Then you said you crammed his tapes.

I went to his satsang, which was supposed to be his last and luckily I got a private time with him – he kept his hand on my head for a long time. Then, a few weeks after that, he left his body and that was the second wake-up call. My mother was the first when she died and then, when Robert died, it was like, 'Oh my God, let's be a little more alert here! This is rare and wonderful and this is not like going to the movies. Time to get serious.' So, I listened to Robert's tapes all day. Luckily I have friends who had 60 or more tapes so they made me copies. I listened to about three of his tapes a day and any other satsang tapes I could get hold of because then I was teetering on the brink of falling into the heart. There would be samadhi for half-day periods but it would never last.

One of the big breakthroughs was in this samadhi state of sedated aliveness, which is the only way I could describe it. There was this very deep calm but it was vibrating with awe and wonder. I looked at the body and I thought, 'I get it, it's just a body, not *my* body.' And then at one point the cat walked by and I thought, 'It's a cat, it's not *my* cat.' So the conditioning of ownership was starting to dissolve just through the grace of going to so many satsang. But it would never last.

I would sit with Francis Lucille, who is so exquisite, and then Gangaji and then I found a beautiful lady called Neelam, who's Polish, from Papaji. About half a month after Robert had left, I was sitting with her and this *shakti* kept rising up and it made my body nervous. Once I asked her about this and I said that it was really scary and strong. And she started laughing and just said, 'Let it have you!' It was helpful to be around the women teachers because it dissolved a lot of concepts of what I thought freedom would look like. It was reassuring as they were very accessible and you could just be friends. So I spent time with Neelam and we went to Sedona – it was very beautiful and this time I was fully honouring presence. There was this decision that I was not going to be stupid about it.

Then one day during an outdoor satsang, there was a shift and it was just literally a falling into the heart. It was so simple and it was so true. I couldn't deny it and no amount of brain activity saying 'no' could cast a shadow over it – it just was.

You said it was like sunstroke.

Well, it was funny because the brain thinks it is your freedom coach. It's saying, 'You're identified today! Oh, that's a judgement!' It was trying to assist me in this goal of freedom – it had read all the books and decided it could be a good coach. So when this shift happened through grace, it said that either I had sunstroke or I had realized the Self! It was so funny. The mind really is a parrot or a little computer, it's not this immense thing to be opposed.

There was just quiet and well-being and still some wondering about the mystery. But everything would get revealed just as grace decided to reveal it. The brain was still trying to figure out the mystery. It was very quiet compared to before but, if it did move, it would move in a little bit of judgement or it would move to assess the mystery. Finally, after about a year and a half, it realized, 'Well, it's a mystery.' And it really quietened. But there was definitely a change in the sovereignty of the mind over the heart or presence. There was a dissolving of the conditioning. Some people have described it as a deepening but that's not really accurate. People often use the analogy of the petals in a lotus – it's blooming.

You often speak about awareness and consciousness but I don't understand the difference. Is consciousness unmanifest Self and awareness a perceiving quality within it?

Yes. Some people might take issue with the words 'awareness' or 'consciousness' and enquire into them separately. Awareness delights in the discovery of its own apparent movement. Consciousness rests behind it and yet they are not two. Awareness arises from consciousness and it goes off to enjoy and explore and then it returns. So that's why in India they call awareness the feminine aspect.

So when we get lost in the drama, what's happened to awareness?

Awareness is still present but it's merged with the drama. You see, awareness by nature is devotion and innocence and it's so curious. It merges with everything. If awareness smells using the senses, it's just mmm – it literally merges with the fragrance. So that is a delightful quality of it. We suffer when it merges with suffering, when each cell is literally in agony, and yet it is still pure awareness, fully immersed or identified. The sweet thing about awareness is that it thinks it is thought and it thinks that it's a body but really it's just conditioning.

When little kids are tiny there's no sense of separation from mommy. Children are always trading roles and playing, for example doctors and nurses. It's like an endless exploration of trading roles and playing with them. As we get older, it gets a little more serious and we forget who we are but it's still just a role. So awareness gets confused by the bundle of thoughts and feelings. It really thinks it's so-and-so, it's a Pamela and then it really feels the stakes are very high. If you think that you're just a body, then the fear of death will be looming every day.

Could you relate the analogy of Rama and Sita and Hanuman and how that ties in with the various mechanisms of the body-mind.

It's nice when you can use a story to illustrate something which seems very heavy in order to make it light. That's actually what fables are about – showing how we are all alike. Everybody has the same desires and dreams, hopes and fears.

So basically, Sita is awareness and she gets kidnapped by a demon king. Then, of course, she forgets who she really is because kidnappers always keep control over their victim. Actually she is really trapped by thought, as represented by the demon king, and thought is not very nice to awareness consciousness. Have you noticed how it always says mean things to you? 'You're too fat,' 'You're stupid,' 'You shouldn't have said that.' It's always threatening with judgement and disapproval. Thought keeps awareness agitated because, if awareness comes to rest, it recognizes who it is. Rama, who is consciousness unmoving, the vast presence, sees that awareness, Sita, has been kidnapped and he sends grace in the form of Hanuman to rescue her. In the story, Hanuman drops a ring, so I suppose that would be Self Enquiry or whatever – you could get really literal about this! But really all the ring does in the form of grace is soothe the system enough so that awareness recognizes who it is and then the spell breaks. Because conditioning is just a spell that's maintained through agreement or opposition. When we go to satsang that spell gets broken.

I have difficulty with the concept that realization is a gracious gift. I can't accept that you've had this grace but I haven't. Is it that the personal self does make some effort of its own to go on the spiritual path, do Self Enquiry, but then it dissolves of itself?

I like the way Robert puts it – it's about the vibatory rate of someone who is resting in the heart. He used to say that the heart vibrates a million times back to someone who's identified because all of the energy is up on the surface, maintaining an artificial persona, defending it, maintaining its opinions. It's an incredible amount of work to maintain a contraction in something that is naturally expanding all the time. So all the energy goes into retightening it – otherwise it would just relax and fall back. Robert put it that you just want to get around the vibratory rate of someone resting in the heart and that will literally dissolve the sense of separation. 'Vibratory rate' has beautiful names – you can call it grace, the hum of life. It's not about what appears to be the satsang giver but that which animates the satsang giver, which is life itself, undiluted. So that's what transmits. It's almost as if any contraction that comes around that vibration cannot withstand it.

Even in the beginning when someone comes to satsang, there might be a discomfort with the silence. Now that is a clue because there is a recognition in the body and brain that something very immense is happening – and it's a little scary. So the way I explain conditioning is the image of mortar around bricks. Mortar is basically made of sand and something else which hardens and it keeps the building in place. It's the same with conditioning – it's hardened through time and agreement and opposition to it. In an earthquake, if there is a brick building, the earthquake literally vibrates the mortar back to its original substance, which is sand, and then the whole building collapses. This sounds terribly deconstructionalist but that's exactly what happens in satsang! The conditioning, that little shell, which is maintained through surface tension, starts to crack and dissolve and all of a sudden that which was resting prior to it is revealed. So it's definitely good to get yourself to satsang.

Robert used to say to read about Advaita or some sage's life for 15 minutes in the morning and 15 minutes before you go to bed, just to return the awareness to truth. It's funny because even this grace that you can find in satsang also arises up from these books.

You spoke of two strands today, bhakti *and* jnana. *Does that mean the two paths are occurring simultaneously?*

Yes, they kind of meet in the middle. It's true – it's all welcome. If you interview someone who is awakened and they didn't have a teacher, they would say that no teacher is required. If they awakened with a teacher, they would say that, absolutely, a teacher is required. So it's the same if a being recognizes that devotion to the guru or devotion to truth or devotion to satsang brought them here to rest in the heart – they'll say to go for devotion. But if someone deeply enquired into truth using the mind and then reached this resting, they will say enquire and find out who you are. But the funny thing is that all this is on the surface. Grace is the one who is working so it doesn't matter what is apparently going on. It's all point of view.

Some observations that disturb me . . .

Things you don't like about satsang?!

It seems with some people that when attachment to ego dissolves, there is paradoxically a self-promotion campaign, a book, a web site, brochures and leaflets full of quotes about how wonderful they are. When I think of Ramana, a community naturally grew up around him – he did nothing. But now contemporary teachers of Advaita are actively managing their own publicity and it's turned me off. You know, the perfection of web sites and all that . . .

They should be imperfect, I agree! Tattered edges, upside down photographs, I know! Yes, these people should just rest in silence . . . Yes, the fun thing unfolds and you absolutely have nothing to do with it. So, in this case, there was an innocent presence, feeling very brand new and very ancient. It was just wide-eyed and present and going about life normally and yet with a completely different experience. I mean, it was just heaven. Of course, when there was some kind of meeting with a harshness in life, there was a contraction still but it wouldn't linger.

I lost my job with the company I had been with for nearly 12 years. I rang up a friend who was a satsang giver and I said that I didn't have a job and I guessed I'd go and work in a dress shop or a health food kitchen! So my friend said to me that I wasn't to go and work in a dress shop or be a cook. And I said that I was and this went back and forth for a few weeks. He said that I should go and give satsang and I said, 'No, I'm not, I know nothing, I'm just resting in what I call cluelessness. Just innocent awe.' About the 15th time he said that I should be giving satsang, there was a bit of a glimmer and I wondered whether maybe this was grace talking to me. So a few weeks after that, someone called up from Seattle and asked if I would give satsang and somehow the ticket got bought and there I was in Seattle. I was sitting with a group of beautiful beings and there was just silence. Then someone asked a question and silence answered the question. Then there was seeing that I really have nothing to do with this.

Then things just happened and Mira came up to me and said that I should have a web site. So what am I going to say? 'No, Mira!' So it keeps unfolding like that. The image I have sometimes is looking down at the feet and, as the feet take a step, there is a carpet that rolls just enough forward for that step. And then there's another step, so it's not like I ever know what's going to happen in the future but that life is unfolding and I just respond to life.

When there is satsang giving, there is no ownership of giving satsang. There's also no ownership of the web page or of the words that are spoken or of any of the books. As a matter of fact, it's not even correct to sign the book 'Pamela Wilson' because first of all she doesn't exist – I can't take any credit.

Some people say that you can intuit who is a genuine teacher and who isn't. There are some teachers who are passing through London and I think yes, there is something very special and profound. With others I have wondered, what the hell is going on here.

Robert used to say to just sit with the one that brings you peace. What's so sweet about what's happening now is that very few of the newer ones would call themselves gurus – they are messengers really. Hanuman in San Francisco says at the beginning of satsang, 'Are there any questions about my master's teachings?' He's not even saying this is *my* teaching. So it's very sweet the way it's happening now. It's just friends sitting with friends and even that is an embodiment of how this teaching is.

There's no separation, no hierarchy, and I'm resting in cluelessness and you're resting in cluelessness and yet the mystery speaks. What happens is that with anything you're interested in, you merge with it – so if you like gardening, after 10 years, you merge with your garden. The same with satsang. There was I innocently going to satsang and my devotion for satsang kept blooming and I merged with it. But the fun thing from the beloved's point of view is that everyone is a Buddha.

I can see that this brain still goes to judgement and there are going to be preferences for which teacher you want to go and sit with. That's natural and that's also grace leading us here and there. Also, in duality there's going to be an infinitely delicious teacher and then there's going to be a really arrogant, ugly teacher. That's duality. You could say it's predetermined but it's all unfolding perfectly.

There are also ideas about enlightened behaviour.

Yes. It's nice to enquire into what enlightenment is. It's just being. Now being is going to express itself in infinite ways because being isn't limited. Papaji said that conditioning sometimes takes up to seven years to fall away. If there's an honesty within the being and a not using of the remaining conditioning, grace just dissolves it all because conditioning is the only remaining defence. This presence needs no defending. So, there's awareness here as well as remaining conditioning and there's compassion for it, so there's a compassion for the conditioning in others.

I believe that even Papaji wrote in a diary once that there was full identification one day.

Yes. I can report that huge chunks of conditioning fell away and I certainly can report that I had nothing to do with that. And there's awareness of some remaining conditioning left. But I figure that grace knows better than this little being.

So who am I and why don't I know it?

Because you're looking through the brain. It's funny, supposing you want to see a bird in the tree, you are not going to get out your blender to look at the bird in the tree! It would be better to get a pair of binoculars, you know! This is the goofiest metaphor but it's like going looking for this vast presence with a tiny measuring device that only looks at objects. We are using the brain, which only can perceive something that's an object or a thing, so therefore it can't find something that's not a thing. And you are what you are seeking. Awareness cannot find itself. It'll find thoughts and feelings and everything like that but since it's using the vehicle of the brain, it's looking for this huge god, an object.

Or perfection . . .

Or perfection but that's an embodied perfection that has matter to it. This silent backdrop – the brain has to keep rejecting it because, if it doesn't, it's just so juicy. It's always looking away from the silent backdrop. It goes outside to find enlightenment. The funny thing is that when it turns around or when it's exhausted enough just to rest inside, it becomes the silence.

What makes the switch?

Well, I would have to say grace but exhaustion helps! Isn't it true? Have you ever worked really physically hard one day and just came home and there's this wonderful sense of exhausted, sedated well-being. Just a feeling of hmm, yes. Everything's good, you know. The brain attributes it to the fact that you worked so hard or you put in a good day's work or you're so incredibly creative that day but what's happened is that it's just come to rest for some reason or for no reason at all, more accurately. And in that, everything is revealed. There is just this quiet sense of well-being that all is well.

For myself, I am exhausted by the effort, particularly the intellectual side of things but I am in a state of limbo, I guess you could say. I've given up meditation and a whole load of other practices. There has been a relaxation of some kind but I don't feel any closer or nearer to any kind of understanding. There's just this wasteland.

Well, very simply, you can just rest there. Can you see that there is absolutely nothing that you can do?

Sometimes I can see that.

OK. Just keep savouring that. There's nothing you can do, OK. So there's this wasteland here, just empty. This is what you're looking for.

The wasteland?

No. Just emptiness. Now, just for a second, this is the fun part. This is where you just apply a little hello and devotion, yeah? So just for a second, honour this raw emptiness just for a second. This is all Parvati did. She sat on a mountain across from where Siva was sitting. No one could get him out of his samadhi. Parvati went into the silence and started to savour it. And then she savoured it some more and then she savoured it some more . . . Then what happened was that her presence or *the* presence rose up so immensely that it matched Siva's own. He opened his eyes and she opened her eyes and they looked across at each other . . . and then they married — awareness and consciousness met each other. So awareness — it goes inside and sees nothing . . .

And that's when the confusion starts.

I know. But right here just be Parvati for a moment. Now 'nothing' is Parabrahman, the unmanifest. So literally, when we seek within, that's the beloved wearing no form. Now the fun part is that when you just introduce a little devotion and hello, what happens is that it starts to reveal itself. So just for a moment, let's go inside. OK. Just start telling this bland emptiness, 'I know who you are. I love you.' Just express gratitude and devotion to it. 'Thank you, I love you. Thank you, I love you.' Be so fragrant with devotion that the beloved comes to you.

I can't trust that.

No, your brain can't. This is just a very ancient way of evoking the beloved. So you can tell it, 'I cannot see you, please reveal yourself to me.' OK. So what's awareness aware of?

There's nothing there.

This is true. Just for a second, could that be OK? Nothing is present, no thing.

I guess what I am looking for is a feeling of being in love.

Now love is resting within the emptiness. It often doesn't reveal itself right away. First comes Brahman or Siva and then, within that, is this dancing love. Sometimes people meet it the other way around but for you Brahman is here.

But it feels very cool and abstract.

Just go and visit our friend Brahman. He's wearing nothing now. But just for a second, as if it were the most delicious love, savour it. It likes to see if our love is unconditional. It becomes quiet and ordinary. Just welcome it when it comes — radiant, resplendent love and bliss. Just allow awareness to move into the right side of the chest. Just savouring and exploring innocently, whatever is present or absent. What's awareness aware of at rest in the right side of the chest?

There's tension.

Could you just comfort the tension. Awareness has little hands that can soothe. It gives it a little massage.

There's also fear.

Could you just comfort the fear. Just have compassion for it. It's just the body's fear. Say, 'You're welcome here, I love you.'

It's like unknown territory.

Yes. That's alright. So what is awareness aware of in this moment?

There's some rest.

Yes, that's it. And just savour and enjoy that.

It's not like bliss or anything. It's just relief.

That's it. Bliss often doesn't come until later. The vibatory rate – it's transformed enough by grace so that it can handle the bliss. If bliss were to just reveal itself right away, sometimes it's just a little too agitating for the body. So first, rest is here. And just enjoy it and let every cell of the body drink of this rest. It feels as if you could drink from it like a delicious wine.

It gets sweeter the longer you rest in it.

That's it, that's it. That's why they have the image of the lotus – it just opens, you get a whiff of the fragrance and then all of a sudden you think, 'Wow, I think I could live here.'

Ramana used to say that there is a tiny flame in the heart. Just imagine an image of your body just resting beside it. Just being warmed and soothed and comforted. Like being near a hearth being warmed and soothed. Just allow the image of the body to rest in it like where the Buddha rests in the lotus. Just allowing the little flame to relax and dissolve anything no longer required, like the past or any suffering or any worries. And then allow that image of the body to dissolve into the image of the flame. Let that rest for a moment. So what is awareness aware of in this moment?

It seems the further you go, there is more peace but there's still fear deep within it.

It's just the body and the brain. Don't let fear stop you, it's just trying to postpone this feeling that's so sweet. Just say, 'Thank you fear for trying to protect me'.

The body is shaking.

But the shaking is *shakti* — it's grace rising up. It's an oceanic presence and all she is doing is loving you. You can be honest, you can say, 'You scare me.' There's just a little bit of nervousness in the body and in the brain. The only time when you fall back and return into this vast presence is when the body falls away, so somehow there's a kind of cellular memory that associates this immense rising up of presence with death. It's nice to know that, so then you can just reassure the body that all is well — 'I'm here, I love you, no one's dying today.'

So can you just see that it is rising up to love? It's life. There's no way that we can keep life suppressed. Could you give it the gift of Paula. Say, 'I have nothing else to give you but myself.'

I feel I'm on the edge of a cliff.

Why don't you jump off? I jumped off. Actually, I was literally pushed off by grace. Everything of value survived. The extraneous bits perished and I didn't miss anything. There was a whole load of extra luggage that had no function other than to maintain suffering. It's just like when you're swimming when you're little and there's no way that you're going to jump into the water. But then a friend jumps in and says, 'Hey wow, this is really fun!' Then finally the desire for that is greater than the fear and you just jump and all of a sudden you realize that this is the best.

Grace will just handle it.

The interview comes to a natural end. Some people who have been hanging around since the end of satsang wander back into the room to collect their things and leave. Pamela puts her arms around me and we hold each other for several minutes. One part of me cannot bear the intimacy; the other wishes to remain like this forever.

I start to pack my things away, feeling raw and new and scared. 'I really enjoyed our conversation,' I say, trying to convey the sincerity of the remark. 'Me too,' Pamela says.

In the hallway the remaining people embrace each other, exchange telephone numbers, find their shoes. I pick up a leaflet from next to the money bowl, which gives details of Pamela's forthcoming meetings. It also carries a poetic koan:

Like water
that comes
from a long distance,
Grace knows the way.

So this fresh water here
can taste
that ancient water
and know.

We all go outside as I take Pamela's portrait in the late spring sunshine. The house is put to rest — doors and windows are locked, the rubbish is put out. Plans are being made for supper in a local restaurant. 'Would you like to come and join us?' someone asks. But I have had my fill for the day and I appreciatively decline.

As I drive away, I again have an experience similar to the one I had when leaving John de Ruiter — a vast space within me, everything happening within me, nothing happening without me. And yet, again, the mind eventually resurfaces with all its quandaries and demands.

An envy arises within me. I am jealous of Pamela's ability to have rejuvenated herself, to have walked with grace and found the ancient and timeless beauty of being. How I so want to be as exquisite as she.

Who is the third who walks always beside you?
When I count, there are only you and I together
But when I look ahead up the white road
There is always another one walking beside you
Gliding wrapt in a brown mantle, hooded
I do not know whether a man or a woman
— But who is that on the other side of you?

'*V: What the Thunder Said*', *The Waste Land*
T S Eliot

Isaac Shapiro

CHAPTER TWELVE

NO GURU,
NO METHOD,
NO TEACHER

Satsang means a meeting with truth.
What is spoken of as truth is That which doesn't change.
We have many different experiences but something
remains the same.
This is what's called truth. That which is always here.
That which doesn't change.

Isaac Shapiro

Travelling from London to Harwich by train is just like any other railway journey in England. The familiar countryside blurs past – fields, houses, factories, trees. A few hours journey by ferry across the Channel to the Netherlands, arriving at the Hook of Holland, the train ride to Amsterdam is a painterly voyage through a Dutch landscape. Suddenly, I don't feel alienated and separate from nature as I did before when spring first arrived. Now I feel as if I could reach out and touch it, only to get my fingers wet with the freshly applied oils from the artist's brush – a palimpsest of rivulets, like God's template, it strikes me how extraordinary it is that just a change of scenery can bring you back in touch with life itself.

The train arrives at Central Station in Amsterdam – the outside plaza is vast and busy and wet. The advancing heavy rain is turning the tramway into brown rivers, which subdivide and run away into different areas of the town. My travelling companion and I hopscotch over them and catch a tram taking us in the direction of the Tropenmuseum. The windows of the tram are opaque with the breath of commuters so I wipe the glass with my fingertips – a Bohemian world emerges through my misty peephole. Tall, thin houses with long sash windows and arrow-headed rooves crowd up against each other, reminding me of a fairy-tale world of cobblers and watchmakers and Rumpelstiltskin. The tram snakes its way through the streets and piazzas. We get off by the museum and find De Muiderkerk, in Linnaeusstraat – a modern church, the size of a cathedral.

Satsang has already started – being late is beginning to be a habit. A shoal of shoes is washed up in the portico. Through the glass doors, I see what must be at least some 300 people sitting in ordered rows around a stage. We slink in, past tables of satsang tapes and books, and find two empty chairs in the back row. I am taken aback by the sheer size of the building – the wood-panelled ceiling seemingly miles above our heads. Isaac Shapiro is sitting on the stage, minded by two large microphone stands. A chair is next to him and someone is sitting there, gazing at Isaac. Isaac smiles back gently and then looks at the audience. Nothing is said. Then the devotee brings his palms together in *namaste* to Isaac, reaches over to give him a hug and trots down the stage steps back to his seat.

For the remaining hour that we are there a succession of people climb up on stage – some looked scared stiff, others as if they are floating in bliss. I don't feel connected somehow to the meeting – waves of laughter sporadically break out in the audience and I can't seem to work out what the joke is. I suddenly feel very English and gather in my sensibilities and restraint. The meeting then ends on the dot of nine. I thread my way past people and seats and introduce myself to Isaac. 'Ah, yes – would you like to come over to our place tomorrow?' I lend him my pen and he writes down the address.

I am strolling through Amsterdam's district of Jordaan – a labyrinth of canals and alleyways, fringed with stylishly converted warehouses and *eetcafés*. I arrive at Lindengracht, a wide street bedecked with antique shops, restaurants and bicycle racks. I enter the apartment block where Isaac is staying and climb the stairs to the top flat. Isaac greets me enthusiastically and ushers me into a stylish apartment with pine floors, white furniture and linen drapes which leads onto a balcony festooning with plants and flowers. Isaac Shapiro is a big hairy bear of a man – his face appears to be crinkled into a permanent smile, his generous nature borne out by a hearty laugh. He makes me a cup of tea and we sit at the dining table. He starts to munch through a plate of coconut cookies with great gusto whilst clipping the microphone to his T-shirt.

The eldest of four children, Isaac was born in 1950 into a white Jewish middle-class family in South Africa and had a regular childhood. Then at 19, he had his first LSD experience: 'I wasn't a drug taker and had no experience with drugs but I read an article on Timothy Leary, who was talking about 1,000 orgasms per second! So I ended up taking LSD and I had an experience of unconditional love – I knew that it was real and that the way I normally saw life was not real. It was almost like my mind was a super computer – I never read any philosophy but suddenly I knew Plato. Unfortunately, the experience passed but I wanted to live like that because it was beautiful.'

This precipitated a change in direction. Up until then, Isaac had been studying gynaecology because, he says, he was 'sex obsessed' but everything in life came under scrutiny. Moving to New Zealand in 1971, he became involved in Mind Clearing, an offshoot of Scientology – a technique using biofeedback: 'That got my mind quite clear and I understood everything but I could still feel that I wasn't finished. I knew that I was source but there were all kinds of stuff still going on in me. At some point, it dawned on me that attention is the key to everything. Where my attention was determined my experience.' By now he had moved to Maui where he started to run awareness workshops, working with people and focusing on the need for quality of attention and its effect. 'Amazing stuff was happening – people who had histories of being crazy got well. We'd be in this no-mind space or God space and people would be dropping into it quite naturally.'

Isaac became very successful – he was becoming famous, making good money. But still something was eluding him. 'I met someone who had been to see Papaji. I was still anti-guru because I could see that this whole mechanism of putting someone up there was painful and ultimately didn't work. But I could see that something had happened to him and that he was different from when I knew him before. Anything that produced that kind of change I was interested in.'

Thus, meeting Papaji for himself in 1991 brought Isaac the ultimate revelation – 'Bring your attention to awareness itself,' Papaji told him. It was the missing link.

For myself, I feel that I am still working towards a so-called point of perfection . . .

Everything is ultimately how it is – there's murder, there's rape, there's war, there's everything. And the only time that we suffer is when we think it shouldn't be that way. Now, I think many teachers have done the world a disservice by pretending that they are not touched by anything – and maybe there are some that aren't but so far I have not met any.

So, it's not a question of being touched or not touched. It's how you deal with the touch. Either you internally try to control your experience and hold it in your body in a certain way, in a familiar way, or you open and let the experience wash through you. And there's no obstruction to the experience – it can just come through you. And the funny thing is that when you just let the experience move through like that, it's experienced as love. So even now, in your body, ultimately the whole world, the whole universe, everything, is only sensation. I mean what you see, what you hear, what you smell, what you taste, it's sensation that is then interpreted through the filters of your mind.

So, right now in your body, there are certain sensations, OK? And what we tend to do is we label our sensations and in the labelling of them, calling them fear or sadness or anger, once we label them we make it into something solid. But the truth is that it is not solid, the sensations are constantly changing and moving. Once we label, we attach a story to it and then we fix it and make it solid.

The label has a judgemental quality.

The label has a judgemental quality and some sense of either wanting to push it away or trying to control it. Even now, you can try it as you are sitting here. Whatever sensations are in the body, just let them go wherever they want to in the body, through your whole system. Try it now – just allow the sensations that are there to move freely. No story, no judgement of it, no labelling of it. They're just sensations and let them move freely and see what happens. Try it for yourself and you can see if it is true or not.

What happens is that the sensations do dissipate.

They go all the way through. What does it feel like?

Relaxed.

Yeah. Simple, no?

But I've heard that so many times and I've practised it so many times and yet I keep needing to be told that.

You don't know what it will be like next time?

Yes! The big thing for me doing this project is that I've had over a dozen interpretations of the same thing — everyone has their own slightly different perspective. In my mind, I've concocted my own version of the truth in a very mental and intellectual way but I just can't seem to make the transition to the teaching being a living, breathing reality.

OK, so in my view it's like this. We say that we have a mind but all it is is a system of thought. There is no mind per se, there is no entity called 'mind' — if there is no thought, then there's no mind. But there's a system of thinking that we are used to, you could say. So, part of that system is the need to understand. So we try and get a world view or an enlightened view that fits it all together. Ultimately it's useless because what has to happen is, instead of experiencing reality or the isness or the now through the level of the mind, there's a way to experience where the mind relaxes and you are just being. And when you're just being and you're not trying to understand and know, the mind can function very well to move you from one place to another. But it's not your predominant way of experiencing the world. Most of us actually know being, but not very much, because we wake up in the morning and we start thinking and we think until we go to sleep.

Most of us hang out in the mental realm all day long. Everything that goes on is filtered through the mind — 'They like me, they don't like me, I like it, I don't like it.' Everything goes through this filter. It takes a little getting used to, living without going down that particular channel. But it's not about fighting the mind, it's about letting the mind continue. It's not trying to change it or fix it or change the content or anything, it's just allowing it to be. And there's something that's aware of the mind.

Right now, whatever it is that you call 'you' in your own experience, can you say what that is? Just this now? Can you come back in this moment to what you feel is you? It's not the body, it's not the mind. Where do you come to?

There's awareness.

OK, awareness. So that awareness is here and that's living life without going through the filter of mind all the time. Touch awareness and just rest there for a second. You've relaxed the mental body, you've relaxed the physical body and now there's the sense of letting the sensations go where they want to. The physical body is not holding anything, just letting things move. The emotional body — that's tied to the mental and physical body. Emotions can come and go freely. You are awareness. Any tightness, you let it be there in the body. It's not about trying to change it or do anything, it's just that you are not focused in that channel —

you are being the awareness. You are that in which all the channels are appearing. So from this awareness itself, what do you have to accomplish, what do you have to do, from awareness?

There's nothing to do.

There's nothing to do. And there's nothing to get to and there's nothing that has to change. This awareness is already here, it's not that we have to get it or learn it or uncover it. I mean, there's nothing to do! It's just a habit you could say to operate in the mental plane or the physical plane or the sensational plane. But it's strong – we are used to it. It's the way we have done it our whole lives and we are not used to just being. Nobody told us! So you know, in my view, there's a lot of making of it into something that it's not. It's very simple.

There are very purist interpretations, such as those of Wayne and Ramesh, who say that even the ability to relax into this awareness is beyond our control, that it's not something that we can actively do. It may be that we don't intrinsically exist but it does seem that there has to be some kind of attitude that should be assumed.

OK. So the way I would describe the same thing is that when the mental plane is functioning, it feels like that's you. There's a sense of the controller or the observer but ultimately, when you examine it, you find that there is no controller. All you find is there is an activity of labelling everything. This activity of labelling everything we call 'the witness' and that feels like the controller. As long as that activity of feeling like the controller is trying to relax, it can't because its nature is not relaxation – doing can't not do doing. Activity cannot know non-activity. That activity itself can never relax because it is activity.

We are just sitting here and, in only one second, you're in being. When I say you're in being, there's no 'you' that's in it – it's just the sense of being at home. And it's not something that you did because being was always here. It's just that instead of attention being paid to the activity of mentation, it drops down. And it's not a voluntary thing that anybody is doing – it's a being. So there's nobody that can do it. But to say in an absolute kind of way that nobody can do it is misleading. The doer you think you are cannot do it, which is more clear than to say you can't do it. Do you understand what I am saying?

It strikes me that the Ramesh way makes perfect sense in an intellectual way.

Because it's intellectual. It take us two seconds to meet in being and then you say in your own experience there is nothing to achieve, there is nothing to get, this is already who I am. Once you know that it's your own experience and you know it's not something you can do through the mind, you can have perfect understanding. But what does it mean? Ultimately it has nothing to do with it. It's great to have it but now, from being, I can ask you any question and, if you speak from being, then you speak with the wisdom of the Buddhas. That's all.

A few friends came around recently to my home and we played a little game whereby we would each take it in turn to be the guru and the teaching came out quite naturally. It's almost as if I'm playing at being ignorant.

Of course. Exactly! All that's happened is that you've activated the mental channel or rather the mental channel has been activated. I mean, there's nobody doing it. Once that's known, once that's really seen clearly, the mind channel activates and automatically there's no interest in it. You know from experience it's really painful to hang out there. So you just get used to hanging out as being. And there's no big bang or special thing, it's just that being is here and it's home. It's not that something can get activated but when it does get activated, there's an appreciation of being. And from being there's an allowing of it – opening rather than jamming you into one of those circuits. So, that's the relaxation into being and then it's just a natural process, it just keeps on doing it – whatever arises, whatever arises . . .

But to say nothing arises – maybe there are a few individuals where nothing ever happens but I don't know, I haven't met any or rather I haven't met any that I can say it's that way for sure. I just know.

It can be a misconception.

I think it can be a huge misconception.

People think that even if there are going to be problems that arise, you're going to be still and open-hearted and that nothing will phase you.

I don't know, I've heard people make all these outrageous claims and I know them personally and that's not what they live. Someone was here last night who'd stayed with Rajneesh three months after he had been booted out of the States – she was married to his brother – and he'd come to stay with them and she said he was a really moody guy but on stage he was this very holy character. You speak to the wives of some of these men or these so-called saints and you get a different picture. I don't think it does anybody a service to pretend that it's different than it is.

Well, it's a lie then, isn't it? If there is the assumption that it's going to be OK and it's not OK, that makes a mockery of the whole teaching.

It does. It's misunderstanding. Ultimately, in being, there is the ability to be with whatever is happening, you know, and it's not a big deal but it doesn't mean that the response doesn't happen. It's just that it's happening and instead of going into a normal channel of trying to change it or fix it, there's an embrace. What I've found is that every time I've tried to change myself or anyone else, there's been immense suffering.

Everything is as it is, people are just as they are. You saw in satsang last night – I don't try and change anybody, I'm just there, everyone can be like they are. There's a miracle in that. Some are people who are coming to rest in that. Now I can't even say that's coming from a doing because I'm not doing anything. People are saying that they are grateful but I'm saying that gratefulness has nothing to do with me. You know, there is gratitude when your being is functioning through you because that's the natural disposition of being.

It was an extraordinary evening last night. I arrived halfway through and there was a guy who got up and he seemed to have rather an odd manner about him. Then this laughter started in the audience, which seemed to be directed at him and, quite frankly, I was appalled by the whole thing.

Yes, but it's just so perfect. Some people are laughing, some people are judging and it's all OK. And what's happening in the OKness of it? People start to catch their own reflection. They see that there's a judgement happening. But if you go and try and say now look, don't judge . . .

Or stop laughing, give the poor guy a break! You know, I've come to this point where I'm nauseated by satsang, having to listening to other people's stuff.

Yes, but once you start seeing that, the judgement comes up in your mind about laughing and you feel the contraction of the judgement – it's just a knee-jerk response. It's not like there's some ideas of 'poor him'. You don't know what his experience is, he might be in bliss. He's there cruising away and you're thinking poor guy! Then you see that's your own judgement and it's no big deal and not even your judgement. It's just there's something in there that said, 'Don't laugh at people, it's not kind.' That little programme was sitting there and was waiting for the moment that it could assert itself. But OK, someone's laughing, someone's acting like that. This mind is judging and you start to laugh at yourself, it's so ridiculous.

The thing is that if you have an idea in your mind that you shouldn't judge, it's another judgement and it brings about internal violence. Every time judgement happens, whip, and every time you see judgement, then you judge that judgement. Then it becomes violence, violence, violence. So, you know how beautiful it can be when finally judgement can come up and it's just a judgement. So the mind judged, OK, big deal, wow! So what! We all know about judging and still it happens but so what. Take the pressure off.

Everything is God except judging? It doesn't make sense. It's just like when you really just experience judging, there's no judgement about it. It's funny — it's love, it's nothing, it's like what's the big deal? Well, this is my experience of it.

There are so many teachings that say, 'Do not do this, do not do that.'

Yes, and it just creates internal violence.

So right behaviour arises when you are in being?

My sense of it is that, from being, the ideas that haven't been examined are still going to come up and play, like you need to be like this or that. But what happens is that as you are simply being, that pattern will come and maybe at some point you will go, 'Oh, it's just a thought,' or 'Oh, it's just a judgement,' and then it's not a big deal. In some way, judging is just judging, and there's not judging of judging.

From being, there's enough space. It's like every time it's seen, there's a bigger chance it gets seen. I mean, I sit in satsang all the time and there's a field generated by people. And people have all these weird and wonderful experiences and recognitions and seeings and I'm not saying anything. I'm just doing nothing.

What I have discovered is that having leaped out of a morally and conceptually-based institution where the teaching was steeped in the words of Shankara and now that I am hanging out with people who like the words of Ramana Maharshi and Papaji . . .

I don't even find that useful anymore, you know. I mean, honestly. Yeah, I like to read them but the difficulty is that when you read something like that, it is always interpreted through the mind. It just stays in the mental channel of trying to understand, trying to get it, trying to get to this perfect state, to whatever the story is and it's not about that at all.

So one can make a concept out of being.

Yeah. We're hanging out here and we're talking a little bit and having some fun and suddenly your body is relaxing, your mind is relaxing . . . So who's the teacher, who's the student? In being, there's none of that, you know. There's just this clear seeing, you could say, that happens or it doesn't happen. And even with clear seeing, what is it that we really know in this instant? Honestly and truly, everything that we think we know is just another idea. So, for me, I would just not be concerned with knowing or not knowing. There's life flowing through this body and doing its thing – breathing it and living it.

Teachers today . . .

I don't even see myself as a teacher. It's like, what can I tell you? I don't have a teaching, I honestly don't have a teaching. Being is not a teaching. To me, just resting in being, everything just seems incredibly funny. So I just enjoy other people and the patterns that come up in me – they seem real for a moment or two but, a few moments later, they don't seem real.

The biggest thing for me at the moment is how disillusioned I feel and how painful that is.

Oh, I'm happy that you're disillusioned!

With teachers in particular. I got a brochure through the post the other day and it had Ramana's photo, Papaji's photo and then this particular teacher's photo with quotes from various people about how wonderful he is. If identity is not such a big deal anymore, why am I getting wads of paper telling me that this guy's identity is not such a big deal anymore. It's ridiculous!

Yeah! It's become a new religion. Really. I don't do my own web site. What happens is that, in my experience, I'm cruising around and people talk about me like I'm enlightened and I'm this or that. And then someone says they'd like to do my web site for me and I say OK, great, because I don't know how to do it. I have no interest actually to do it. And then they do something and that's their idea of what it's about.

Some people will be attracted to it and have a projection onto it and other people have a negative projection. I've had both. I get asked whether I'll do an interview for a magazine and I think, 'Oh my God, this has become like another priesthood.' There'll be this whole story into me. It's like give me a break, I don't have an interest in it.

The whole 'Advaita-thing' has made me angry because I've invested my energy, my time, my money, my belief.

That anger now, just feel it, let it wash through your body, let it go wherever it wants to go and what happens? Just like that. So ultimately people are doing this, people are doing that, people are pretending to do this, to do that.

Maybe we could talk about your time with Papaji, which is quite well documented in Roslyn Moore's book?

Each time I tell my story it comes out differently. There's no actual story of what really happened – it's just a joke, in my view. So what slant do you want?!

Well, just the bits about drugs and sex.

I never had sex with Papaji!

Was there some restlessness that drove you before your meeting with Papaji? For myself, there's always a restlessness . . .

Now, now, now . . . from beingness, what's true? The rest is just a story. It's a nice story. So, my meeting with Papaji, what do you want to know about it?

What did you know to be absolutely true when you met him? Did something happen, was there some kind of 'crack'?

It didn't happen like that for me. I went to see Papaji and nothing dramatic happened. We had a nice time together – he played with me, I had a few meals with him at his home. The key thing was he said to me, 'Oh, you have done very well, now bring your attention to awareness itself.' So I thought, 'OK, what does that mean? I'll have to just experiment within myself.' But somehow it made sense to me. It never occurred to me that to give attention to someone's story was both painful for them and for me but to just rest my attention on them was good. Just resting in being. So an endless exploration of bringing my attention to awareness followed – where's awareness, who's doing it, all those things came up. But it got examined in a pretty intense way because that's my personality.

And the more it got examined, the more I could see there was no one here. This movement of attention was just a movement that happened, pretty much through the force of habit. It wasn't anybody controlling it per se, it was just habitual movement. So I played with it and it became clearer and clearer in this being, you could say.

I had been doing work with people and what happened was I went to India and I said I'm not doing it anymore because I could see that I was more interested in resting my attention in awareness. People said that they loved what I was doing before and, if I had found something better, I should tell them because they'd been waiting all year to see me. 'OK', I said, 'I'm not really qualified but let's do it!' And people liked it so I just honoured my commitments that I had already made and thought that when I'd finished with these people, I'd go and hang out with Papaji for a while and let this deepen.

When I went back to India, Papaji said, 'Oh you've found the diamond, I want you to start giving satsang.'

There is a belief that recognition of awareness has to be sanctified in some way by a guru.

Yeah. It's a funny thing. There were all these people around Papaji and they would relate to him as their master and some of them thought, if they really worshipped him, maybe it would wash off on them. All these people with funny kinds of purposes.

It is as if people have a fundamental need to devote themselves to something.

Most of it, I could see, was to be wanting something, to be worthy of something, to get something.

Feeling special.

Yeah, or being in association with someone special. There's just a whole range of things that go with it. I could sense that. There was an expectation that I would see it in the same way and be involved in the same way but for me it wasn't like that. Quite a few patterns played out. I wanted attention from Papaji, I wanted to be seen and that was all very painful. For me, most of the time being around Papaji was painful because these patterns would play.

But in the meantime, satsang was happening. I could see things were happening and people were getting it or whatever you want to call it. I didn't really know what was going on ultimately and there were certain patterns of wanting to claim that or wanting to think that I knew something and all of that stuff.

There's quite an irony there — ego is supposed to have dissolved and yet there is a claiming of that state.

Yeah!

How did Papaji play with you?

Oh, he was a master at exposing patterns that were going on without words by just being around him, you know. He'd say one thing or look at you in a certain way. There was this one guy who came to a satsang of mine and he just had this experience where he fell down and he was laughing and laughing. That used to happen in Papaji's satsang a lot and I thought, 'Ah ha. Great, that's now happening here. I can't wait till tomorrow when he goes and tells Papaji about this.' He told Papaji and Papaji said that was an intellectual understanding only and it was not real at all. Then the same guy was rolling around on the floor laughing and Papaji said, 'Very good.' So I was thinking, 'Oh my God, I'm misleading people'. So afterwards I went to him and asked what was going on and he said it was the same but that he was only playing with me. It was great because it just exposed that I thought I had done something, hoping that Papaji would acknowledge what had happened with this guy. So I was seeing how I wanted recognition of wanting to be special.

I would go to Lucknow and sometimes I wouldn't have to ask to come into his house. He would allow that for a while and then I was told I had to wait at the gate and not be let in — it was push and pull for a long time. My experience was very ordinary and pretty painful because I was seeing things about myself sitting in satsang. There were endless judgements coming up and discomfort — there's my friend weeping in bliss and I'm thinking, 'Oh God what am I doing here? This is a mad house'. And yet I would leave Lucknow and certain patterns would be gone and I didn't know how.

So I was aware that some mysterious process was going on but it was beyond my mind — I didn't know what was happening. Then you could start saying this is the guru's grace or who knows what. We don't understand but it seems to be tied to Papaji. What to do about it? I found if I went there, I would meet people who had been living with Papaji and, from my perspective, not much had changed. It seemed a fair amount had happened in me and they couldn't see it in me, so who knows?

Inasmuch as Advaita is a democratic belief system, there can be a form of subtle hierarchy going on — you know, the teacher up at the front, the inner sanctum of helpers, the PR people. I've been 'close' to a teacher and got sucked into the idea that I was someone special. It brought up a lot of vanity and all that stuff.

Yeah, it's good to see it!

Just being, absolutely simple and easy and that's beautiful. Here we meet and there's just a laughter in the heart – it's sweetness, yeah? We could sit here if you like and really be and have some far out experiences! And it can be like that and it's no big deal.

I guess it's all so ordinary really. It's funny, you go off on a journey and then you arrive at a place where it's the same as when you first started.

It's all the same but different. There's not that contraction, the sense of seriousness.

But I still feel kind of numb inside. There isn't a sense of lightness, let alone euphoria.

But is that now?

Well, no, but there's often a sense of everything being meaningless in a negative way, which is not some existential witnessing or whatever.

That's not beingness. That's like the mind says it's meaningless and so you numb out. Or the thought is, 'It's meaningless,' so you see experience through the thought that it's meaningless. If you are actually living in meaningless, without the thought of it, it's actually quite lovely. So it's just a filter. It's no big deal.

Love – is love just beingness?

Yeah, yeah.

I don't feel love all the time.

Yeah, but it's like you wake up in the morning and the kids are making a mess and the phone is ringing – in those moments, movement is happening quite quickly and life is happening like that. But that's different to if I'm sitting here. There's a different quality, you know. Or then you're writing about being or I receive a nasty email – it's just like waves on the ocean. Sometimes it's very blissful and you can get drunk on it, other times it's very ordinary and that's just life.

What about ethics? There doesn't seem to be a definition ultimately of what is right and what is wrong.

Exactly and that's just being, right?

But in beingness, do you kind of know what right action is?

Even that we don't know. We don't know, we don't know. From within a certain perspective it looks like right action but how do you know?

Things change all the time.

It appears like this in this moment and then like that in that moment. For most of us, as we first start to experience being, there's a sense that you could love anybody and make love with anybody and I've lived like that. I had a period where I was just wild and now I live with a woman, I'm married, I've got kids but it doesn't mean that attraction doesn't happen or thoughts of having sex don't happen. But the thought will happen and then you can see that OK, if I do that then . . .

There will be a repercussion . . .

You can't even say that there will be a repercussion – you don't even know if it will happen like that. Something says, 'I will do it,' or 'No, I won't do it,' or whatever happens in the moment. But then we try and put a right action or a wrong action on it but it's like, in the end, nothing much is happening! There is always a tendency for some sort of subtle morality to go on. There's this cosmos and there are these little blobs of protoplasm not knowing what's going on.

It's interesting how this wonderful sense of freedom is turned into a concept to justify certain action. A man said to me once that in relationship, women can become possessive and jealous and according to the teaching, there is no such thing as relationship. So for him, it was OK to have free sex and multiple partners.

But what's wrong with possessiveness and jealousy? OK, say you'll sleep with other men and let him get possessive and jealous!
   So we've covered sex, drugs, rock 'n' roll, what else . . . ?

As is so often the case, my fractious mind settles down during our discussion – the list of questions I have painstakingly prepared now seems utterly ridiculous.

I suddenly look down at my cassette recorder and realize that it has stopped turning – oh my God, every journalist's worst nightmare. 'Well, it would appear that the recorder has decided we've come to the end of our interview,' I lie casually.

We step out onto the balcony overlooking the main street below. 'Don't you get sick of all the travel, living in other people's houses all the time?' 'Not really – I love satsang and I love meeting people. We only travel for about half of the year. The rest of the time we stay at our home in Byron Bay in Australia.'

His wife, Kali, and their two young children are due back any minute – domestic reality returns. I make my preparations to leave. Isaac shows me to the door – we put our arms around each other and I seemingly disappear for a moment into his ursine body. 'Will you be coming tonight?' he asks. 'Oh yes. Maybe I should come up on stage too!' I joke. 'Yes, why don't you come up?' Isaac looks at me intently . . .

Back on the street, I stop and fumble around in my bag, grab my cassette recorder and press rewind and then play. It chugs pathetically but I can just make out a distorted, high-pitched stream of words. Oh, what a relief.

And back in satsang at the De Muiderkerk, I sit at the back of the hall, wondering whether I should go up on stage. Every time I'm on the verge of plucking up the courage, someone else has already taken the seat next to Isaac. The satsang comes to an end. Isaac looks around at everyone in the audience. I then feel he is looking at me – well, at least, it feels that way, though no doubt it could be something more interesting behind me. I'm sorry that I didn't come up, I think as I look at him. That's OK, I think he says. I smile and look away.

> *Questioner: I seem to have a clear idea of what needs to be done but I find myself getting tired and depressed and seeking human company and thus wasting time that should be given to solitude and meditation.*
>
> *Maharaj: Do what you feel like doing. Don't bully yourself. Violence will make you hard and rigid. Do not fight with what you take to be obstacles on your way. Just be interested in them, watch them, observe, enquire. Let anything happen – good or bad. But don't let yourself be submerged by what happens.*

Q: What is the purpose in reminding oneself all the time that one is the watcher?

M: The mind must learn that beyond the moving mind there is the background of awareness, which does not change. The mind must come to know the true Self and respect it and cease covering it up, like the moon which obscures the sun during solar eclipse. Just realize that nothing observable or experienceable is you or binds you. Take no notice of what is not yourself.

I Am That, Talks with Sri Nisargadatta Maharaj

Vartman

CHAPTER THIRTEEN

THE BEAT
GENERATION

My first sight of Vartman is at the Resource Centre, Holloway Road in London – an increasingly popular rendezvous for visiting satsang teachers in London, chosen, I assume, more for its seating capacity rather than its atmosphere. The chaotic pile of shoes outside one of the minimalist conference rooms feels rather like a recalcitrant kick in the face of this sanitized and soulless place. Inside, 40 or so people are seated on expensive and official-looking chairs, neatly arranged in rows facing a raised dais, where Vartman sits on a couch. I arrive to find him in mid-flow. Sitting in his white *kurta* shirt and loose *pyjama* trousers, his long face, high forehead and black hair, which is pulled back into a ponytail, make him look like he is descended from a Mogul warrior caste rather than being a native Australian. Although he appears relaxed – emphasized by his Antipodean accent – he speaks slowly and precisely, pausing awhile after a sentence or two, speaking again, then pausing until someone asks to sit next to him.

Vartman is joined on the couch by a middle-aged man, keen to get something off his chest. 'Since awakening . . . ,' the man begins. I inwardly groan. What I'm beginning to notice is that as soon as someone starts to eulogize about enlightenment, I immediately switch off. Although Vartman responds openly to him, he also appears to give no time to his list of spiritual trophies and looks away, saying nothing. The man finishes what he wants to say, raises his hands in *namaste* to Vartman, who mirrors the gesture, and then returns to his seat. Another, much older Indian man then comes up on stage. He is so softly spoken that I have to strain my ears to hear him. He speaks of an inner turmoil, problems in dealing with people at work. Vartman leans towards him, offering words of comfort and encouragement. There is not one person who is not touched by the humility of this sweet old Indian man, so that even long after he steps down, nobody appears to want to disturb the moment as it is. In situations like this, I can understand why Christ said, 'Blessed are the meek' – you can just feel why.

Vartman's wife, Susanna, is sitting in the front row. Vartman motions to her to come and join him, which she does with her guitar. Susanna is Swedish and explains, in perfect English, that she wants to sing to us a song in her native tongue. Vartman holds the mike and we listen to a beautiful ballad about love. At the end of it, Vartman brings the satsang to a close and then asks an assistant to put on a CD of bhajans – perhaps we would like to all have a dance? The music starts – a droning *Om* underlaid by a techno rhythm – and Susanna and Vartman burst into life, dancing and twirling around the room. A few brave souls get up and join them but the predominantly English audience hold tight onto their seats. Vartman and Susanna's youthful vibrancy is infectious and a part of me is impressed by their beatnik approach. And yet another part of me is simply not in the mood. It's difficult to put my finger on what it is exactly but I just can't seem to muster the enthusiasm I had before. Before, when I used to be so inspired by going to satsang – the magic, the buzz, getting all dressed up as if I were going out to a party, scanning the audience for friends to have a good gossip with or looking for someone to fall in love with. God, I feel so tired of all of this, so bored of running around, expending all my energy in the hope of a spiritual fix, spending money on transport and giving donations I really can no longer afford . . .

The interview is arranged for the following afternoon. I drive to Highgate in north London and park in a secluded street just off the busy high street. It is late summer and the city heat has made the air dry and taste of pollution and car exhaust. I ring on the door and a young man opens it. I say I have come to interview Vartman. 'Great', he says, invites me in and then passes me into the street, closing the door behind him. I am left alone in the dark hallway and feeling somewhat perplexed. Hello? I call into vacant rooms leading off from the passage – nobody appears to be at home. I find my way into a bright kitchen at the back of the house. Suddenly, a slim silhouetted figure wanders towards me out of the darkness of the hall. I cannot make out who it is owing to the contrasting light. Then Vartman emerges, like a hologram, extending his hand to shake mine. 'Hi, I'm Vartman. Pleased to meet you.'

I am surprised that Vartman is not quite so tall as I remember him from the previous evening. Now he has come off my metaphorical pedestal and stands before me, he has reassumed his 21st century demeanour with his sports gear and a pair of sunglasses hanging around his neck. He makes us both a cup of green tea and leads me up the staircase to a balcony at the back of the house, overlooking the small gardens and backyards of north London. I'm glad that I don't feel anxious and am immediately at ease with Vartman as we sit under the piercing blue sky, talking and drinking our tea.

Chetan Vartman was born in Adelaide in 1967. He was introduced to meditation at the age of 10 by his sister: 'We lit a candle and watched our breathing – there was something in it that was just connected. I've kept meditating virtually every day ever since and that got me interested in Buddhism.' Meanwhile, he trained as an economist, working as a management consultant as well as running a number of his own businesses. By the age of 25, he had made it – big car, big house, big bank account. 'Although I'd always had some call towards the Buddhist teaching, I still was trying to find happiness mainly through money, success and wanting to experience everything as much as possible.'

But after many years in search of new experience, he'd finally had enough. By 1995, his first marriage was breaking up and so he went to a marriage guidance counsellor who sent him along to meet Gangaji. 'That's when I pretty much saw yes, this is what I was looking for. It just seemed so beyond anything I could get bored with. That was the main thing I was running from – boredom.' Thus, he embarked on a final journey for that ultimate experience, 'This big bang, this golden light, this choir of angels . . . ,' travelling extensively through Europe and America, then meeting Papaji in India in 1997. The following year, he went to the Osho Ashram in Poona, India, where he was given the name Chetan Vartman, meaning 'Consciousness Here Now'. There he met a woman called Dolano – though she had been around Osho for nearly 20 years, it was within two weeks of sitting with Papaji that she had found who she truly was. Dolano invited Vartman to sit with her, sensing he was right on the edge. Through their repeated enquiry, Who am I?, Vartman was finally able to let go.

On your web site there is a dialogue between you and Gangaji. In it, before things really shifted for you, you speak of a period of being 'flat'.

Yes, that was back in 1995, I think. I said to Gangaji, 'Every time I stop and enquire Who am I?, I just get this flatness.' And she looked at me and said, 'Are you willing to be flatness for the rest of your life if that is all there is?' And I said, 'Yeah sure,' but it was like no way – that to me was boredom. I wanted fireworks and angels and golden light and something that my mind could get really excited about and this was absolutely nothing for the mind. So that kind of drove me into this search that took me to Papaji in 1997. I remember that was kind of near the end because I was just so frustrated. Even these incredible great groups I did and experiences I had like balling my eyes out and killing my parents in therapy – it still wasn't filling the emptiness. And so in 1997, I bought a gun and bought a bullet and said, 'If I don't wake up in one year, I'm going to kill myself.'

You were quite serious about that?

Yes. I was just so depressed – I don't know if I would have done it but I was just so desperate because everywhere I looked, everyone had what I thought I wanted. But they didn't seem very happy inside to me – I call it divine discontent but it was more like greediness. I just wanted what I knew in my heart was possible, otherwise I wasn't interested in living. So that's what took me to this really serious searching. I worked enough in my businesses to keep them ticking over so that I could search full on for that year. I went back to India again to Papaji's ashram and I did a group called *Satori*, which is seven days of Who am I? and that really cleared out many concepts of who I thought I was. But I still wasn't willing to accept this flatness as who I am, as who we are.

A woman called Dolano saw me in the ashram and said to me that I was ready to accept this. Then for five weeks, every second day she would back me into a corner and, through her pointing really clearly and pragmatically, I just saw that I had no choice, that I had to finally come to accept this or not. She said, 'Go to the park and just enquire one more time – if what you find is the same as the last three years of enquiry, then just accept it and rest in that and stop looking outside of that.' And that's just what stopped the whole search. There was just this incredible opening to the fullness of this moment instead of trying to alter this moment for something more exciting for my mind.

I very much appreciate what you say about flatness. I have that same experience pretty much all the time. Even satsang has lost that specialness . . .

For a lot of people.

I know there's nothing to be done but how can that flatness become something alive for me?

It can't seem alive with the mind – that's the whole trick. To the mind, it's just bloody flatness. So you have to recognize it without the mind, without something you can sense. When I was willing to let the greediness of the mind try and get it, then it was just like, OK, what is actually here? And it's like this incredibly subtle, ever present openness, which is just so bloody great! Then it's like, man, this is perfect, this is exactly what I want, I don't need anything more than this. Then it just opens and opens and opens to unbelievable depth. The mind can still have any of its playthings but it's rooted in what I call unreasonable happiness – it's peace beyond peace. It's also so beyond mind and everyone knows that but somehow, in my experience, until we're willing to accept it, we just keep running and running and running looking for it.

Satsang is quite new to Europe and yet in one, two years, what I'm seeing is that initially people got really excited about it but now there's this kind of like one question, one answer, and it just doesn't lead anywhere. That's what really interests me – how courageous are people to live beyond the recognition of nothingness? It's one thing to recognize your nothingness, that you're untouchable, you're that which doesn't change. But then to be fully willing to be in the world, in that which *does* change, which is also who we are – body and flesh and everything that goes with that – that's what makes it really interesting. That's what I call playtime where, all of a sudden, you are recognizing that you are consciousness in a body and let's see how much the world can test me to try and collapse me. Let's practise – this horrible word that we don't like to use in spirituality – let's practise continually opening to the harshness of life because it is pretty shit out here, you know!

The world is a bloody mess and just to say that the world is an illusion and nothing is real and then back out into the nothingness – it's been done and it's been a very useful step in human evolution. But now what I'm seeing is people being called back into life to fully live it. That's something we always lose at because we never beat life – it's the most exquisite game and that seems to me to be the only meaning or reason to life.

This concept about there's nothing to do – I have found, particularly within myself, that it has become a means of justifying non-activity, like a righteous apathy.

Yes, external laziness . . . It's quite pathetic.

I mean, a lot of people who are into Advaita haven't got jobs, which is fine, but I have found that for myself it can come with the justification of saying that it isn't my choice to be unemployed, so it's OK to be hanging around all day doing nothing. It's just turned into a joke.

That's where the mind tries to copy consciousness. Yeah, it's true that we are non-doing, pure receiving consciousness but when the mind tries to copy that, it says, 'Ah good, I can just not do, just be open and dispassionate and therefore I don't have to work, I don't have to change anything,' and it becomes this excuse for laziness. And then you just get this whole bunch of spiritual people who are basically wasting their lives.

It can become an excuse for not taking responsibility for oneself.

Yeah. I make this distinction between internal laziness and external laziness. What people try and do on a spiritual path is internally they are fighting, judging, resisting feelings, they're blocking thoughts and yet externally they are being really lazy. And the truth is, it's reversed. When we are absolutely internally lazy, we aren't resisting the movement of feelings and thoughts. Then, in that non-resistance, what normally comes, though not always, is a lot of external activity. All of a sudden, that person won't be collapsing in fear and their lifelong passion will start to push them and drive them. They'll start writing a book, they'll start a teaching centre or they'll have some children. They'll start a business or they'll do something that perhaps before they were resisting inside just because of the psychological fear of it.

In the recognizing, 'I am consciousness,' those fears become a little bit unbelievable. And then incredible, beautiful – I guess what Buddha would call right action – just effortlessly starts to happen. All of a sudden, these people who are willing to take that next step, they start leading really meaningful, exciting, productive, worthwhile lives.

A lot of people who follow this particular teaching of Advaita have moved away from Buddhism, which essentially seems to be saying the same thing. Why is that?

Buddhism is one of the biggest religions in the world. Although there is a lot of dogma to it, it is incredibly close to the truth. Christianity often completely loses the true essence of who we are. A closer religion is Buddhism and, for the mind, it's socially acceptable as well because of its non-violence, right action, purity in living – all those things that the mind can quite clearly say, 'Yes that's spiritual.' But in any religion, if there's dogmatism to it, eventually mind is going to find limits to it. We have to finally go outside of mind. The only freedom is to transcend the limitations of thinking, understanding, beliefs and dogma.

But Buddhism is quite prescriptive in telling you how to live a good life.

Yeah, and when you're trying to live from your mind, then great, get all the guidance you can possibly get. But when you've recognized beyond mind, then any shoulds, any prescription on how to live, becomes a constraint, becomes a straitjacket on pure action, on action in surrender.

Which is much more spontaneous.

Which is much more spontaneous, it's totally authentic, there are no rules, there's no particular way it looks. It's just, 'Thy will be done', acting through a body, not being constricted as much by fears, wants, needs, limitations of mind.

Keeping on the Buddhist theme — I saw recently a video of the Dalai Lama speaking in London at the Royal Albert Hall. He started off the talk by saying, 'I would just like to say I am no different from you, I am your human brother.' I was very impressed by his humility. I believe also in Buddhism there is the concept of the Great Lie — that to say that you are 'enlightened' or 'realized' or whatever you want to call it, to profess something you are not, is a really terrible thing. The overall impression I get from the Buddhist way is that Buddhists are incredibly humble and meek in this respect. What I am trying to say is that I have a problem with somebody who sits up the front and says there has been a realization of their true nature or some kind of variation on that, however semantically stated. For me it creates separation and an implicit suggestion that that person is different from me.

Absolutely. I don't think I have ever said that I am enlightened. I mean, it's pathetic to say it. And even if it were true, why would you say it? The whole thing with what enlightenment points to — and who even knows what enlightenment means anyway — is that there is no separate 'I' that can be enlightened. It's just the seeing through of a thought. I mean, what's so great about that? It's like, that's it. You just see through a thought, which you were previously believing in and then you check it out and you see that it's not true. I mean, congratulations, big wow! But seeing that it's a lie stops suffering because all suffering is revolving around is the thought that there is a 'me' who is being judged, a 'me' who is good, a 'me' who is bad, a 'me' who is getting it right, doing it wrong, getting jealous and all this story builds up around a thought. It's just seeing that that particular thought is not valid, even though it still may create reactions in the body.

Even though anger and all these other feelings may arise, it's seen as kind of like, so what? And then to be worshipping something that you know is not true just becomes a bit crazy and it winds down. I really agree with you that the whole thing of 'I've got it and you haven't' is like spiritual snobbery.

The Ramesh line of thinking is that there are people who have got it and those who haven't.

But Ramesh is really straight. He just says this is my concept. It's just a concept. If it helps you to stop suffering, pick it up, check it out. If it doesn't, just discard it. He's really straight like that. It's more to do with our belief in what he is saying — it's reflecting that. He's not suffering!

And he's making a lot of money out of it!

Is there a problem with him making money?

Well, I guess not really. Look, all I want is to know the truth and be happy. I have met many people — inasmuch as they are telling me the same thing, they are all telling me a slightly different way to get there. There's lots of confusion. That's all I know really. I am also becoming more and more sceptical and disillusioned about all of this.

I think it's great because what it's doing is that it is going to throw you back to yourself more and more. You're going to have 15 different opinions plus plus plus and you are really going to have to check it out yourself. And that's where a lot of people don't want to go, they don't want to go into themselves so deeply and check out what's really true for them here. Now whenever I do that, I just get to nothing, I have no idea. I haven't understanding or really firm conviction about anything and yet, I'm talking to you here and what I'm speaking about sounds really convincing. And yet if you were to ask do I absolutely believe that, I would say no because tomorrow I will probably see something deeper — I'll go, God, I was just speaking about a bunch of crap yesterday. So it's the willingness to be totally disillusioned the whole time and it's just like what feels authentic in this moment?

But my question to you was what about Ramesh making money?

Well, I just think that spiritual people ought to be a bit poorer really!

That's a good belief! So, if you're going to get more spiritually developed, you're going to get less and less money. Well, that's a pretty good reason not to get spiritually developed! I think what Ramesh is doing or any of us are doing is no less spiritual than sitting in a bar with a beer, I mean absolutely not. To think that we're really doing anything more holy is again more spiritual bullshit. It's like, he's working, he's helping people and he's collecting some money for that. Good on him.

Last night, you were talking about masculine and feminine energy. Could you expand on that?

In creation, God is what we could call masculine and feminine. It's this void of nothingness which traditionally they call the male aspect — it's the pure potentiality. And in that, you have mother nature, creation, everything that you see, touch, taste, smell, anything, which is the feminine aspect. It's like form as compared to non-form. What all this is, is both of them — the yin and the yang. It's the everything and the nothingness co-existing together. That's who we are.

The fun thing about seeing this work in humans is that through form, we can be accented one side of God more than the other. You can be accented a more masculine side or a more feminine side. You can be more attracted to the nothingness and the freedom and the openness and the spaciousness and the non-touchability of the masculine. Or you can be this flowing, powerful, every possible expression, love, depth, radiance of the feminine. And that's why we see this attraction. When someone's really flowing and radiant, they're incredibly attractive to someone who's in their clarity, their masculine. There's this incredible attraction.

Everything comes back to divinity. Even a relationship, the attraction there is not for a good friend to have around or someone to rub genitals with. It's because there is this incredibly divine attraction of God appearing to separate itself, to create these polarities, which attract each other. Unless we really see how it works in relationship, that gets lost and it just becomes hard to make a relationship even remotely work.

Watching you with Susanna, sitting up at the front together, was incredibly powerful. It reminded me of the image of Rama and Sita — the perfect union of the masculine and feminine in human form. But it also made me feel very jealous because that kind of union is so rare and there is such a yearning within me for that union. It's not that I don't want to be alone — it's something much more profound than that.

Exactly, it's this most intense attraction of God to itself. But the more we filter that through mind and neediness, the more kind of twisted it gets, until you get down to a man looking at a porno movie. It's still the divine attraction back to God, it's just that it's filtered and twisted through a whole bunch of more superficial mind. But everything here is this play of light and darkness. And the beauty is, when you find it in yourself, there's no need to find it in someone else. From that, everything is perfect as it is and whole and complete. So then hell, why not find someone to play with because it is so much more intense when you can taste these different ends of Oneness. When you can see it in someone and live with them and are being devotional to your partner as the female aspect of God, it's like wow — it makes life totally worth living.

It's true. All great literature, music, art — it's all about love and relationships.

And for me, as my principle of 'I am nothingness,' all this is the big woman to me, this is my divine partner. This is why I'm looking at the sky and saying, 'God, I love that.' And it can be more manifest in one particular woman but it doesn't need to be about that person. So it's never about the partner or about the relationship – it's never about finding the right one. It's about finding the right relationship towards what's actually going on here.

But there is this idea of finding one's true soul-sex mate.

And that's a nightmare because if you' re trying to find your soul partner, a particular person, then you're probably going to compromise. What was interesting meeting Susanna was that she was probably the first woman I had ever met who really was completely uncompromising. She was much more in love with God, whatever that means, than man. She wanted to deepen in her relationship with God rather than in her relationship with a particular person. So therefore I couldn't manipulate her, I couldn't twist her, I couldn't make her do what I wanted her to do by holding things back from her. Therefore I respected her.

It's funny how things are often the reverse, the other way round. There's nothing more attractive than someone just being themselves, wanting nothing from anybody. Similarly, there's nothing more unattractive or repelling than someone who wants something from you.

Yes, that's why on retreats we often talk about the different paths of deepening. In suffering, the problem is holding onto the beliefs of who we are, which we haven't fully checked out. But once we recognize they're not actually true, then we can just be this internal laziness of not resisting the feelings as they are arising. And in that, every feeling, every thought, is welcome here – total OKness with everything. But from that, the spiritual paths tend to be quite different. There'll be some with a masculine accent and some with a feminine accent. And that could even be a man with a female exaggerated quality or a woman with a male exaggerated quality.

Like for the man, it probably would be more meditation, finding his purpose in life, getting some direction and clarity, testing himself on how he could be open and loving. But to the woman, it's generally more nurturing, an openness that might be dancing or singing, playing with children, being in nature. It's not challenging herself, it's just being really open to the fullness of who she is, where she's just so happy in herself. She's just glowing with that *shakti* of God. And of course, men are just like flies around a woman like that!

So what to do about the yearning for male-female union, which has become a fixation?

If you're arguing with what is in the moment, you're arguing with God by saying, 'I don't like the way it is now. I should have a partner.' But as soon as we do that, we're a victim and then we're just going to feel powerless. So it can always simply be, 'OK, I'm being fixated, can I find what I am looking for in me? Can I find this stillness, this openness, this clarity that I'm looking for out there, can I find it in me?' Because you *can* always find it in you — I am complete here. And any feeling of not completeness is just a feeling that hasn't been checked out very deeply. The ball is always in our court — we are never a victim to what is.

To return to the subject of satsang. It used to be such an exciting place to be for me but it no longer interests me. In fact nothing interests me that much anymore.

That sounds very developed. Satsang is a trap. This is total theory but it seems to get people into this nice, feel-good space where you get to sing some *bhajans* and hang out with your friends and feel some bliss and opening. It all starts off so nice but it is a trap for the mind because nothing really happens until we're totally disillusioned and absolutely bored with the openings and the contractions and the bit of bliss and is it this guy or is it that guy. Once that becomes so boring and meaningless then it's perfect because then there's only one place left to turn.

But then the mind makes a thing even out of that. I'm at that stage of disillusionment and now I am thinking this could be it!

Yes. Of course, it is it.

But I don't feel it.

No, you won't feel anything. You talk to anyone — all the people you've interviewed — they're probably all saying the same thing. They went through this extreme disillusionment. I know John de Ruiter talks about this the whole time. He had one year of real, opening bliss and then it was just hell. He said he was just so tested to be OK with flatness, deadness, nothingness, lifelessness — to be in this well that was dried out. And that's totally my experience. I think that's all of our experience, knowing it's just not possible to find it with the mind — 'I just can't do it, I've looked everywhere, I've tried everything and I just feel like I'm growing out of this'.

I feel like I'm coming out of a really immature phase — not that I feel I'm becoming more mature though . . .

It feels like it to me.

Well, perhaps, but I feel I've been very childish.

Yes. The whole world is childish. I mean, how many adults are there on this earth? A hundred? 'I want this, I want that, give me some excitement, give me some nice feeling, give me my soulmate, give me some bliss, give me some . . .' We are all just looking for our parents or God or something to come down and make us feel perpetually good and it's like this pathetic hobby, which we can't win. And realizing that is really spiritually mature.

We collect up the empty cups and go back down to the kitchen. We then step out into the backyard where I take Vartman's picture in the partial shade of laundry drying on a clothes line.

I then ask Vartman whether he gets tired of travelling so much. 'No. Susanna does a bit. She says I'd sleep on rock and eat concrete and be happy. For me, it's really great. I love the changing scenery. But I'm really looking forward to our break. It's been two and a half years pretty much of continual teaching.' He goes on to tell me that he hopes to hang out in Tibet or Nepal for a while before returning to Sweden with Susanna, where they have plans to set up a retreat centre.

'Good luck with the disillusionment,' Vartman says as I collect my things together and we say goodbye. He stretches out his arms and he gives me a hug. He then escorts me through the hallway, wishes me well and closes the door behind me.

On the passenger seat of my car is a leaflet advertising Vartman and Susanna's forthcoming retreat in Sweden – last minute research just before the interview. It reads:

> *Do you want to open to the totality of life, the truth of who you are? In every moment your deepest possibility is to naturally live as boundless stillness of consciousness, and the fullness and perfection of love. And to play in that as the apparent opposites of masculine and feminine expressions of life.*

I reflect on what Vartman had to say about relationships – not just between man and woman but between me and the very universe itself. To accept that there is ultimately no one called Paula with a separate identity does not mean that I will cease to interact with the people around me. Without the context of a hidden agenda, what could be more exquisite than to taste and enjoy the divine relationship, like the lovers Siva and Parvati, Krishna and Radha, Rama and Sita – the perfection of the masculine and feminine expressions of love.

> *There is a strength in supreme love which defies reason and laughs at death itself, and Rama suffered himself to be persuaded – partly because his love was great as hers and every passionate word she spoke found ready lodgment in his heart and partly because he was confident of his ability to protect her. It was settled that Sita should accompany Rama to the forest.*

Ramayana

Gangaji

CHAPTER FOURTEEN

SAN FRANCISCO
RENAISSANCE

I have never been to the West Coast of America before, in the main owing to my fear of flying. Being in an aeroplane never seemed to bother me in my youth; in fact, I positively relished the opportunity of going abroad, visiting new places and foreign lands. The older I get however, the more frightening the whole experience becomes – images of being in a plane crash, seconds away from my bodily death, come up to torture me every time I set foot in an aircraft.

The woman next to me in economy class starts to get in a kerfuffle because she can't sit with all the seven members of her family in one row. I nobly offer my seat and the relieved stewardess offers me a replacement in business class. Somehow, having more space around me, feeling less physically constrained, my anxiety about the flight subsides and I actually start to enjoy the eight-hour trip to San Francisco. When our jumbo jet eventually circles over Golden Gate Bridge, I peer down on an ant's world of buildings and freeways – a stainless steel matrix, shuddering in its mathematical proportion and beauty. When I think of the logistics of flying, I can hardly believe that my body is thousands of feet high up in the sky, suspended in space, cradled only by the conceptual projections of an aviation engineer's dream.

It's a strange experience arriving on foreign soil – everything looking the same as well as being completely unfamiliar. Still trying to shrug off the drugged inertia of the flight, I pick up my hire car and drive straight into the city's afternoon rush hour traffic. Stinson Beach, where the interview is to take place and where Gangaji lives, is a small coastal town about two hours' drive north out of San Francisco along Highway 101. There doesn't appear to be a direct route out of the city so I drive, tired and apprehensive, through a metropolitan labyrinth.

As twilight falls, I travel over Golden Gate Bridge and turn off the highway towards Stinson Beach – a long and winding road taking me up and up into the hills, emerging along the coastline. Journey instructions from Gangaji's Customer

Services inform me that the road has breathtaking views of the Pacific Ocean but I have to take their word for it – there are few houses or signs of life and the route is pitch black. Physically exhausted but feeling exhilarated by my adventure into the unknown, I arrive at my lodgings and plunge into a deathlike sleep.

My room, or rather small apartment, is part of a motel complex about five minutes' walk from the beach. Having arrived in the dark, I have no idea of the layout of the town. Although it is now September and out of season, the weather the day after my arrival is balmy and clear. I set out to explore my surroundings and stroll along the main high street – a short road comprising mainly restaurants, a gift shop and the local grocery store. I bear towards the coast, passing through an empty car park – the cries of children and dogs' bark still faintly audible in the gentle wind blowing around the vacant hamburger stalls and deckchair stands. I walk along a sandy path, leading through grassy banks, littered with driftwood and bits of fast-food wrappers. And there before me, framed by bluffs on either side, emerges the sea . . .

I sit down on the damp sand – I am quickly surrounded by artful wasps, reconnoitering the dunes. A salty miasma of damp seaweed fills my nostrils; the crash and hiss of the surf fills my ears. The Pacific Ocean stretches out before me, right to the very edge of the world. Fishing boats on the horizon sit like mosquitoes on the ocean's skin. The water is azure blue, blanketed by a violet haze that merges into intense cobalt above. Way out in the distance, waves are breaking, like lace fringes on a liquid counterpane. At the water's edge, there is a zebra's coat of foam and spume.

The achingly painful beauty of this moment overwhelms me.

I know that this is it.

But the moment is too perfect. It is too glorious. I want to hold onto something or someone to help me continue to experience it. I want to share it.

A nostalgia takes hold – a stench from the past.

The moment is lost.

Returning to my room, I prepare for the interview. In these modern times, most of my information is taken from the Internet. Gangaji's web site is sleek and informative – there are extracts from her books, details of forthcoming events, TV listings of satsang broadcasts on the US cable network. I have also brought with me *You Are That! Satsang with Gangaji* and turn to a chapter entitled, 'Facing the Fear of Death':

> *The way that death and fear of death are usually seen in our culture is a clear indication of deep misalignment with truth.*

Because of our conditioning, physical death is seen as the problem. In actuality, facing the reality of the death of personal identity is an immense opportunity to directly encounter eternal, undying presence.

There is a strong, conditioned belief that you are a psychological entity located in a body. In truth, there is no real psychological entity except as an image or a thought coupled with physical sensation.

When fear of death is directly investigated, it is discovered that only form is born and dies. Consciousness is free of formation, free of birth, free of death.

Gangaji's office is about a mile out of town on the main road leading northward. It is an unassuming wooden building next door to a video rental shop, a gym and an ice-cream parlour. There is a small sign on the door on which is written in red letters 'Leela'. The interview is scheduled for two o'clock – it only takes about 15 minutes to walk from my motel but it feels like three hours. I try to walk slowly, watching my breath, feeling my feet on the ground, all in an effort to remain calm and composed. But a spectre of fear is creeping up beside me, like some evil djinn, ready to kidnap the peace of my mind. The door is opened by a friend of Gangaji's, who makes me a cup of tea and whose sweet conversation makes me feel more relaxed.

On the dot of two Gangaji arrives, introduces herself and we go and sit in a back room overlooking a small garden. Gangaji is a slim woman in her late fifties, with platinum-white hair, which is tucked away in a clip. She is wearing a simple grey trouser suit and matching slippers. The room is tastefully adorned with candles, a bowl of fresh red roses and small framed photographs of Papaji and Ramana Maharshi. On the wall there is a much larger black and white picture of Ramana – his gaze looks back down at me; open, steady, forgiving.

Antoinnette Roberson Varner was born in Texas in 1942 and raised in Mississippi. She was not particularly happy as a child – both her parents were alcoholics. At the age of six, she started having the experience of her body disappearing. Not understanding at the time what was happening, she was taken to a psychiatrist who prescribed the drug phenobarbital, which she was to take to counteract the effect. Thus life moved on. In 1964 she graduated from the University of Mississippi, and then married and had a baby daughter.

But by 1972 things had started to change. Moving to the San Francisco Bay area, she decided to pursue a spiritual path. Initially she tried psychedelics, which gave her a taste of existence in total acceptance and surrender. She then decided to take Bodhisattva vows, practised Zen and *vipassana* meditation and helped to run a Tibetan Buddhist meditation centre. She also travelled to England to study acupuncture, returning to establish a successful practice of her own. By now, she was married to her second husband, Eli, and, on the outside, everything appeared to be going just fine. But by 1988 it became apparent that underneath it all, it wasn't.

Moving from California to Hawaii, Gangaji's persistent longing for personal fulfilment prompted her to pray for a final teacher. On a trip abroad, Eli was to meet H W L Poonja in India and implored her to meet him for herself. Gangaji finally met Papaji in April 1990 on the banks of the river Ganga, where she was given her spiritual name.

Gangaji is almost businesslike in her matter-of-fact manner – she sits cross-legged on a chair, simply waiting for me to start our conversation. She has large sea-blue eyes that look straight into me – unthreatening and yet utterly uncompromising. Although her body remains still, it is her southern voice, rich and melodious, that seemingly contains all possibilities for movement and expression. Half of me is petrified. I feel I am sitting in front of my conscience. I wait a good few moments to catch my breath and begin.

I sat on Stinson Beach yesterday and it was so beautiful and I thought, this is it. This is all I need to know, there is nothing beyond this. There's nowhere to go, there's nothing to do. But then a nostalgia came in and I wanted to experience that moment with somebody. I felt incredible loneliness and it all kind of lost itself.

Yes. This is the trickery of the mind. Papaji said to me once that when someone begins to awaken – the experience of I don't need to go anywhere, this is it, this is beautiful, this is more than enough – all the gods and demons of the past come to reclaim them. So this nostalgia is a trick, it's a trick, and if you believe it, which it sounds like you did, you begin to tell a story about it. Your story is about no one to feel this with, loneliness, which actually means you're left alone again, whereas before it had no meaning. Do you experience it now? We can actually have the opportunity of looking at how to meet something like this.

Well, at this moment in time, there is intense fear.

Oh well, that's good enough! I don't know what the fear is generated by in this moment in time but fear must be met. When I say 'meet', I don't mean get rid of fear or get rid of the nostalgia but as Self Enquiry. Even forget 'Self' because we have some idea of what that is. What I mean is as real enquiry – to really enquire into anything in this instance. And there has to be a letting go of preconceptions of what will come from that enquiry, either hope of what will come or fear of what will come. So it's actually a scientific enquiry. Right now, just drop your consciousness into the fear, just let your consciousness go into the fear, rather than staying somewhere away from it.

I perceive fear as a bad thing, so I want to deny it.

That's right – that's the pattern. So, I'm asking you to recognize the denial that comes from the perception it's a bad thing and, for our purposes, just to drop that. Just to not know what fear is. That's what I mean by it's scientific because then there's an openness of mind. So I'm really speaking about your mind dropping into fear – your open mind, not the contracted, 'Oh this is bad, I have to get away.' So just as an experience, you open your mind and let it fall into fear. What do you experience?

It dissipates quite naturally but then it comes up again.

That's fine, let it come up again. But now you know you're waiting for it. The secret here is not to get rid of it, it's not about pushing fear away. Fear needn't be pushed away. This is the lie that we have been taught. Fear has a very appropriate response physiologically for the organism. But when it becomes a psychological fear, when it becomes a pattern or a barrier to experiencing the natural expansion of your being, the boundlessness of your being, then it must be met. Obviously, I'm not saying if you cross the street and a truck is coming you should stop and meet your boundless being – that would be absurd! But this inappropriate fear, this unwarranted fear, is really a fear of death. And the fear of crossing the street is also a fear of death but we are haunted by our fear of death in ways that we needn't be haunted. We have never really faced death, so we give this fear a label that it's bad, I need to get rid of it. Whereas really this is the fear that appeared to Ramana – it's the same fear. It appeared to Ramana and, by some grace, he was able to stop and experience it. That's real Self Enquiry and in the experience of it, the fear dissipates and there is something that is perceived that wasn't perceived before. The invitation is to experience that all the way because there is something under that.

I know that intellectually.

Yes, but I'm not speaking intellectually, I'm speaking experientially. That's why I'm interested now that this fear is here and that you are willing to, in our time together, drop into it, drop your consciousness. Is it back?

It's hovering. It's not as bad as it was.

Invite it in then. Invite it in.

I find there's a residue in my body though I feel much calmer now.

That's right. So drop your consciousness in the calmness. What's there?

It goes away!

And what's here when these states quite naturally go away with enquiry? What's left?

Calmness.

Yes, so what is the boundary between you and this calmness?

I don't really know.

OK. Can you find one?

Not now.

'Now' is all we're dealing with. Now is all we can deal with in this moment. Obviously in the past there has been experience of huge boundaries between who you are and whatever. But in this moment, now, if you examine you will find no boundary because there is no boundary there. The boundary is only there when we believe our perceptions of boundary and then create a story from those perceptions. And those perceptions and stories are fed emotionally. But the feeding of that emotionally is based primarily on the fear of death, the death of this organism. The gift of Ramana is actually facing that death. Stopping the usual, normal habits of mind of pushing the fear out or conquering the fear or making sure I don't die, I'll deal with that later. Just to stop and die, right now.

The fear is in the body and there is this clear seeing but then the fear just seems to come back.

So what? What's the problem with it coming back?

It comes back and it creates a boundary again.

So what's the choice then?

To not believe it?

Yes, that's a choice but not to believe in it is still dealing with believing it or not believing it. But you always have the choice to fully experience it, to drop your consciousness into it. So, either you have a choice to withdraw your consciousness from it, which continues on the assumption that it is real and that it has meaning and that it is saying something very important that you have to obey. Or you have the choice to actually experience it fully with your consciousness, which is listening to it in a deeper way than you have ever listened to it and discovering the treasure. So this is the essential choice. It doesn't matter if it comes back a million times a day — when you recognize that you have that choice, then fear is not the enemy. Fear has never been the enemy.

Well, I have constructed a life that avoids it.

That's normal but your life now is not constructed to avoid it because you keep putting yourself in the face of people just like you who are telling you it is possible to stop. It is actually possible to face what has been feared, what one's whole life has been based around avoiding, what one's whole culture avoids, especially in the West.

I just feel that my life is a wasted opportunity somehow.

It can be. Most lives are wasted opportunities because here we are in this precious experience of being human with intellectual power, with reflective consciousness and with choice. And most of this is wasted. What we choose is to feel as safe as we can feel for as long as we can feel and then we die. But there is no safety — the body is subject to death, it is subject to danger. But the great teachers throughout time have offered us an alternative — choice and the invitation is there clearly.

You say you have experienced it when you take that choice, when you actually allow your consciousness to fall into what it is you're avoiding. And it may not just be fear, it could be despair, anger, helplessness, it could be this abject loneliness that you're speaking about. Rather than scurrying away from it, if you fall into it, there is a huge discovery that is always here. And it's actually very good if you have lots of opportunities for discovering this is always here. So if it appears and you only have this once, so what? Some people have more fear than others, it's the way the nervous system is wired, where certain imprints have gone in — but that's secondary. What's primary is that you have the opportunity, by some great blessing in your life and the choices you have made, to follow that blessing, to follow it deeper, to really know who you are. To discover it in a way that, no matter what happens, it's irrevocable. The discovery is the discovery and whatever emotion appears, whatever mind state appears, whatever thought appears, whatever person appears, that can't be shaken.

I think I really want it.

So what's the hesitation?

I don't know. This project — there have been wonderful moments of seeing but then incredible frustration and anger. Anger directed out to the teachers themselves — so many concepts within myself about how teachers should behave . . .

It's all about yourself, isn't it? Isn't it really anger at yourself? Or anger at God? Anger at the universe? Anger at the imperfection of human beings? Isn't that yourself?

Yes.

So, it's possible, just for an instant, to stop telling the story about you and your failings and some teacher and their failings and just experience this anger and see what is under the anger. And what's under that and what's under that and what's under that. This is the promise of Jesus that the Kingdom of Heaven is within. But people have no idea what that means — 'within'. This is actually showing you that within is letting go the story that projects the mind outwards. And the mind will find us enormous targets — the universe has lots of targets! Everybody is messing up in one way or another but if we are willing to just stop and experience within our own selves that frustration, that anger, that humiliation, that energy, then there is a great treasure out there waiting, a great treasure. It doesn't mean that your opinions have to stop, it just means that something else, something bigger, is discovered.

I've been so entrenched in the theory.

That's the problem.

Advaita theories like do I exist? Can I make a choice?

The Advaita theory in general? Well forget it! Advaita fundamentalists everywhere! They're caught in a box and it's the fundamentalism in every religion that causes the most problems because it demands conceptually a freedom and a perfection. But freedom and perfection are not conceptual. Anything that is a concept is bound by the mind. The mind is beautiful — I love the mind — but it's limited. The truth of the freedom that you are, of the perfection that is always alive waiting for its self-discovery, is in this willingness to be imperfect.

In myself, as a woman, there are all the issues of how I look, how I speak, am I well read enough, funny enough . . .

Yes, so what is the hope there?

I want to be loved and I want to be respected and I want to be popular.

Yes, and what will you have then?

I think I will feel more complete.

That's right.

And then I won't feel this loneliness.

So, this is all about avoiding loneliness in search of completion. What I am saying is, if you are fully willing to experience that loneliness, you will find completion. You can spend the rest of your life searching for these things – love and respect and understanding – and you'll get what you have discovered so far. But you can never get enough love to make you feel complete, you can never get enough respect to make you feel complete. You've certainly experienced love and respect in your life but it's not enough. But the willingness to actually experience the loneliness reveals that at the core of loneliness is the completion. It's the same as experiencing death. And it won't be found in theory because that is a concept. So I always start by saying I am not an Advaitist, I am absolutely not an Advaitist. I had never heard of Advaita when I met Papaji, thank God! And I don't speak in Advaitic terms because I find them very stilted, like if I were speaking in biblical terms or some other religious terms.

It's possible, just like this, as human being to human being, to see what is deeper than woman to woman or deeper than Westerner to Westerner, what's deeper than human to human. What's deeper than this species, you know. What's looking out of these eyes and meeting itself in your eyes and inviting itself into the deeper meaning in this nervous system. So this nervous system can experience, while still experiencing human incarnation, the radiance and the truth of being that does not need human incarnation for its beingness. And this loneliness which you speak of and the fear that you speak of are pathways to that.

But the psychological experience of fear is overwhelming.

It's only overwhelming when you're running from it. Doing that feeds it power and then it's like a horror movie. Running from fear takes a lot of energy. This takes no energy at all. This is effortlessly opening. What it does take is a willingness — that is the resolve — to know the truth rather than continue to feed the neurosis. So, you're very aware of the neurotic patterns but I sense with you that there's still some hope that one of those patterns will actually reach completion.

Yes.

So maybe you need to experience some more of the futility of that hope. I certainly can relate to that. I mean, I did everything I did to get the love and completion I was receiving and I was receiving quite an amount of love and respect. I had a great relationship, I was treating patients, but so what? It didn't touch this ground of my fear of loneliness and my searching desperately to get that fear to go away, to get that loneliness to go away. Because that's a divine fear, it's a divine call but no thing can give it, no person can give it. It will only be satisfied with itself.

I have read about the lives of many teachers and I have felt very jealous of what they discovered.

But you told me yourself you have had many moments.

Yes, that's true.

So you have to tell the truth.

But it hasn't 'clicked'.

It has clicked but you've turned away from it. It has clicked.

Why do I turn away from it?

Because you still have hope that being like you thought you were will get you what it is you thought you wanted. There has not been a big enough disillusionment with the patterns of your mind. It's there all the time but as these gods and demons of the past attack, you bow to them. So in this moment right now, you can say yes to yourself, not knowing what that will look like. You can be true to yourself. There are many teachers who can provide you with their transmission, their field of grace, but you have to say yes. That's the only difference between you and me — I said yes. I said it with my whole being, regardless of the consequences. I had no idea what that yes would mean. It was terrifying to say yes, to say yes so completely that I just pushed everything onto the table – yes, take it all.

I thought I had said yes.

Well then you've left some string where you can pull the yes back. So it has to be yes, regardless of what appears, regardless of what emotion appears, regardless of what thought appears, regardless of what phenomena appear, because what you are speaking of are thoughts and emotions and states, and they change. Some are good and some are bad. But who you are doesn't change. And in your willingness to experience any thought, any emotion, any state all the way in, you have the capacity to experience that.

The Advaita idea is that you have no choice in turning towards freedom.

But you have to forget that because the mind just uses that to justify itself. That's why you should forget everything you have learned, especially Advaitic theory because mind can use that very quickly. 'Oh, no choice, OK.'

And that enlightenment is predestined or pre-programmed . . .

Enlightenment, or whatever you want to call it, is already here and you have full choice to recognize that. And you know it.

Yes and I am scared of it.

Yes. It's scary. It's big. It's bigger than you can control. But so what? So what does that mean, 'I'm scared of it'? Does it mean you then slink off and start denying it again for more suffering through your denial? You're too smart a girl for that.

When I see people who have made that leap I envy them but, when it comes to myself, I just can't seem to do it.

So maybe you're more infatuated with your suffering than you are with your freedom. Then the key is to tell the truth. If you are more infatuated with your suffering, your envy, your story, whether I had it or lost it – then go into it fully, tell the story. Then at least you can consciously suffer! But this suffering and then this story about the victim seeping in – this is absurd.

I know that I am infatuated with myself.

Yes but not with yourself, but with your suffering. That's narcissistic suffering. Who you are is complete. Your image is incomplete so you can spend the rest of your life's energy feeding this image. Or you can discover, in an instant, the truth of who you are and then the rest of your life is an emanation of that. It is a radical invitation but you keep putting yourself in a position to hear it.

And then I deny it.

Well, that's your choice.

I've come all this way to meet you and I don't really know what else to say.

But you got it on the beach. That's a moment of pure beauty, of grace. Perhaps it is choiceless that that moment appears because they don't appear to everybody and it's a mystery how it appears. But where the choice is, is in saying yes to that, so that when the moment passes and the experience passes, the yes remains. So the allegiance of one's life is to that, not to the image.

I read an excerpt from your book, freedom & resolve, *in which there was a woman who woke up in the middle of the night in a state of panic. It has been the same for me — ever since I can remember as a child, I wake up in the night, not being able to breathe, thinking I'm about to die. The fear of death is very deep.*

Yes, it can go even deeper than any verbal or conscious storytelling. But this is the lifetime. So, whether you believe in past lives or the manifestation of past lives, just in your ancestry, what's in the genes — there's a lot of really horrible things that have happened which gets passed on in the genetic material as well as everything else. So, the opportunity of a life lived in truth is the willingness to meet that, whether it's called meeting one's karma or meeting the genetic propensity of this end result of many millions of years — this is all the same.

But there's still a knot within.

So what? Why would you shift your energy to that knot rather than into the radiance that's shining? Are you afraid of the radiance? Are you afraid of actually being complete? What have you been searching for all this time? Are you afraid of actually being love? You are the love you have been searching for. You know why you are afraid — because that would mean that the search is over. And you think that what you have gained has been from the search rather than from the love itself.

But I feel I am not worthy.

Well, you're not worthy. Nobody's worthy. That's the beauty of it! You cannot be worthy of that. When you look at your history or anyone's history — we have all caused so much suffering even in just this lifetime. No, we don't deserve it and still it is here. So the yes I was speaking of — we don't deserve the grace as it appears but the yes is this willingness to deserve it, the willingness to serve it. You know, if you haven't had an experience, it doesn't make sense but you have had.

That's what makes it more painful.

That's right. Thank God for this pain. It's a beautiful pain. But you want even more of that pain. Finally that pain does not let you budge an iota on the truth of your being, whatever *vasanas* or habits or thoughts appear, whatever physical, mental, emotional appears, you know the real suffering is in the denying of the truth itself.

There's always a kind of self-deprecation. It actually feels quite virtuous in some way.

Yes. Self-righteous. That's right. You deserve that but you don't deserve the grace! You deserve the beating! And since you deserve it there is some pleasure in it. And the truth be told, it's actually an erotic pleasure. So there has to be a moment of recognizing that, not only are you being beat by yourself, by your super ego, you're enjoying it. And not only are you enjoying it but it's eroticized. That's a moment of truth where you really, really get that. Then when the opportunity appears to engage in that, you at least know the truth of it. It is a masochistic tendency. But you have the opportunity to say no. It's a kind of addiction.

So what do you want? What do you really want?

To be honest, I don't really know.

So, this is what you have to discover because what I sense is that there are lots of fragments of desire. And you have had experiences and, just now, I just saw that you have the capacity to experience what is just appearing and to discover what's under that. But I also see that you have not collected your energy to really say truthfully what you want, absolutely, finally, at the risk of all. So that's the maturity that's waiting because that's what gives you the strength. You want a little here, a little there, so it's really a gathering of the power of desire. And that comes from telling the truth.

How long have you been drawn to these issues?

Since I was about 21. I was bullied at school, which started those feelings of alienation, isolation. So I started to read like crazy — it was a wonderful security. I think when you start to read literature it naturally takes you to consider deeper values, spiritual values. Then I got involved in an organization that taught Advaita very theoretically. One of the things we were taught was that the only way for a woman to 'realize herself', except in rare circumstances, was through a man — either through obedience in marriage or obedience to a male teacher.

My goodness — another form of bullying. This is fundamentalism. It takes the values of the culture of a particular time — a patriarchal culture — and then infuses that with the power of spiritual discovery as if that were the reality. Well, this is very familiar.

Then I met Catherine Ingram who showed me the possibility of something else. I just feel now that I am drifting around — up and down, left and right.

My teacher told me to stop. And I had drifted around enough and tasted enough and yet had not had enough fulfilment. I saw something in Papaji's eyes, which was beautiful and cosmic and inviting. He said stop. So I stopped. I said yes. But that wasn't the end — I mean, there was lots of stuff that happened. But the pivotal, crucial moment was accepting the invitation to stop. Of course, at first I didn't even know what he meant by stop. You mean stop everything?! But what if I need to go?! So that's all really I can say. Stop. Stop hating yourself, stop torturing yourself, stop worshipping yourself. Stop hoping, stop fearing, stop searching, stop believing, and then you will see, naturally.

It's very obvious, but . . .

Stop the but. So right now — this whole thing is arising, it's familiar, it's not like it's a created new thought. Just stop. Don't follow it. Just be still. You see and then there's just that much more capacity. So really we're speaking about the capacity to bear the bliss of being, the beauty of being, the love of being.

We sit for what feels like hours together in silence, though from my watch I realize it is only about 10 minutes. The cassette recorder clicks off and I jolt at the noise. 'Good luck,' says Gangaji leaning over to rub my knee. We go out onto the verandah to take her photograph. 'Write to me if you want if there are any more questions. Now that there is this connection.' She then disappears with the speed with which she arrived. Gangaji's companion gives me a copy of *freedom & resolve* — I thank her profusely both for the book and for making me feel so welcome.

As I step out and walk away, one part of me is deeply humbled, the other is utterly humiliated. Anger arises and I think, I've spent so much money just to get here, I've flown so many miles just to hear things that I already know. I do want freedom, I really do. I retrace my steps to the beach. The sky is not as clear as it was when I last sat by the shore. A light autumnal breeze stirs the heavens. Clouds pulsate and scud across the sky. What do I really want? What do I really really want? To be free. Can I be free here and now? Yes I can. So what's holding me back? Me! Gangaji had told me the truth. She had not patted me sweetly on the back, telling me all would be well. She told me I have a choice and it is in my hands whether I accept that choice or not. No wonder Papaji had made Gangaji the carrier of the Ramana lineage – she just cuts through everything to the core.

I look out again to the sea. America – the land of freedom and plenty. California – the place where Eastern teachings were flourishing, inspiring teachers and artists and poets. Stinson Beach – the moment where I must choose to face death in order to be immortally free.

> And just for a moment I had reached the point of ecstasy that I always wanted to reach, which was the complete step across chronological time into timeless shadows, and wonderment in the bleakness of the mortal realm, and the sensation of death kicking at my heels to move on, with a phantom dogging its own heels, and myself hurrying to a plank where all the angels dove off and flew into the holy void of uncreated emptiness, the potent and inconceivable radiancies shining in bright Mind Essence, innumerable lotus-lands falling open in the magic mothswarm of heaven. I could hear an indescribable seething roar which wasn't in my ear but everywhere and had nothing to do with sounds. I realized that I had died and been reborn numberless times but just didn't remember especially because the transitions from life to death and back to life are so ghostly easy, a magical action for naught, like falling asleep and waking up again a million times, the utter casualness and deep ignorance of it. I realized it was only because of the stability of the intrinsic Mind that these ripples of birth and death took place, like the action of wind on a sheet of pure, serene, mirror-like water. I felt sweet, swinging bliss, like a big shot of heroin in the mainline vein; like a gulp of wine late in the afternoon and it makes you shudder; my feet tingled. I thought I was going to die the very next moment.

On the Road
Jack Kerouac

Ramesh S Balsekar

CHAPTER FIFTEEN

THE GODFATHER
OF SOUL

You can see Elephanta Island, home of cave sculptures depicting Brahma, Vishnu and Siva, whilst sitting in the Sea Lounge of the Taj Mahal Intercontinental Hotel on P J Ramchandani Marg in the Colaba district of Mumbai. In front of the island is a much smaller one, Mandwa Island, and when they are viewed together from the hotel's first-floor window, the islands give the impression that they are equidistant from the shore – like two almond-shaped eyes peeping over the horizon's edge.

I can hardly believe I am in India. Having dreamed of coming for so many years, as well as just having flown halfway around the world in the opposite direction to America, here I am, finally – tired, bewildered and yet utterly exhilarated. Although I am staying at an old colonial-style guest house, I have come to the Taj, only a minute's walk away, for afternoon tea. After my arrival in the early hours of the morning at Mumbai's international airport, I am taking the opportunity to relax and acclimatize myself to the sweltering heat, the bitter-sweet smells and the flamboyant madness that is India.

The Taj is the most exclusive hotel in Mumbai – it reminds me of the Savoy Hotel on the Strand in London; an edifice of such opulence and grandeur, all the while haunted by tramps and beggars in the arcades around the building's rear entrances. And here at the Taj, amidst its ground-floor arches running around the perimeter of the hotel, prostitutes and dope fiends skulk in doorways, peering out of the shadows ready to offer you sentient pleasures and all at a very good price. Such are the contradictions of India – luxury and poverty, the privileged and the dispossessed, all within a hair's breadth.

So, this is nearly the end of the journey, the denouement of my journey in the peripatetic quest for some kind of understanding, the understanding of who I am. I look out to sea again. Tourist pleasure boats bob in line along the quayside.

Garlands of yellow flowers and detritus float nonchalantly on the grey-green sea. Towards the horizon, a milky mist veils the view – urban pollution has become a permanent fixture of nature here. In the street below life carries on regardless – taxis and rickshaws, bicycles and horse-drawn traps, tourists and beggars, children and stray dogs. These are the dramatis personae of Mumbai.

Even though I prefer to travel on my own, arriving alone in India can be a gruelling experience. The first thing that hits you as you walk out of the airport terminal – bleary-eyed and physically drained from your eight-hour flight – is not only the stifling heat, despite it being well after midnight, but the sight of the sea of men in their white cotton uniforms awaiting your arrival, who seethe towards you, shouting and haggling for your attention.

I find the queue of small, black taxis and I squeeze onto the rear seat of one of them, my rucksack still strapped to my back. I daren't take it off – not for fear of having it stolen but for fear of someone kindly offering to carry it for me . . . and very cheap at the price. As we pull away, the dark brown face of a young boy pops into the open window. He starts lamenting, 'English lady, English lady.' He thrusts out his small hand and then points to his mouth. This is something I'm going to have to get used to, I realize – the signs of poverty shoved right up in my face.

The ride to the Colaba district takes about an hour. It is probably the most disturbing car journey of my life. The road winds its way through a shanty town of such abject poverty that I can barely look through the window. Ramshackle and ragged shops and buildings prop each other up, clamouring for attention from the passer-by with their bright neon signs, all written in what looks like Sanskrit. As we drive along to the constant tooting of the taxi's horn with the warm wind in my face, there is an indescribable smell – a sweet faecal odour that seems to get right up inside my nostrils and down to the pit of my stomach. On the pavements, people are lying asleep only a few feet from the wheels of passing cars, oblivious to the traffic. I start to wonder whether there can be the luxury of Self Enquiry in the face of so much suffering? Could you truly be wondering about the complexities of Advaitic theory when having to deal with the prospect of not knowing where your next meal was coming from?

We arrive at my hotel at about two in the morning. I pull out wads of notes from my purse to pay for the journey – I must seem like a millionairess as I fumble with the alien currency. Dealing with money is going to be something else I am going to have to get used to. The hotel proprietor stumbles half asleep out of a small room, I apologize for waking him and he takes me up to the third floor in an antiquated lift that groans all the way up its shaft. The room is nondescript, except for the green-black mould creeping across one wall. I disentangle my rucksack from my body, hang up my mosquito net and settle into bed.

But I cannot sleep. I am far too excited, as well as feeling incredibly vulnerable. What if something happens to me – what if I get attacked or I catch some awful disease? The hours pass by . . . Eventually dawn breaks. The first thing I notice are the birds – but this is not the birdsong of European daybreaks, sweet and harmonious and heralding the new day; it is the dirge of rooks and crows, screeching over the rooftops, proclaiming their carrion meals under the sweltering heat of the sun.

It is now just before nine in the morning, the day after my arrival. A Dutchman staying at my hotel is also going to see Ramesh and he escorts me to the bus stop just around the corner. Bus 83 is a huge long white coach, which stops for barely longer than is absolutely necessary for the waiting passengers to leap on. I am last in the queue and my companion scoops me up from the street as the bus sets off. We sit at the back and pay our fare to the Breach Candy district – the princely sum of six rupees. The bus is packed and the journey is physically agonizing – it lumbers on at an alarming pace, with no attempt to avoid the potholes in the road, each trench sending its passengers inches from their seats. Because I am still tired and dazed by the heat and jetlag, the funfare ride makes me laugh at every jolt. But India is not unlike any other commuter city in rush hour – people turn around and stare at my giggles and wonder what all the fuss is about.

We journey through a densely populated and overdeveloped, sprawling metropolis. Remnants of the the British rule in India are visible everywhere. The architecture is the city's living history. The bus takes us into the 'better' end of town, where we get off – Ramesh's street leads downhill to the ocean's edge. Near the end of the road, a small crowd of people have gathered on the left-hand pavement – this is the drill, I discover. At nine-thirty, a slim jolly Indian man with a sleek black moustache joins us. Called Murthy, he is in his early forties and puffs seductively on a cigarette, greeting everyone by name. 'A new face,' he chuckles. I explain who I am and the reason why I have come. He nods enthusiastically. 'All your questions will be answered by Ramesh,' he laughs. 'There's no need to go to anyone else.' Murthy has been coming for many years, shepherding devotees in and out of Ramesh's house, knowing that he, at least, needn't go anywhere else. At twenty to ten, we all cross the road and enter Sindhula Building. We go up in the lift which jolts to a halt outside Ramesh's apartment. There are shelves for our shoes and I dutifully place my Dr Marten's on the rack.

We file in through the hallway which leads into a large bright room furnished with ornately carved occasional tables covered with photographs of Ramesh and his family, vases of flowers and a beautiful bronze carriage clock, its crystal weights rotating back and forth – an ambience more akin to the bourgeoisie of Europe than the home of an Indian sage. On the other side of the room there is a hammock, where a young woman is swinging back and forth with such a look of glee on her face that she reminds me of Alice in Wonderland. My heart is beating like a drum. This is it! I am really going to meet Ramesh Balsekar. I have a card from the Ramana Maharshi Foundation in London, signed by some of its members, and wait nervously to give it to him. And then here he is . . . and how small and delicate he is! I offer the card to him as a way of introduction. 'Oh, thank you,' he says, with the sweetest smile that makes my heart break. He has such an aura of purity and innocence, he reminds me of a choirboy in his white Indian clothes. He places his hand on my cheek and says, 'How lovely to see you. What is your name? Paula? Please, come.' He escorts me to a small room off the hallway. He then disappears whilst Murthy reappears, explaining to me that new visitors must sit in the 'hot seat'.

The room fills with about 20 people, sitting either on chairs or on the floor. The window looks onto the Arabian Sea – from the street the sounds of taxi horns and people's voices can be heard. A crow sits in the open window, peering in and wondering what we are all doing. On the walls are pictures of Ramana, Nisagardatta and Ramesh. On the window sill are quotes by Ramesh, etched onto wooden plaques. 'All there is is Consciousness and Consciousness is all there is,' declares one. 'It is not an action – it is a happening,' says another. Through windows looking into the next room, I see a tall wiry Indian man, Singh, who is plugged into recording equipment through bell-shaped earphones, lending him the appearance of a nightclub DJ.

At ten o'clock, Ramesh appears. He walks briskly into the room and sits in a chair in the corner. He puts his hands together in *namaste* and looks around the room acknowledging everyone as old friends. Immediately, Ramesh picks up the conversation with an Indian man where he presumably left off. Has he understood what was being discussed yesterday? Ramesh reiterates his points to the man and then turns to me. 'So, Paula, you come from London?' Now it's my turn to be under the spotlight. I am handed a microphone. Ramesh proceeds to ask me questions about my personal life, my interest in the spiritual path. This is the only time, other than with Gangaji, that I have been quizzed about myself. Talking about my history makes me feel uncomfortable, however I soon lose any nervousness. Ramesh makes you feel nothing other than interesting and special.

FIRST SATSANG

So, Paula, what is your understanding now of what Paula is seeking? Would you use the word salvation?

Well, not even that. Just peace.

That's right. Salvation is just a word.

I used to think I was looking for God. It seemed that Advaita was the end of the road and the end of concepts. That kind of seeking has quietened down but, in my heart, I don't feel I am any closer to any kind of understanding.

So, it seems to me that the answer is very clear. What you are seeking is to be rid of frustration. That's what the spiritual seeking comes down to. 'I don't like being frustrated.'

Yes. I wish it were more holy, my search!

I know! The real problem with the spiritual seeking is that it has certain words, which are astonishingly misleading. What does one mean by salvation, Paula?

Salvation from frustration?!

Frustration! And what does frustration mean? Frustration means not being able to be comfortable with myself and not being able to be comfortable with others. You cannot be comfortable with yourself if you are not comfortable with others. So, what is the end of frustration? The absence of frustration means being comfortable with myself and comfortable with others.

But this teaching says that everything is consciousness. So that means that this frustration is as God wills it. Is even the fact that I cannot accept my frustration also God's will?

Yes.

So why am I here?!

Because God does not want that frustration to remain for the rest of your life.

But he put it there.

Yes.

So why doesn't he get rid of it now?

You will be rid of it only when God wills it, Paula. Therefore if God put the frustration there, what makes you think he has put it there for all time? What makes you think that he does not intend to get rid of the frustration in the next two or three days?

Well, I'd have nothing to worry about then would I?!

That's my point! Now, we are talking about Paula being comfortable with herself. What is Paula? Paula who wants to be comfortable with herself is a personality, is an ego, isn't it? An identification with a particular body-mind organism and a form and the name Paula. Identification with this name and this form. This identification means really a persona, personification, a personality. So what is Paula? A personality which has identified itself with a particular body and a name. Now, what is that personality? Personality is based on the body-mind organism and my basic concept is that Paula, the ego, is based entirely on the programming in this body-mind organism. And by programming I mean you have no choice in being born to particular parents, in a particular environment.

Therefore you have no choice about the genes, the unique DNA, in this body. And by the same token, the conditioning that this body has received in the environment in which she was born and raised, every moment from day one, at home, in society, from school, in church. All the time, the conditioning being this is right, that is wrong, if you do this you commit a sin, if you do that you will earn a merit in the eyes of some computer, which is keeping a very close touch of all your sins and good deeds.

I can understand that we are products of conditioning but something in me says isn't each individual person a glorious manifestation of God? I'd like to think that I am something more than just mind-body programming.

Think of it, Paula. Is it truly anything other than the programming? As a stranger, you walk into a party, you look around, you stand for a while with a drink in your hand and listen to the conversation. Have you yourself not felt drawn to a particular group rather than to another group?

Yes, definitely.

And then Paula says, 'I like this group more than another group.' So how has that happened? Why does Paula feel inclined to go to a particular group? Because, my answer is, what she sees is approved by the conditioning.

But what if there is a beautiful sunset outside the window? Is that still a form of conditioning?

If I'm drawn to something beautiful?

What you think is beautiful is according to your conditioning. You may consider watching the sunset as something beautiful. What someone else considers beautiful, and is drawn to, is because the conditioning is different.

Why is there conditioning then?

The conditioning is because of the programming in the mind-body organism. Every human being is a unique individual, is a unique instrument or computer – the DNA is unique. My point is that science accepts that the DNA in each individual is unique. There are no two human bodies with the same DNA. That is why I am saying that God has created each human being as a unique creature, as a unique instrument.

So the conditioning is the way that that person has been shaped?

That's right. And my point is, why has God created each human being as a unique instrument or computer? So that he can function through each of the six billion human instruments and bring about such actions or events or happenings as there are supposed to happen. The instrument, because of the ego and the conditioning, thinks that it is his action or her action. But my point is that, at any moment, any action that happens through any body-mind organism is something which is supposed to happen at that moment at that time and place through that particular body-mind organism, according to God's will. Or if some people don't like the words God's will, according to the cosmic law.

In other words, what I am saying is, all actions happening through all the body-mind organisms at any one time is exactly what is supposed to be, according to the cosmic law. No human being does anything – that is my basic point. All actions through all human beings are happenings, created by God according to the cosmic law.

Scientists think that there is a spiritual gene.

Quite right. So, for Paula to be interested in spiritual seeking, the programming in this mind-body organism, the genes and conditioning, is such that this kind of seeking can happen. And there are thousands of mind-body organisms, the programming of which simply prevents this kind of seeking happening.

So from the point of view of consciousness, it doesn't matter if you are ignorant or awake. It's just the way it is?

From the view of consciousness, there is no 'you' at all because you would be something existing apart from consciousness, if we truly accept that all there is is consciousness, all there is is the source, the One without a second, by whatever name it is called.

But I do appear to exist.

Indeed, indeed. You appear to exist.

Whatever I say at any time is a concept, it is not the truth. So, if you keep listening to me, the thought will keep on coming, 'I like what Ramesh has to say, it gives me a sense of freedom but how do I know it is the truth?' Therefore I make it perfectly clear that whatever any sage has said at any time is a concept – a concept being something that some may accept and some may not. It may appeal to some intellects, it may not appeal to other intellects. Anything that any scripture or any religion has said is a concept and that is why we have religious wars. Concepts of one religion are not acceptable to concepts of another religion.

If everything that everybody has said is a concept, is there such a thing as truth at all, which nobody can deny? Can there be any truth that no one can deny? What do you think, Paula? It's difficult to find, isn't it, and yet no human being can deny that he or she exists! I am. I am. Not as Paula but I am, irrespective of the body, irrespective of anything. I am, which is the impersonal awareness of being. The impersonal awareness of being, which no one can deny, is the only truth. So consciousness that was not aware of itself, consciousness at rest, became consciousness in movement and at that moment, the manifestation came into being – this impersonal awareness of being, I am. Then this impersonal 'I am' identified itself with each mind-body organism and the ego came into being – the ego with a sense of personal doership. We use the word ego so easily. What do you mean by ego, Paula? Have you ever thought about it? What would your answer be?

Identification with a body-mind organism?

Merely identification with the body-mind organism? When the ordinary man or woman is called by their name, he or she responds but so does the sage! If a sage were called by name, whether it is Jesus Christ or Moses or Ramana Maharshi or Mohammed, he would respond. That means that, even in the case of the sage, identification with a particular form and a particular name must be there for that body-mind organism to function. So what is it that distinguishes the sage from the ordinary being?

He believes he is not the doer?

That is the point. So, that which distinguishes the sage from the ordinary man is the sense of doership in the identification of that particular name and form. So, to me the ego is identification with a particular name and form as a separate entity.

But as long as I believe I am the doer, which God put there in the first place, it doesn't matter if the ultimate truth is to believe that I am not the doer because I am thinking the way that God wants me to think.

That is correct.

So it's irrelevant whether truth exists or not, or whether the sage exists or not. In my own experience, in my own programming, I think I am the doer and that's the way it is until it's changed.

So, in the programming of a limited number of body-mind organisms, God has created this kind of spiritual seeking. What I am also saying is that there is no seeker of any kind of seeking, whether the seeking happens for money, for fame, for power, for God or truth or whatever you call it.

When this is truly understood, that there is no doer, how can there possibly be any pride or arrogance? When something nice happens, the news about it is the input and a sense of pleasure arises both in a sage and an ordinary man. Where is the difference then? The difference is for the ordinary man, along with the sense of pleasure, is the enormous amount of pride. My life's ambition has been fulfilled! I'm a Nobel Laureate! The sage finds it amusing that he should be considered Nobel Laureate at all. He knows he hasn't done anything. So, in the ordinary mind, a sense of pleasure is accompanied by pride and arrogance. In the case of a sage there is no pride or arrogance even for something nice that has happened.

Then something that is not so nice happens. The news comes in that an action done by a particular mind-body organism is not acceptable to society, for whatever reason – that is the input. A sense of regret arises. In the case of the sage, as with an ordinary being, a sense of regret arises and a wish that it had not happened but the understanding is that it is not his or her act, which has been disapproved by society. Therefore there might be a sense of regret but there will not be a sense of guilt or shame. Why should I feel guilt or shame if I know deep down that it is not my action? Even if the result is of a punishment, then I accept that punishment.

Therefore basically what I am saying, Paula, is that if understanding happens by the grace of God that I am not the doer, that no one is the doer, then for all actions happening to this body-mind organism, I can have neither pride or arrogance, nor guilt and shame, you see.

Now, what happens in life? I have to accept pleasure or pain, reward or punishment — that is the price one has to pay for having to live in this world, whether you want it or not. But what is absent is pride and arrogance, guilt and shame. So if there is an absence of pride and arrogance, guilt and shame, would you not say that you are comfortable with yourself? And if you also accept that no one else is the doer, then action that happens to some other mind-body organism that hurts you — even if that other person wanted to hurt you and is happy that you have been hurt — he doesn't know what you know. He would not have been able to hurt you if it were not God's will according to the cosmic law. So the hurt is accepted as part of your destiny or God's will. Knowing that no one can hurt you, there cannot be any sense of malice or hatred. Whom will you hate when you know that no one can do anything? Nobody is the doer. Therefore how can you have a feeling of malice or hatred, of jealousy or envy? So not having a sense of malice or hatred or jealousy or envy for anybody in the world makes you comfortable with others.

My life is not about doing actions but how I feel about doing action.

That is exactly the point. What have we been looking for? Not having frustration. That's where we started. Not having frustration means being comfortable with myself and being comfortable with others. If I know that I am not the doer, then I accept whatever happens as part of the cosmic law, without pride and arrogance, guilt and shame. So accepting of that, without pride or arrogance, guilt or shame, means I am comfortable with myself and therefore I am comfortable with others. And all that just by being able to accept nothing can happen unless it is God's will!

So, no frustration, comfortable with myself, comfortable with others, all because of one's acceptance — 'Thy will be done'. And even that acceptance can only happen with the grace of God! And for that to happen, God has already created the programming in certain body-mind organisms, which makes that possible at some time or other, when it is supposed to happen. That is the whole teaching, Paula.

SECOND SATSANG

Let me begin. What I am saying is that there is only one source, unchanging, eternal – it may be called consciousness, it may be called energy, it may be called God. But my basic point is that there is one source from which has emerged this totality of manifestation that can be perceived by our senses. And the manifestation is nothing but a totality of objects, therefore the human being cannot essentially be anything other than an object. A human being is a uniquely programmed object through which the source or God functions and brings about such actions as are supposed to happen according to his will or according to a cosmic law.

In other words, what I am saying is, at any moment, the four words in the Bible – Thy will be done – is the basic and essential concept in life. Thy will be done. The meaning is very simply that nothing can happen unless it is God's will, you see. So if something has happened, whatever it may be, the human being may decide good, bad or indifferent. But if something has happened, it could not have happened unless it was God's will. That is the basis of what I say. Anything else, Paula?

In deep sleep, the sense of individuality goes and only impersonal awareness remains. Why don't I experience this impersonal awareness in deep sleep?

Because in deep sleep there is no duality. The manifestation exists in the duality. Duality is only in manifestation. So in deep sleep, the impersonal awareness excludes all duality. The impersonal awareness means absence of duality.

But I have heard it said that a jnani in deep sleep is aware of deep sleep and I don't understand why that should be.

I don't either. Deep sleep is deep sleep. And even in the case of a sage, the identification with the name and form as a 'me' is still there. And that is what comes up as soon as he wakes up.

So even if a jnani is in deep sleep and somebody calls his name, he will wake up.

Sure. Therefore identification with the name and form is there.

So how is deep sleep different to being awake in the waking state?

Being awake in the waking state – that is an important point, Paula. Being awake for the sage in the waking state does not mean the dropping away of identification with the name and form. The sage still has to live his life in the world, therefore there is identification with the name and form as an individual entity, separate from the rest of the world. So the sage has not lost his separation from the rest of the world as an individual entity. He has lost the separation with the rest of the world with this understanding – that his own body-mind organism and all the other separate body-mind organisms are merely objects through which the same energy of consciousness functions.

So, when the understanding is that it is the same consciousness or energy or God functioning through my body-mind organism and Paula's mind-body organism, when the understanding is absolutely deep, that means there is no separation. But there is separation as far as the appearance is concerned, as objects are concerned.

I have confused personal doership with identification but they are different.

Right. So the sage is called by name – he responds which presumes the identification with a particular name and a particular body. So does the ordinary man. If the sage responds to his name being called and an ordinary man also responds to his name being called, where is the difference? The difference lies in the fact that in the case of an ordinary man, besides the identification with the name and form, there is the deep feeling of personal doership, which is obliterated in the sage. In the case of a sage, there is total acceptance that there is no individual doer, that everything that happens to all the body-mind mechanisms is created by God. The sense of personal doership is removed from the ego, so what remains of the ego after the understanding is mere identification to name and form to enable that individual mind-body organism to live the rest of its life in the world.

So if you weren't identified with your body, your name and form, you wouldn't feel the need to feed yourself, clothe yourself, or anything like that. It's the identification with your body that makes you care for it in order for you to continue to live.

Yes, and live and do whatever the body is supposed to do, with the understanding that what I think I do is not me doing it, that I am not doing anything. So, to put in different words, the sage as well as the ordinary man participates fully in this movie of life. If there is something tragic, there may be tears in the sage's eyes, like the ordinary person. If there is humour, he will laugh as wholeheartedly as the ordinary man. But the only difference is, while the ordinary man sees life as it happens as real, the sage is never unaware of the screen of reality of consciousness on which this unreal movie of life is being shown. So, while the sage participates in life, he is never unaware of the screen behind consciousness or impersonal awareness on which this movie happens.

THIRD SATSANG

Why does judgement arise?

The basic point, Paula, that I am saying is that once it is possible to accept by the grace of God that no one is the doer, then immediately there is no question of judging anybody. There is no question of judging yourself nor anyone else. And because of that there is peace. You see, the peace is not to be achieved. Peace is already there but it is covered by continuous conceptualizing, judging, blaming. What goes on from morning till night – conceptualizing, objectivizing, he is doing good, she is doing bad. That is what makes one lose the peace, which is already there. So, it is not a question of achieving peace but it is a question of something leaving that is preventing that peace from being felt. It is astonishing, amazing, how this one simple concept – 'I am not the doer' – that nothing can happen unless it is God's will, brings peace. Thy will be done.

You talk about the thinking mind and the working mind. The judgement comes from thinking mind?

Thinking mind is the sense of personal doership in the ego.

Which still comes from God?

The ego itself has been created by God or the source. Why do you suppose, Paula, God has created ego which makes everyone who has the ego so unhappy and uncomfortable? Why do you suppose God created the ego?

It enables human beings to manifest in this world?

No. For manifestation to happen, the ego is not necessary. The manifestation has happened because the potential energy has activized itself. Consciousness at rest has become consciousness in movement. The manifestation has arisen and the functioning of manifestation is also a happening as the energized energy or activated consciousness. The ego has been created by God because, without the ego, life as we know it cannot happen. The Hindu maya, life as it happens, like a movie, like a dream, cannot happen unless there are inter-human relationships – likes and dislikes, hate and love, frustration and fulfilment. So the inter-human relationships cannot happen unless there are egos. Life cannot happen unless there are inter-human relationships and inter-human relationships cannot happen unless there are egos. Therefore God created egos so that life as we know it can happen.

At the same time, God also started the process of destroying the sense of personal doership in the ego in a limited number of cases. So that life goes on, there are a few people who are seeking the meaning of life or seeking freedom from the very inter-human relationships, which are a cause of misery.

But why is it like that? It's a bit like the story of Charlie and the Chocolate Factory. *There are these children and a few of them get a golden ticket in a chocolate bar, entitling them to go and visit Willy Wonka's Chocolate Factory. But there are only a handful of golden tickets and it is seemingly by chance that someone can get hold of one.*

Because if everybody had the chocolate, if everybody had the chocolate of enlightenment, if everybody had the chocolate of understanding that he is not the doer, then the egos wouldn't be there functioning and bringing about inter-human relationships. And if inter-human relationships didn't happen, life wouldn't happen. So it is for life to happen, which is called maya. It is also called God's game.

Now your question is – when Paula suffers, what kind of a game is God's game? Many times Paula is unhappy – do you think that makes God entertained? That is Paula's question, isn't it? The answer is, Paula, it is God who has written the movie, he has written the script for the movie, he has produced and directed the movie, and most important, he is playing all the characters in the movie and God is witnessing the movie. Where does Paula come in? God is playing all the characters in the movie and it is God as consciousness who is witnessing whatever is happening through individual body-mind objects, which have been created through which God can enjoy as consciousness whatever is happening.

But if I'm God, why don't I know that or feel it?

Because that understanding is clouded, covered, hidden by the ego.

By God?

By the ego, which has been created by God. As part of life, God has started the process of the destruction of the sense of doership in the ego in a limited number of cases so that life should go on. So, the sage participates in the movie of life – tears may arise if he sees something tragic or he may have a good laugh if there is something comic according to his programming. He witnesses all that and accepts whatever is happening, accepts the misery and the pleasures of life as something happening to that object, which was created by God.

The only question which cannot be answered is on what basis does God allot pleasure and pain in each body-mind organism? On what basis does God bring about whatever happens in life? That is something an individual cannot know for two reasons. For Paula to know God, or whatever you want to call it, Paula has to be the subject and God the object. Therefore in wanting to know what God is doing, Paula has usurped the subjectivity of God and, worse still, turned the pure subjectivity into an object, which the pseudo-subject wants to know. If ever there is an original sin, this is it!

We think God is playing dice with the universe because we do not have the full information that God has. Niels Bohr had a theory of modern physics called the theory of uncertainty, which I am told is basically that, at any moment, there are thousands of probabilities about what is to happen through whatever body-mind organism, whether a thought or an action. Out of the thousands of probabilities, one probability collapses and becomes an action – which probability collapses, we don't know but according to Niels Bohr, only God knows. He said it is not like God playing dice with the universe however it is not possible for us to have all the information, which God has. So we may think that one of the thousands of probabilities collapses into actuality but God knows exactly which probability is going to be turned into an actuality when and where.

FOURTH SATSANG

When consciousness was at rest, it was whole and complete, One without a second . . .

Yes, there was nothing. When consciousness was at rest, the energy was in its potential state – there was nothing to become complete or incomplete. Only when the potential energy, the potentiality, activized itself, when consciousness at rest became consciousness in movement, everything began.

So then consciousness created something within itself and you say that was a spontaneous happening for some reason?

Because it was its nature.

So why is it that something contained within consciousness has no knowledge of itself? Why is it that the subject created an object within itself?

The conceptual answer is potential energy activized itself to know itself. Consciousness at rest became consciousness in movement so that it could know itself.

Like a reflection in a mirror?

Yes, exactly. For you to see yourself, you take a mirror. Potential energy, the nature of potentiality, is to activize itself. Otherwise it wouldn't be potential, Paula, it would be dead matter. So, the nature of potentiality is to activize itself at sometime and that's what it does. The potential energy activizes itself in a burst of unimaginable energy and then that energy finally exhausts itself. The activization goes back into the potential until the potential activizes itself once more.

I can understand the definition but I don't understand why life is like this.

Because the activized energy, the basis of activation, is inter-connected opposites, beginning with sage, man and woman, Adam and Eve. The basis of the manifestation and its function is inter-connected opposites. One cannot exist without the other. So, in the Hindu mythology, Siva is the source. So when Siva activized himself into the manifestation, Siva turned himself into Siva-Shakti. Shakti is the power of the female energy. Even according to the Hindu mythology, there is duality – Siva became Siva-Shakti, the male and the female. Since then, everything in the manifestation is inter-connected opposites.

I guess my underlying understanding is it is as it is. We can conceptualize it and define it scientifically, but . . .

Yes, the main thing is who is trying to find out? Who is trying to find out? The one who is trying to find out is that consciousness itself. Therefore the seeker is really not someone or something different from what is sought. Consciousness is seeking itself. Consciousness, which has activized itself and become movement, having become activized, wants to know its source.

But, in any case, all of it is a concept.

As I listen to Ramesh and look at his face, I turn my attention to a black and white photograph of Ramana Maharshi on the wall behind him. I look back again at Ramesh and realize that they are one and the same, both in body and in essence. I then notice a mug on the table next to Ramesh – 'Best Grandad in the World' it reads on the side. I almost burst out laughing.

Around ten past eleven, the talk comes to an end. Ramesh waves his hand to the door and a small Indian woman comes in. She sits on the floor in front of Ramesh and starts chanting *abhangas* or *bhajans* whilst chiming together two small bells. Ramesh closes his eyes and claps his hands and then clicks his fingers to the music as the rest of the room joins in.

Gurur Bramha, Gurur Vishnu
Gurur Devo Maheshwara
Gurur Saakshaath Parabramha
Tasmai Shri Guruvenamaha

My Guru is Lord Brahma, Lord Vishu,
And Lord Maheshwara (Lord Siva).
My Guru is the Supreme Self Incarnate.
I salute my guru who is God Incarnate.

When the singing comes to an end, a few people get up and kneel in front of Ramesh, *namaste*, then prostrate themselves with their hands placed on the floor or on Ramesh's naked feet. On every other visit, I have simply sat still and watched this charming ceremony – now I too get up and bow before Ramesh, putting my fingertips on his long worn out toes. 'Thank you, Ramesh,' I say. 'You are most welcome, Paula,' he replies.

As our interview is scheduled for the afternoon, I return to my hotel room in order to rest and prepare myself for our conversation together. This is the final opportunity to air all the doubts and confusions I have about the theory of the teaching. And who better to ask than Ramesh? Indeed, I still feel that my mind needs to be satisfied with knowing the answers to specific intellectual points. And although Ramesh would also agree that what he says is still a concept, my mind yearns to crack the metaphysical arguments so that they can finally be put aside and laid to rest, once and for all.

It is now late afternoon. I decide to take a taxi which collects me from the hotel's entrance – a spanking new black Padmini deluxe 137D, adorned along the dashboard with pictures of Shirdi Baba with a string of mala beads hanging from the rear-view mirror. I want to take some flowers for Ramesh's wife, Sharda, and try and explain to the driver that I need to find a florist. He doesn't understand a word of what I am saying. But I am in luck – one of the few words of Sanskrit that I remember from elementary Sanskrit lessons I took a few years back is *'pushpum'* meaning flower. I say it almost proudly – *'pushpum, pushpum,'* adding a Hindi accent for greater effect. He understands and laughs loudly, whilst his head rotates on its axis, like a spinning gyroscope. We roar off and arrive in the Breach Candy district about half an hour later. There is a flower vendor just outside the Breach Candy Hospital. The driver pulls into a side road and I leap out.

Ramesh greets me as if I were his long-lost granddaughter. I offer my yellow roses to Sharda who is relaxing in the bedroom. She is thrilled and gives me a loving cuddle. Ramesh and I then go and sit down in the lounge and an Indian lady appears with some refreshments. Ramesh offers me a biscuit, takes one for himself and then dunks it into his coffee.

Ramesh Sadashiv Balsekar was born in Mumbai on 25 May 1917. 'Ever since I was a child, ever since I can remember, I had the intuitive feeling everything is going to happen exactly as it is supposed to. The result of knowing that, for me, made life very simple.' Born into a Hindu Brahmin family, Ramesh was surrounded by traditional spiritual practices – at the age of 12, he made a promise to his mother that he would daily chant the *Ramaraksha Stotra*, which he continues to do even to this day.

In 1936, Ramesh went to study commerce in England for three years at the London School of Economics and, upon returning to Mumbai, obtained a post at the Bank of India as a clerk: 'When I started working, I saw absolutely no reason to pamper and flatter whomever was my boss. I knew with the deepest possible acceptance that if I were going to get a promotion, no power on earth could stop it. And if I were not to get a promotion, no power on earth could get it. No matter how much bootlicking I did, I am not going to get it.'

With this philosophy as his principal guide, when Ramesh was instructed to accept a posting out of Mumbai he refused – his father was ill and he was needed to help out at home. Knowing that to go against the boss's wishes would mean the loss of his job, he immediately wrote out a letter of resignation. However, his boss, realizing that Ramesh was a man of noble character fulfilling his domestic duties at the expense of his career, not only allowed Ramesh to continue working in Mumbai but, from that moment onwards, took him under his wing, advising and helping with his career in the bank. So much so that Ramesh received promotion after promotion, culminating in the highest position of the President of the Bank of India, a post he held for 10 years until his retirement at the age of 60 in 1977.

Ramesh's first guru was a Hindu Brahmin from Poona. 'He was a genuine teacher but, within a week or two, I knew that what he said about Advaita was acceptable but he was too much inclined towards being a Hindu.' However Ramesh continued to seek his guidance for more than 20 years. 'Then the book, *I Am That, Talks with Sri Nisargadatta Maharaj*, came out. There was a review of it in the magazine, *The Mountain Path*, which is published by the Ramanasramam. So I read that review and it had such an impact on me that I went to see Maharaj straight away. And the first day I knew – I am home, this is where I belong. I went to Maharaj in 1978, exactly a year after I retired.'

Ramesh started to translate Maharaj's talks from Marathi into English right up until Maharaj's death in 1981. The following year, when an Australian man turned up at Ramesh's home early one morning, he started holding talks of his own. The next day a few more people came and so it went on until today. Indeed, every morning, each day of the year, Ramesh speaks about Advaita. As he says himself, 'No one is invited and everyone is welcome.' Ramesh has been married for 60 years to his wife, Sharda, with whom he has had three children.

What was Sri Nisurgadatta Maharaj like?

He was quick of anger but had nothing in his heart. He was a loveable old man really but this fiery temper was always there and it confused many people. And he used to smoke continuously so people used to miss something. They would say how can he be a sage, how can he be a *jnani* — he smokes all the time, he shouts at people, he gets angry!

You went every morning to his talks and translated for him?

Yes, I went every morning but I didn't go in the evening because, after the talks, there was a *bhajan* — not the kind of *bhajan* we have here but the traditional *bhajan* where they sing and they bang the bells and the cymbals and so on. I was there once and I couldn't stand it! So Maharaj said, 'Why don't you come in the evening?' So I said, 'Maharaj, two reasons. What I learn in the morning is heavy enough for me to last for the day and quite frankly I can't stand the noise, I can't stand the noise!' He smiled!

After going for six months, sometimes he said to me to do the translation. So I said OK and the translation that I did was much appreciated by the foreign people because the other translator didn't have the knowledge of English that I have. So, there was a certain amount of deep understanding and a control over the English language and everyone was delighted. Maharaj could see that.

Was there a moment in time for you when the understanding arose?

There was a specific occasion. It was the festival called Diwali, the festival of lights. There was no talk in the morning because the tradition was that, on that day, a group of seven or eight volunteers would come and do the spring cleaning once a year. A friend of mine suggested having the talk at his place. Maharaj thought it was a good idea, so that day we had the talk at my friend's place. And, since he was busy looking after the people, Maharaj suggested that I do the translation that day.

And it happened on that particular occasion. Somehow, something happened and the translation was utterly spontaneous. Normally the translation was hard work. Maharaj had no teeth so his words were not terribly clear! Sometimes I had to ask him, 'What did you say?' And once he said, 'Are you deaf?!' I was 61 and he was 80 so I said, 'I'm getting deaf because of my age!' and we both had a big laugh! So first I had to understand his words and the meaning, then I used to have to translate them into English because he spoke in the local language, Marathi. So it used to take some time between his talk and my words coming out. But that morning he could hardly finish and the words would be flowing out of me, you see. In fact, I knew what he was going to say. I could hardly wait for him to finish before the words started. And at the end of the talk my friend said, 'You are in great form today, Ramesh!' I said, 'In what way?' He said, 'You talked louder, with authority, you make gestures which you never made before and it was spontaneous.' So I said, 'I know, I felt it too.' And Maharaj also knew it. So that particular day, I knew that something had happened. The words came out spontaneously. So that was the morning that I could pinpoint that something had happened.

That was beyond your control?

Absolutely. Totally.

So did you carry on translating for Nisargadatta?

Oh yes, until he died. And a curious thing happened. About a month before he died, on a Sunday, a group of people had come from a place about 200 miles from Bombay. And at that time Maharaj was ill and was lying in bed. So he told them, 'Ask your questions and he will answer them,' pointing to me. Everybody was surprised. But they didn't want that, so no questions came. So of course I gave no answers. That was the first time he had authorized me to talk on his behalf. So then Maharaj said, 'What's going on?!' And then he was angry – nothing was happening. I said, 'Maharaj, they don't want to listen to a speaker, an instrument, a recording machine, they want to speak to you!'

I took it as an authorization to talk only on that morning but I did not take it as an overall authorization to talk on the subject. So afterwards, I never talked and he knew I didn't talk. He knew people would come to me but there was no serious talking taking place. So, two days before he died, suddenly he got up on his elbow and shouted at me and said, 'Why don't you talk?' He shouted and then he fell back, so I thought that was the end but it wasn't! He lived for two days more but he had shouted, 'Why don't you talk?' and the meaning was clear – 'I authorized you to talk, why don't you talk?'

From that day, I talked whenever it was necessary and that's how it started. One man came and he was a medical student and I talked to him. He read my book, *Pointers*, and he said he had to come here and that he was very grateful and could he come again. And I said yes, so the next day he called from the railway station and said, 'I am here, I am coming, I have four people with me, is that alright?' I said sure, so those four people came and then it grew. It was only because people came here that I started talking. I didn't advertise or ask people to come to me. God sends them to me and God makes me talk.

So, to turn to the teaching, in the West everybody thinks about philosophy as 'I think, therefore I am.' But in the East, it's the other way round, 'I am, therefore I think.'

Absolutely correct.

So, what I really want to ask you is this. What is the final truth?

The final truth is only one thing and that is, in the absence of consciousness, there is neither you nor me, he nor she. Therefore, consciousness is the very basis of everything. In the absence of consciousness, there is no manifestation and no functioning of manifestation – therefore there is no life. The very manifestation depends on the existence of consciousness. That is the first truth.

Why did Western philosophy go off at such a different tangent?

Western philosophy has been attaching too much importance to proof being obtained. I think, therefore I am. Here, we say I am, therefore I think. The West says, I believe it if I see it, you see. In Eastern philosophy, believe it and then you will see it!

The teachers I have met, for example you and Wayne, talk about the teaching in a very precise, conceptual way. But there are teachers who come from Papaji for example, who say I should forget concepts – just be here now.

But what do they mean by 'be here now'? If just 'be here now', then there is no question of any talk, any conversation.

Anything anybody has said or will say is bound to be a concept because some people will accept it and some people won't. The only truth is the impersonal awareness of 'I am', not as I am Paula or Ramesh or so and so. I am this impersonal awareness is the only truth. And when you are in that impersonal awareness, nothing happens. So, 'be as you are' happens when there is no thinking. That's all there is. 'Be as you are' simply means there is nothing to be done – don't think, don't do anything, be as you are.

But in life, you have to think, you have to make decisions, you see. Decisions have to be made as if you are an individual entity with volition. What happens in life is that you're making decisions all the time. And what is our experience, everybody's experience? Our experience is that we make a decision – sometimes it turns into an action, a happening, sometimes it doesn't. Whether a decision turns into an action or not is not in our control. That is everybody's experience. But we still say, 'I am in control of my life.'

I can understand that there is no free will – that everything is God's will, I can accept that. But to come to the understanding that I am not the doer, is that also God's will, that understanding?

Whether you are able to accept that you are not the doer and that no one is a doer is itself God's will.

But I read that Ramana Maharshi said that the only choice that you do have is to turn in – that implies a form of choice on the part of the individual.

I know it does! Then, the question would be, those who do not turn in, have they decided not to make this enquiry – you see what I mean? What I am saying is they are either interested or they're not interested. Those who are interested are told to find out who wants to know, Who am I? Those who are not interested are not concerned because they are not programmed to have any interest in this spiritual seeking. So the question of making a choice doesn't arise. By 'choice' what Ramana Maharshi probably means is that you have the choice to go by any path and you will go by that path which is indicated by your programming. So you are free to make the choice which way you will go, whether you will go by this Self Enquiry or whether you will go by *bhakti*, repeating God's name, or by social work, like Mother Teresa. You have the choice but that apparent choice, upon investigation, is found to be based on your programming.

So it's apparent choice to turn inwards.

Apparent choice. So the choice you are supposed to have – which path you are supposed to take – is only an apparent choice because that choice is invariably based on your programming, genes and conditioning.

Something I have struggled with in the teaching is this kind of paradox — at the phenomenal level, I exist, but on the noumenal level, I don't.

You cannot know at the noumenal level, that is the point. At the noumenal level, you are only consciousness. At the noumenal level, there is nothing other than consciousness. So, whatever you are thinking about can only be at the phenomenal level. That is why, if you recollect, I always say why do you want Self-realization? Why do you want Self-realization, Paula?

Because I think it is a good thing to have!

The reason I am asking is, when there is Self-realization, 'me' wanting Self-realization as an individual entity with a sense of doership does not remain. So, that is why my point is when you want Self-realization it is because you expect that realization will make you or give you peace or happiness in life.

Wayne says you want to be around when Self-realization happens.

That is the whole problem, you see. Self-realization means the absence of the 'me' wanting Self-realization. 'Me' as the doer, as an individual entity with a sense of doership. When that is totally gone, that what remains is merely identification with the body-mind organism to enable that body-mind organism to function in life, knowing that whatever happens in life, there is no one doing anything. The basic understanding, Self-realization, enlightenment, is — according to my concept — that there is no individual doer. There is no action that is done by an individual entity. All action is a happening because it happens to be God's will or if you don't like the words God's will — and some don't — let's say nothing can happen unless it is according to a cosmic law. And that cosmic law no individual can ever know.

There are other teachers and religious traditions that say you need to relax, you need to meditate, you need to do this, that and the other.

And that is the conditioning I am talking about. Everything has to be done the right way. There is a right way and there is a wrong way. So, the right way according to the English man may not be the right way according to a French man. Therefore there's truly nothing right or wrong.

So what about things like morality or ethics?

Again, you merely do what you think you should do. That is the only criteria you can go by. I mean, in the state of Kerala in India 100 years ago, it was considered improper for a lady from a good family to wear anything on top. It was only the woman of loose virtue who wore anything on top, so that she could attract the attention of somebody. You see the logic of it? You take a nudist magazine – the first time you open it, you have a shock! You turn the pages and see 10, 20, 30 women with nothing on top. But then you see anything covered or half-covered, it attracts your attention more.

Yes, it's because of the mystery.

Yes, what's behind that.

Like the teaching can be mysterious.

Yes. Whereas something that is bare, open – you don't look at it, you see. So again, what I am saying is environmental conditioning makes you think what you think. So what you think you should do at any time is almost entirely a matter of genes and conditioning. The natural design and programming in that body-mind organism.

In biology, the genome – the complete chromosome blueprint of the human being – has recently been discovered.

In the last year or so, more and more research is being done into genes. One of the latest things – if you are a homosexual, blame it on the gene.

Or a murderer or a philosopher or a seeker.

Yes. And then the latest one I heard – it's quite amusing but research shows it. If you're inclined to cheat on your partner, blame it on your genes! You cannot help not being faithful to your spouse.

Ramana was asked about adultery, wasn't he?

This particular case you mention about adultery is not contained in many books on Ramana because, if it were included, then it would be construed that Ramana condones adultery. What he means is whether adultery is to happen or not, is not in your control – that is what he means. This particular account is of a young man, recently married and it was exactly the same time in Kerala when the women went bare-breasted, in the early part of last century. So he comes to Ramana very sincerely and he says, 'I'm newly married, I love my wife but I'm afraid of committing adultery.' In other words, 'I am afraid of committing the sin of adultery because I am tempted by the breasts of a young neighbour of mine.' Ramana Maharshi must have realized that the man was sincere and an honest seeker with a certain amount of spiritual effort already done. So he tells him, 'You are always pure. You cannot commit any sin.' Then he says, 'Even if adultery happens, there is no 'me' to think about it. You have not done any action. Nobody can do any action. Whatever action seems like action is a happening, which could not have happened unless it was the will of God. So, if adultery happens, you need not think about it as you having committed the adultery. It happens because it was supposed to happen and you need not think about it afterwards.

There are many people who say they know about the truth and appoint themselves as teachers or gurus. And yet, all the time one hears about financial and sexual abuse associated with these people. Is that still God's will?

It has happened, so it has to be God's will. Hitler could not have happened unless it was God's will. Mother Teresa happened because it was God's will, Saddam Hussein, Stalin, Mahatma Gandhi, Jesus, Ramana Maharshi happened. Everything, all happening because of God's will. And why so many false gurus? Because in the *Bhagavad Gita* there is a verse, which says, 'Among thousands there is one seeker and among thousands of seekers, there is hardly one who knows me in principle.' So that thousands of seekers fumble about in confusion, they need false gurus. So, false gurus happen and according to the destiny of those who are supposed to go to the false gurus, they go.

It is difficult to accept.

It's not easy.

What about the theory of reincarnation? It struck me that people like that theory because it makes life appear to be fair and just — this person is suffering because of bad karma in a previous life, whereas that person is having a great life because of good karma.

So, my point on this question is simply one thing. Paula is only in this life, with this body-mind organism. There was no Paula in an earlier life. There was some other ego in a previous life, which doesn't exist in this life — the ego died with that body. And that ego does not know anything about Paula's suffering or enjoyment of life. And Paula is not going to know any ego in a future life.

The theory of karma simply means theory of causation. Cause, effect, cause, effect — a chain of causation. So the karma theory is right — karma basically means action but not a personal action. Causation is right but not someone's causation.

But Ramana talks about birth and death. He says that for the jnani *who no longer believes he is the doer and whose mind has therefore become inactive, he remains unaffected by birth and death. But for the ordinary man, Ramana says that after the death of the physical body, the mind remains inactive for a while but then it becomes active again in a new body. This seems to imply a so-called 'rebirth'.*

So, what it means is a fresh birth happens.

Just another mind?

Just another body-mind organism — another birth.

Not the migration of a specific mind?

That is my point because there is nothing to migrate. My point is nothing can get destroyed, so all your hopes and failures and frustrations, they all go, let us say, into the pool of consciousness — all thoughts, all aspirations of all beings. When a new conception happens, what goes from the pool of consciousness into that conception, nobody knows. It may be that, in a particular case, 70 per cent or 80 per cent of the aspirations and frustrations of one particular life may go into the other life. But it may be one per cent. Nobody can know.

So that would explain why some people do have recollections of a previous life.

Yes. What I am saying is that they may have a recollection of a previous life. Therefore what I say is there have been births, there will be births, but no rebirths. And Ramana Maharshi has said there was no rebirth and this is the truth.

So finally, Ramesh, who am I?

The 'I' that you are talking of is really the 'me', isn't it? You see? Paula is merely the name given to a body-mind organism, which is a programmed instrument through which the 'I', as the source, functions. 'Me' is the name given to a uniquely programmed instrument through which 'I', or the source or God, functions and brings about such actions as are supposed to happen according to the cosmic law.

Ramesh is utterly courteous and generous throughout our hour of conversation together. However, I am conscious of the fact that he begins to grow tired in the growing shadows of the late afternoon sunshine – I feel instinctively that I must bring our interview to an end, as much as I would like to go on all night. As I take his photograph, he asks me if I have read his book, *Sin and Guilt: Monstrosity of Mind*. I confess that I haven't – he disappears, returning a few moments later waving a copy in his hand, which he offers to give to me. 'Would you sign it for me?' I ask. 'Sure,' he replies, walking over to his desk and then scribbling an inscription inside the cover. 'With warmest affection and love, Ramesh S Balsekar, Oct. 9, 2000,' it reads. I am deeply touched, I tell him. Ramesh then wishes me every success with the book and says that he is looking forward to reading it. 'I hope that I have given you enough material to work with.' Ramesh walks me to the lift and once again he cups my face as we say goodbye. What a privilege, I think, to have met such an extraordinarily wise and humble man.

Peace reigns in my heart as I journey back to Colaba. I return to the Taj for an evening drink – a delicious sweet lassi, made of chilled yoghurt. Life continues to play itself out in the view from my window of the street below. I am filled with such an indescribable sense of well-being. Not exhilaration, not even bliss; rather a feeling of total acceptance, of a quietly joyous resignation to the fact that everything is as it is. Nowhere to go, nothing to do. Just here and now, as God deems it so.

As the day wears on, I too start to feel tired with the heat and the earlier adrenaline surges of excitement. I return to my room to rest and I drink litres of mineral water and eat a couple of small overripe bananas. Tonight, my penultimate night in Mumbai, I am finally beginning to adjust my sleeping pattern. It is just after nine in the evening and I retire to bed and fall into a deep and satisfied sleep . . .

There is someone in the room. I cannot see their face but it is a presence I am aware of. I am not afraid. 'The only choice you have is to turn inwards,' the presence says. But it is my voice . . .

I awake with a start. The crows have started screeching in the new day. I lie in bed looking out of the window, out onto a surreal landscape of exotic trees and hotel rooms with verandahs full of drying clothes. The search is over, I think. There is no need to see anyone else. All I need to do is turn around and see.

My final full day. I stroll around the bustling streets, through crowded and noisy markets, absorbing all the sights and smells of urban Indian life, watching phenomena manifest and dance in front of my eyes. I buy some Assam tea and masala spice in a nearby shop and then return to my room for a siesta. Suddenly I don't feel so well. I am aware of a growing pain in my abdomen – a gripping ache that seemingly replaces the peace of the day.

By evening, I am wracked with physical pain.

Bhagavan Sri Ramana Maharshi

CHAPTER SIXTEEN

RENDEZVOUS WITH
RAMANA

*'Rama, this enquiry, 'Who am I?' is the quest of the Self and
is said to be the fire that burns up the seed of the poisonous weed
of conceptual thought.'*

Yoga Vasishtam

I haven't slept a wink. My body is weeping sweat and the pain in my gut has had me
writhing on the bed all night, culminating in an acute upset stomach. I feel terrible.

Once more, day breaks. The sounds of India seep into my consciousness as I
lie in my alien room – strange noises fill the air but not so much the coughing of
heating pipes, rather booming Indian television and the strains of toilet flushes.
The taxi arrives first thing in the morning to take me to Mumbai's Santa Cruz
domestic airport. I have booked a ticket with Jet Airways, India's first commerical
airline, to take me to Chennai. I am told the journey to the airport should take
about an hour by cab but the driver thinks he is Stirling Moss. The road ahead
subsequently turns into a racetrack – buses, rickshaws and fellow members of the
human race all serving as chicanes, which he swerves around with terrifying speed.

My fear of flying also rears its ugly head once more, augmented by my weary
aching body. I am thrown around the back seat of the taxi not daring to look
through the windscreen – it never ceases to amaze me how Indians are unafraid of
passing traffic and can walk nonchalantly within millimetres of moving vehicles.
We arrive at the airport within half an hour. 'You drive very fast,' I say ironically.
But the subtlety is wasted and he turns around and beams delightedly. Indeed his

pride is such that he demands a significant tip for getting me here so quickly.

What with my overcompensating for delays, I am hours too early. I go through the laborious bureaucratic checks and rechecks of check-in. Then I am told that I can catch the earlier flight to Chennai if I want. Ah ha! This is God telling me something, I think. Fear of flying . . . arrive too early at airport . . . offered different plane . . . what else can it mean except that I am being saved, obviously, from disaster on original plane. 'Yes, great,' I say, 'I'll take it.'

Santa Cruz is a busy domestic airport and there are scores of people milling around awaiting flights. I walk around looking for a vacant seat – again, the usual sea of staring faces. Until now it hasn't bothered me too much, I have simply looked away. Now I am feeling at a low ebb, the penetrating eyes start to distress me deeply. I start to imagine what it must be like to be famous, to be constantly the centre of attention. I think, in the grand scheme of things, I am glad to be a nobody.

Flying in India is the subject of many jokes – everything on an aeroplane is held together with elastic bands and Elastoplast, they say. Now I am sitting in one, the joke is not quite so funny. But it's OK. I'm in God's hands. All is well. The engine starts up and we taxi to the main runway which, like the streets of Mumbai, appears to be strewn with potholes. But it's OK. I'm in God's hands. All is well. The plane pauses, waiting for its slot. Then the engines fire up and we're off. My heart kicks into overdrive. We are hurtling faster and faster along the runway, gathering up speed, ready to reach into the sky . . .

Suddenly, the plane brakes violently. I am thrown forward in my seat. My head whips down nearly banging the seat in front of me. I throw my hands out to restrain myself. Jesus holy Christ.

THIS IS IT.

The plane stops dead.

Silence.

I daren't imagine what's happening. Oh please, I don't want to die. Not like this.

Then the captain's voice can be heard – it is a well spoken, English public school accent. 'Perhaps we are all wondering what has happened . . . Some technical problems . . . We need to sort out the paperwork.' Somehow the sound of a Western male voice takes the edge off things though I would have thought that finding an engineer was the more expedient approach to the problem.

As I look around the cabin, I appear to be the only one who is concerned about our safety. The plane is filled predominantly with well-dressed Indians, business-men presumably, who reach immediately for their mobile phones to convey the bad news that they will be delayed for their rendezvous. The stewardess walks past me along the aisle – I reach out my hand to her, 'What's happened?' 'I don't know, I'm afraid,' she says with that reassuring smile, well practised over many years of having to deal with the general public. 'Is it safe?' I enquire. 'I hope so!' she replies, still seemingly unperturbed. Am I really the only one getting in a panic? Do these people genuinely have no fear of the inevitable – that everything is ultimately God's will . . . even plane crashes?

After an hour, we finally take off, lurching up over the Mumbai landscape heading eastward. I breathe deeply, trying to relax. As I do so, tears well up in my eyes and stream down my cheeks. I am feeling utterly wretched and sorry for myself. Not only do I feel like death warmed up, I am sick of being stared at, tired of wondering whether I can eat this or drink that. I am so very far from home and I feel absolutely alone. For all the sense of relief that Ramesh's teaching had brought, when push comes to shove, it has all gone out of the window. But surely this is supposed to be the moment when I need the teaching the most? Never before have I felt so attached to my body, to my feelings and my mind.

The waves of paranoia eventually subside and I fall into a fitful sleep. When the plane arrives in Chennai, I am utterly relieved. I stagger through the airport with all my baggage and photographic equipment, bracing myself for the next stage of my journey. Before leaving London, I had emailed the Ramanasramam with my flight details with the return promise that someone would come to the airport to collect me. Somehow I can't quite believe that anyone in India can be that organized. So where's the taxi? I bet it hasn't come. But it has come! There, just outside the airport terminal doors, on a large white sign written in red and gold handwriting is my name, Paula Marvelly. My beautiful, lovely, beloved name. After what I have just been through, it is the beatific vision.

My chauffeur has been waiting for nearly three hours. He didn't want to be late so set off in good time. He leads me to his taxi – a brilliant white Ambassador car. He proudly opens the door for me and I climb in the back. We then pull away and enter the busy main road out of Chennai towards the south of India.

Fatigue and a growing surrender to the inevitable take hold – the passing madness and chaos, the heat and smell and noise through the open window swirl around my brain. As my vitality fades, I start to slip away into a quiet secluded space in my mind. Darkness and blankness consume me. Resistance failing, I lie on my rucksack and disappear into nothingness . . .

When I wake up, everything is changed. I have re-emerged into another world. Now, having shed the skin of sleep, I rise up to greet an Arcadian vision. If I had just died and gone to heaven, this would be it, I think. Never in my life have I seen a panoramic landscape of such vivid luminosity, such radiant colour and texture, such exquisite proportion of field and rock and tree.

I feel like I am on a magical mystery tour. My taxi roars along the dusty road, its horn tooting cheekily. I see paddy fields and mountains and lakes rising up before me like the changing set designs in a theatre. Then suddenly, here is a small village, where the men stand in groups discussing who knows what and the women brush out their small reed-thatched homes and tend to their domestic chores. They remind me of the Tahitian women depicted in the paintings of Paul Gauguin – exotic, mysterious and yet a breathtaking expression of nature's vital force.

We have been on the road for nearly three hours. Then the driver indicates to the horizon over to the right of us: 'Arunachala!' he cries. There, in all its magnificence and splendour, a shrine made from earth and rock pointing towards heaven, is Siva's 'sacred red mountain', the home of the great sage, Bhagavan Sri Ramana Maharshi.

The setting sun in the west casts an opaque gauze of light over the landscape. Arunachala is silhouetted against the sky giving it the appearance of not being made of matter but a phantasmogorical image hovering in the air. I can hardly believe I have made it here. After going to hell and back, I have been rewarded with paradise.

The scenery gradually changes from provincial to urban life. Stark white buildings, worn out and dishevelled, replace the idyllic rural huts and crowd up against the main road taking us into Tiruvannamalai in the North Arcot District of Tamil Nadu. The village is a labyrinth of streets, houses and shops decorated here and there with religious symbols, garlands of flowers and multi-coloured bunting. The street is filled with people meandering about herding cows around in every direction, and trucks and rickshaws trying to thread their way through this seemingly random display of human life.

By about five in the afternoon, we arrive at the Ramanasramam. It is situated on a road running out of Tiruvannamalai. It is less ornate and more understated than I had imagined. There is a high stone wall running along the perimeter with lattice gates at the entrance, which is surrounded by beggars and street vendors. We drive into a forecourt surrounded by banyan trees. I get out and the taxi driver escorts me to the general office where I am greeted by a suave Indian man wearing a white shirt and a dhoti. He is called Sri Nivasamurthy or more affectionately, the Doctor, and is the ashram's GP. He greets me cordially and asks me to sign a huge leather-bound ledger. I am handed the daily schedule and requested, politely, to attend as many of the events mentioned as possible, as well as remembering to dress modestly within the ashram. I then return to the taxi and we leave the compound, journeying to the women's quarters, 500 yards or so down the road.

My room is simple and yet utterly exquisite. It reminds me more of an apartment in the Mediterranean than a devotee's cell. The floor is tiled and the walls are plastered with a light blue wash. There is a bed, covered with a purple checked counterpane, and a desk and chair. There is a small bathroom, including my very own Western-style toilet and a selection of water taps and buckets for washing. Through the grilled window at the back, I can see luscious umbrella trees covered in creepers and a large brown pond or tank, surrounded by tropical foliage and flowering shrubs. At the opposite end are some steps leading up to a green metal gate and the sanctum of the ashram beyond.

Hanging on the wall next to the desk is a black and white photograph of Ramana lying on a couch, wearing reading glasses. He is studying a letter, whilst a small rabbit has snuggled up beside him. Beneath the picture is a long quote written in Tamil, under which is a translation:

> *Like the string that holds together the gems in a necklace, You it is that penetrate and bind all beings and the various religions. If like a gem that is cut and polished, the separate mind is whetted on the grindstone of the pure Universal Mind, it will acquire the light of your grace and shine like a ruby whose brightness is not flawed by any other object. When once the light of the Sun has fallen on a sensitive plate, will the plate register another picture? Apart from you, O Aruna Mountain bright, auspicious, does any other thing exist?*

Sri Arunachala Ashtakam 5

The electric fan purrs overhead as I unpack. Such has been the assault on my senses that I have not had time to think about my body and its various demands. Now I am safely installed in my room, physical sentience returns with a vengeance. Supper is at seven but I just cannot face it so I lie on the bed to sleep . . .

I awaken to a lightning flash and the crack of thunder. I can hear the sound of shouting and chanting as well as the banging of drums and tooting of car horns in the near distance. I have no idea of the time but it is dark outside. It is also raining and the water drops are pounding on the windows and grilles. Why is it in India everything seems to be so much more alive and real, so much more intense? I cannot for the life of me imagine what is happening outside except that there must be some celebration, some invocation of the gods. But for so long? It is well past four in the morning before the cries fade into the distance and the rain subsides to a drizzle.

The following morning is bright and fresh. My mind is clear and alert, despite the body feeling weak and dizzy. A distance seemingly separates me from the actions that my body performs – washing, getting dressed, making the bed. Everything is flowing with an ease and effortlessness, devoid of the usual running commentary of self-consciousness, retribution and angst. It is half past six and I walk into the ashram, taking a path that leads parallel to the tank, where monkeys are playing in the trees and dragonflies are darting through the grass. I enter the ashram through a back entrance, leaving my shoes at the gate. I emerge just behind the Main Hall but I cannot go in as it has been flooded by the night's heavy rain and numerous people are now bustling about with reed brushes, sweeping out the water.

As I stand outside the entrance, I notice a group of Westerners and ask them what all the noise was about the previous evening. 'It was because of the full moon – people make the 14-kilometre circuit of the hill. And if you make a wish while you are doing it, it is supposed to come true.' 'You have come at a very auspicious time,' another one of them continues, 'for not only is today Friday the 13th but the 13th of October is also Papaji's birthday.' When I reflect on my short time in India, everything seems to have been done at an auspicious moment. Am I just lucky or do Indians have the ability to turn any normal situation into some kind of divine coincidence?

The most popular time to come to Tiruvannamalai is, however, during the November full moon, known as the Karthikai Deepam Festival. Legend has it that Siva appeared as a column of fire on Arunachala Hill. The story goes that, owing to the disputes between Vishnu and Brahma about which one was the greater, Siva manifested himself as a blazing column. He then told them that the one who could find the upper or lower end of the column was the greater of the two. Vishnu, representing ego or individuality, transformed himself into a boar, burrowing downwards in search of the base; Brahma, meanwhile, representing the intellect, changed himself into a swam and flew upwards to seek the column's summit. On his way up, Brahma caught a flower falling from a mountain tree and, returning to Siva, declared that he was the winner, claiming that the flower had come from the top of the column.

Vishnu however, forgetting his mission, became absorbed in meditative contemplation. Returning finally, he admitted his failure in the search, acknowledging that Siva was indeed without beginning, middle or end, being the Supreme Spirit. Despite his not completing the task, Vishnu was nevertheless pronounced the victor in recognition of his insight. And it is this legend that is still celebrated every year with a huge fire, called the Lingam of Fire, which burns for many days on the summit.

Sri Ramana Maharshi also acknowledged the sanctity of the hill, saying that it was the heart and spiritual centre of the world. He recommended that devotees make the circuit of the hill, called *pradakshinam*, advising them to make the journey slow and deliberate, 'Like a woman in her ninth month of pregnancy.' Indeed, there is an old saying that the hill is wish-fulfilling, though paradoxically the highest wish of all, as Ramana pointed out, is the state of no longer wishing for anything.

I take the opportunity to walk around the ashram – I am pleasantly surprised by how unassuming it is. There is none of the somewhat kitsch, brightly coloured Hindu iconography dripping from the walls that one usually associates with Indian ashrams: only simple hermitage structures of white painted stone and thatching. Even the sparingly used ornate carving on the roof of the Main Hall depicting gods, goddesses and wheels of fire and lotus leaves is subtly executed – detail which I would have failed to notice if I hadn't been observing the flight of one of the many resident ashram peacocks soaring over its turrets.

People start to drift in the direction of the dining hall for breakfast. We pass into a small courtyard where there is a huge well. Ordinarily, the water is 40 feet or more below the rim but owing to the night's heavy rain the water level is nearly at the top. People are peering over the ledge to look at it. Sri Sundaram Ramanan or simply Mr Ramanan, the ashram President, and the Doctor stand at the foot of the dining hall steps next to the well, greeting all the ashram residents as they pass into the hall.

Palm leaves are arranged in rows on the red tiled floor, which is worn and scratched by the hundreds of devotees who have been served food before us. We all file in and then sit down on the ground. From the kitchen, men appear carrying large metal buckets. They start walking up and down each row, distributing food. One brings *idli*, a soft rice cake, and another vegetable curry, which he pours onto my palm leaf with perfect precision from a ladle suspended high in the air. Then others come around with buckets of sweet hot coffee or buttermilk, made from the ashram's own dairy – the cows are direct descendants from Ramana's favourite cow, Lakshmi.

On one side of the room, there is a small altar to Ramana. There is also a small bowl of flowers as well as a picture of him sitting on the ground eating, his hand cupped holding food. One or two people kneel before the picture before they take their places on the floor. The rest of the hall is like a portrait gallery of the world's geatest holy men and women. As well as numerous pictures of Ramana, other portraits include Jesus, Nisargadatta Maharaj and Papaji, as well as an array of other male and female teachers less familiar to me.

Conversation is not encouraged in the dining hall. I consume as much as my stomach will allow, all the while trying to master eating with my right hand. Even with a simple meal on a palm leaf, there is a code of conduct – to indicate I have finished, I fold over the leaf. I then get up and leave, stopping at the water tank to replenish my water supply.

I desperately want to explore but know instinctively it is important to rest and recover my strength. I therefore spend most of the day dozing in my room, listening to the strange sounds around me, trying to just go with the flow . . .

I am in a car being driven very fast. I am in San Francisco on a road running along the side of a mountain. The landscape tips over. The car and the driver fall over the edge . . . I am left clinging for my life on the ledge of the mountain. Then the ledge turns into an aeroplane. The back door is open and I am hanging onto it, swinging from its hinges. The plane is about to crash into the sea . . . I am being chased by a dark-coloured man. I am sitting on a balustrade. The man pushes me off and I fall backwards into a deep cavern, which is filled with black oil. I fall into the oil and sink deeper and deeper. The oil fills my lungs. I cannot breathe . . .

I wake up and leap out of bed, panting and thrashing about like a madman. It takes a few moments to realize where I am. It was all just a dream, I tell myself. But it was so very real whilst it was happening. And now, another dream surrounds me. When will I wake up from this one, I think?

The following day, I join other devotees in the Main Hall for the morning milk offering to Sri Bhagavan at his Samadhi Shrine. Opened by Indira Gandhi, it is a large, slightly austere auditorium, with a marble floor and cream and green painted walls. At the end is Bhagavan's shrine – a life-size statue of Sri Ramana sitting in the lotus position carved in a black onyx-textured material is centred on a raised stage, surrounded by a balustrade. Incense billows into the air from burners and multifarious coloured flowers are scattered all over the shrine. There are also portraits of Bhagavan drenched in garlands and various gods and goddesses standing like sentinels, protecting their Lord, whose body is entombed under the altar. Rather than being cremated as is the usual tradition in India, Ramana's body has been preserved so that people may still benefit from his divine presence.

The hall is adorned with photographs of Ramana, sitting on tiger skin rugs or walking with his stick. There are also the famous large black and white portraits, taken by G G Welling, a photographer from Bangalore. The story goes that when Welling was about to take the photographs, Ramana asked whether there was sufficient light, to which Welling replied, 'Bhagavan, you are the light!' By the hall's back entrance is the most well-known picture of them all – a head and shoulders shot hanging in a mahogany frame. Somehow he does not look like a native Indian – his features are more reminscent of a Westerner, with his snowy-white beard and closely cropped hair. His face is mesmerizing – so full of compassion and possessing a childlike innocence. His eyes follow me around the room but I am not unsettled by this, rather I feel that his gaze affords some form of protection, a forgiveness almost of all the bad things I have done in the past. If only a mere photograph can have such an effect on me, what would it have been like to look right into his eyes, to have been so close to his physical presence?

An Indian man starts to sing sacred incantations and then people kneel or prostrate themselves on the floor. A flame in a small dish is then waved around the shrine – a ceremony known as *arati*. He turns towards the congregation and everyone gathers around him, putting their hands over the flame and then placing their palms on their heads. Under the burning wick is turmeric and vermilion-coloured powder, which I mix between my fingertips and then rub onto my forehead. Everyone then files clockwise around the shrine – some walk slowly and reverentially, others with a spring in their step. When we finish the turn, an Indian man holds out a ladle of milk *prasad*, which I receive in my cupped hands. I drink the sweet liquid, though half of it streams down my face.

Throughout certain periods of the day, the Vedas are chanted in front of this shrine. The sound has a drone-like quality – both somnolent and hypnotic. Indeed, it is the Vedas which form the written source of Ramana's non-dualist teaching. They are the oldest scripture known to mankind, dating maybe as far back as 5000 BCE and predating even the Bible. The Vedas (meaning knowledge) are made up of four texts – the *Rig Veda* (hymns and the main Vedic philosophy), the *Yagur Veda* (sacrificial formulae), the *Sama Veda* (melodies) and the *Atharva Veda* (spells and incantations). Each Veda consists in turn of four parts – *Samhita* (hymns and prayers), *Brahmanas* (sacrificial rituals for householders), *Aranyakas* (meditations for forest dwellers) and *Upanishads* (philosophical debate). The Vedas are believed to be divinely inspired scriptures, known as *sruti*, which are revealed through the writings of poets, priests and philosophers. Indeed, Hinduism, Buddhism and Jainism, as well as their indigenous offshoots, all owe their philosophical roots to the Vedas.

In order that the teaching be more accessible to all, allegorical renderings or *smrtis* were compiled. Rather than being overtly stated, the philosophy of the Vedas could be implied through storytelling. Written as literary epics, the *Ramayana* and the *Mahabharata*, which incorporates the *Bhagavad Gita*, therefore were able to make the teaching more available to a wider audience.

Nevertheless, scholasticism still prevailed and the doctrines of six distinct schools of Indian thought started to emerge and to be documented. Despite their metaphysical roots coming directly from the Vedas, the principal school, Uttara Mimamsa, developed its system based on the philosophy found primarily in the Upanishads, thus becoming more commonly known as the school of Vedanta, meaning 'the end of the Vedas'.

In order to clarify the vast array of interpretations, many commentaries were written on the philosophy of the Vedanta, which was now concentrated into a specific text, called the *Vedanta Sutra* (or *Brahma Sutra*), compiled by Badarayana, a pupil of Gaudapada. The most famous commentators on the *Vedanta Sutra* were Shankara (8th century AD), Ramanuja (11th century AD) and Madhva (13th century AD). And although their commentaries were also rooted in the same Vedic philosophy, they developed their own distinctive systems of interpretation, namely Shankara's non-dualism (Advaita); Ramanuja's qualified non-dualism (*visistadvaita*); and Madhva's dualism (*dvaita*). It is Shankara's Advaita that has prevailed, becoming the most widely accepted commentary on Vedic philosophy. His interpretation can essentially be reduced to the following three, seemingly paradoxical, statements – Brahman is real; the universe is unreal; Brahman is the universe.

It is said, nevertheless, that the teaching was revealed long, long before any recording in the Vedas. As well as manifesting as Arunachala mountain, Siva also appeared in human form as the primal sage, Dakshinamurthi – a young illuminated teacher who would teach in silence, initiating and guiding his elder disciples by direct transmission of the Self. Legend has it that throughout the ages, Dakshinamurthi has been sitting on the north slope of Arunachala, underneath a banyan tree and that anyone who approaches him will attain Self-realization. Indeed, Ramana acknowledged the sagacity of this primal teacher, proclaiming that his own teaching, that of Shankara and Dakshinamurthi are one.

In spite of the seemingly complex history of non-dualistic thought, the Ramanasramam, home of contemporary Advaita, is easy and relaxed. There are the Westerners in their orange T-shirts and white cotton trousers, Indian men in their *dhotis* and *kurthapyjamas* and Indian women in their brightly coloured saris, looking like reincarnations of Hindu goddesses. Everyone glides about wrapped in a state of serene peace. What a blessed life it would be to exist just like this, I think – reading, writing and contemplating the teachings of the wise. How difficult it is to find tranquillity in the midst of daily activities whilst living in the West. How the din and the noise of urban life appear to be such an obstacle to finding one's true Self.

At eleven, there is the feeding of the poor in the ashram. The Doctor presides over large bowls of rice and vegetable curry, as the courtyard by the main entrance fills up with every example of human life. It is a moving sight to behold – sadhus, beggars, the disabled and dispossessed, form a loose queue for their daily food offering. Thin, skeletal bodies, daubed in holy ash – their orange robes and mala beads, dreadlocks and matted beards, making them indistinguishable from one another. But their beady eyes and gracious acceptance of what is given make me feel humbled by their presence.

I wander around the other rooms of the ashram complex. Adjacent to the Main Hall is the Shrine of the Mother – Sri Ramana's mother, Alagammal. Her body is also entombed in honour of her own apotheosis on 19 May 1922. The room is small with a central shrine, around which I make a turn, noticing the many statues of Ganesh and Siva, festooned with flower petals and dressed in beautiful fabric, making them look like children's dolls.

Leading from this room and running parallel to the Main Hall is the New Hall. Built in 1949, it is where Ramana gave satsang during his illness and the year before his death so that it could accommodate all the people who had come to see him and wish him well. I much prefer this room – it is far less ostentatious, being decorated only with grey stone carvings and pillars. On the stone floor are mandalas and yantra etched onto the floor in white chalk. There is also another ebony-coloured statue of Ramana, surrounded by railings, and on the wall is an old Victorian-style clock, more reminiscent of one you would find in a British railway station rather than an Indian ashram.

Then I notice a large white board, more than 10 feet high, propped up against the left side wall. 'Death Experience of Bhagavan Sri Ramana Maharshi' it reads in large black letters. I stand transfixed by the text written out before me:

It was about six weeks before I left Madura for good that the great change in my life took place. It was quite sudden. I was sitting alone in a room on the first floor of my uncle's house. I seldom had any sickness, and on that day there was nothing wrong with my health, but a sudden violent fear of death overtook me. There was nothing in my state of health to account for it, and I did not try to account for it or to find out whether there was any reason for the fear. I just felt 'I am going to die' and began thinking what to do about it. It did not occur to me to consult a doctor or my elders or friends; I felt that I had to solve the problem myself, there and then.

The shock of the fear of death drove my mind inwards and I said to myself mentally, without actually framing the words: 'Now death has come; what does it mean? What is it that is dying? This body dies.' And I at once dramatized the occurrence of death. I lay with my limbs stretched out stiff as though rigor mortis had set in and imitated a corpse so as to give greater reality to the enquiry. I held my breath and kept my lips tightly closed so that no sound could escape, so that neither the word 'I' nor any other word could be uttered. 'Well then,' I said to myself, 'this body is dead. It will be carried stiff to the burning ground and there burnt and reduced to ashes. But with the death of this body am I dead? Is the body I? It is silent and inert but I feel the full force of my personality and even the voice of the 'I' within me, apart from it. So I am Spirit transcending the body. The body dies but the Spirit that transcends it cannot be touched by death. That means I am deathless Spirit.' All this was not dull thought; it flashed through me vividly as living truth which I perceived directly, almost without thought-process. 'I' was something very real, the only real thing about my present state, and all the conscious activity connected with my body was centred on that 'I'. From that moment onwards the 'I' or Self focussed attention on itself by a powerful fascination. Fear of death had vanished once and for all. Absorption in the Self continued unbroken from that time on. Other thoughts might come and go like the various notes of music, but the 'I' continued like the fundamental sruti *note that underlies and blends with all the other notes. Whether the body was engaged in talking, reading or anything else, I was still centred on 'I'. Previous to that crisis I had no clear perception of my Self and was not consciously attracted to it. I felt no perceptible or direct interest in it, much less any inclination to dwell permanently in it.*

This is the final barrier to Self-realization, I think – the fear of bodily death. This is the source of all my latent anxieties, all my worries and concerns. This is what my life has been constructed to avoid dealing with, in some way trying to make death an option, or at least something to deal with only when I am good and ready. But everyone has told me – in the facing of that fear, I will indeed die but it won't be the type of death I am afraid of. It will be the ultimate death, the extinction of my sense of individuality, the death of the idea that I am the doer. Only this, paradoxically, will lead to life beyond death, a life of freedom from fear, a life of blessed immortality and everlasting peace.

In the afternoon, readings are made in this room from Ramana's teachings. A learned-looking Indian man squats on the floor in front of a large book, from which he sings out a line in Tamil, followed by an English translation. I can barely make out what he is saying in either language but the melodious cadences are a joy to listen to. I then decide to leave and walk over to a small hut opposite the Main Hall. It is where Ramana slept while he gave satsang in the New Hall during his illness and where he finally died: 'The place where Sri Bhagavan attained *maha nirvana,*' it reads on a black plaque with gold lettering above the glass doors. Inside is a small collection of Ramana's things – his walking stick, timepieces and metal dishes and pots.

Still meandering around the ashram, I find the bookshop, next to the office. Many people have written about Sri Ramana Maharshi – the first and foremost being Paul Brunton, then a journalist, whose book, *A Search in Secret India,* made Ramana's teachings popular in the West. Others include Arthur Osborne, Major Chadwick and S S Cohen, W Somerset Maugham and C G Jung. More recently, David Godman, who still lives in Tiruvannamalai, has made accessible the teachings of Ramana by not only editing *The Mountain Path,* the journal of the Ramanasramam, but also by collating his teachings into one easily manageable book, *Be As You Are: The Teachings of Sri Ramana Maharshi.*

The shop is filled with shelf upon shelf of Bhagavan's teachings and biographies, translated into most of the world languages. I have a specific list of titles that I wish to purchase and buy *Talks, Day by Day with Bhagavan* and *Letters from Sri Ramanasramam* as well as two biographies by B V Narasimha Swami and Arthur Osborne. I then return to my room to look at them all.

In a small village called Tiruchuzhi, 30 miles from Madurai, on 29 December 1879, a child was born by the name of Venkataraman to poor Brahmin parents, Sundaram Ayyar, a petition writer, and Alagammal – the very same day as the December full moon celebrations, Arudra Darshan, were taking place. The second of four children – with an older brother, Nagaswamy, a younger brother, Nagasundaram, and a sister, Alamelu – he was raised a Saivite, though he remained indifferent to religion and even study, preferring sport and games. Venkataraman took elementary classes at Tiruchuzhi and then went on to study at primary school in Dindigul, a nearby village. From there, he attended classes in Madurai at Scott's Middle School and then finally, the American Mission High School, where he learnt English.

It was in 1895 that two significant events unfolded in the life of the young boy, sparking the flame of desire for Self Knowledge, the answer to the question, Who am I? An elderly relative came to visit the family and Venkataraman, asking where he had been, was told that the relative had just returned from Arunachula. The name of the hill had a deep effect on the boy, its sound evoking a longing for something mysterious and magical. Similarly, it was also around this time that Venkataraman discovered a copy of *Periapuranam,* a book describing the lives of 63 Tamil saints and their love for God. So inspired was he by the work and hearing the scared word Arunachula, that it precipitated a spiritual crisis when Venkatraman was only 17. The internal monologue Venkataraman subsequently held within himself as he was taken over by an intense fear of death has become such a famous spiritual soliloquy that it now has pride of place in the ashram.

And indeed, if even the very act of turning towards God is part of one's destiny, then this event in Venkataraman's life was as it should have been. For a curse had been placed on the family that every generation would produce an ascetic. A wandering monk had once visited the house but was not given due respect and, upon leaving, he declared that each generation of Venkataraman's family would produce one member who would become a monk, having to wander in search of food. It would appear that the omen had come true.

Venkataraman contined to live in the house but was rebuked by his uncle and brother for behaving like a sadhu whilst enjoying the comforts of a householder. Thus, on 29 August 1896, while copying out English grammar for homework, his soul rebelled against the seemingly pointless exercise. He thus decided to leave his home and go to Arunachala. He wrote a short note, explaining his decision: 'I have, in search of my father and in obedience to his command, started from here. This is only embarking on a virtuous enterprise. Therefore none need grieve over this affair . . .' He arrived in Tiruvannamalai on 1 September 1896.

The first place of residence for Venkataraman was in the thousand-pillared hall or *mantapam* of the Temple of Arunachaleswara in Tiruvannamalai. He shaved his head, tore his clothes to shreds, wearing only a loincloth, and threw all his money away. He then took a vow of silence, thus becoming a *mouni*. The young 'Brahmana Swami', as he was now referred to, attracted a lot of attention, both reverential and mischievous but he was always protected and fed by pious locals. Indeed, he was to spend many, many years living in various temples and caves on and around Arunachula, always under the protective guise of a devotee. Virupaksha Cave was always his chief residence however; shaped like the sacred mantra *Om*, it contains the remains of Saint Virpakshadeva and thus was a fitting residence for the Swami.

In 1907, a learned scholar and poet called Ganapati Sastri came and visited Brahmana Swami to ask him what was the true nature of *tapas* (spiritual practice). The Swami told him, 'If one watches whence this notion "I" springs, the mind is absorbed into that. That is *tapas*.' Upon hearing these words, Ganapati Sastri's heart was so filled with joy that he composed five stanzas in praise of the Swami, wherein he contracted the Swami's name, Venkataraman, into Ramana. In a letter he also wrote the following day to relatives and disciples, he said that the Swami deserved the title 'Bhagavan Maharshi' meaning 'Lord, the Great Rishi' since he had never heard such depth of understanding as this before. Thus, the name Bhagavan Sri Ramana Maharshi became the adopted name for Venkataraman Brahmana Swami.

It was not until November 1922 that Ramana took up residence at the foot of the hill in what is now known as the Ramanasramam. Initially, the ashram was only a small collection of thatched huts and hermitages but it has grown into a sizeable compound of stone buildings, marble halls and shrines. Indeed, as a devotee, it is still possible to stay in the ashram but you need to give at least three months' notice, such is the demand.

Up until his death, Ramana never left Arunachala, remaining in the ashram and receiving devotees from all walks of life. He led a simple life – he would rise between three and four in the morning, listen to chants in praise of Bhagavan or Arunachala and then greet visitors who had come to sit with him. He would occasionally help with the ashram chores, such as chopping vegetables, cutting and polishing walking sticks, stitching leaf-plates and binding notebooks, but he would always take an afternoon stroll on the hillside. In the evening there would be meditation and the recitations of devotees, followed by dinner. The day would come to a close at around nine.

At the beginning of 1949, a small nodule appeared below Ramana's left elbow. In February, the ashram doctor removed the lump but within a month it returned, much larger and more painful than before. Diagnosed as a sarcoma, it was operated on but the wound did not heal, resulting in another growth appearing higher up the arm. Doctors feared that Ramana was in great pain but he always dismissed their concern: 'There is pain,' he would admit, 'but what has that to do with me.' He would also add, 'You attach too much importance to the body.'

On 4 December he was unsuccessfully operated on for the final time. Devotees, in the growing realization that Bhagavan was nearing the end of his life, asked what they would do without him, to which he replied: 'They say that I am dying but I am not going away. Where could I go?' By January the following year, he was too weak to remain in the New Hall and was moved to the small ante-room opposite. Finally, on 14 April 1950, when his body was wracked with physical pain and disease, devotees started to gather in the courtyard chanting *Arunachala Siva*, sensing that the end of Bhagavan's life was drawing near. Upon hearing the music, Ramana smiled, tears of bliss streamed from his eyes and he drew his last breath. His *maha samadhi* was at 8.47pm. And, at exactly the same moment, a large star was seen to trail slowly across the sky towards the peak of Arunachala.

The life of Bhagavan Sri Ramana Maharshi was immaculate humility and benevolence. He showed compassion to all beings – animals, thieves, people from all castes, religions and creeds. He refrained from getting involved in worldly activities; he never handled any of the ashram money nor did he answer letters addressed to him, though he would always welcome anyone into his presence.

He also wrote down very little of his teaching – indeed the only verses which arose spontaneously were *Eleven Stanzas to Sri Arunachala* and *Eight Stanzas to Sri Arunachala*; the rest of his poetry being produced specifically at the request of a disciple to elucidate a particular point. Put together as a collection, it only forms a slim volume – indeed, his most well known work, *Forty Verses on Reality* or *Ulladu Narpadu*, together with its forty supplementary verses, constitutes just over ten pages of written text. 'All this is only activity of the mind,' he remarked to a visiting poet. 'The more you exercise the mind and the more success you have in composing verses the less peace you have.' Nevertheless, he did meticulously edit the books published during his lifetime to ensure accuracy of meaning, leaving no room for misunderstanding or misinterpretation.

No possessions, no money, I reflect. No hypocrisy or hidden agendas, no egotism or conceit. No relationship scandals, no money scams. No abuse of power, no deceit. Absolutely nothing about the way in which Bhagavan Sri Ramana Maharshi lived his life can be misconstrued. How I wish I could have met him, received his blessing, his *upadesa*, his smile. How I wish I could have been in the presence of an embodiment of human perfection on this planet earth.

Indeed, the Buddha asserted that in the end everything must be given up. Should this not be taken literally, as Ramana's life seems to suggest? I appreciate that living in the Western world, a hemisphere so locked into economic and material functionalism, money and possessions are an intrinsic part of life. But it is not easy to use that argument simply to justify having the things around us. If we truly, truly renounce everything, would not all our needs be provided for, no matter where we lived, as the life of Ramana proved? When asked about this point however, Bhagavan was quite specific – nothing needs to be given up, he said, merely the thought, 'I am the doer,' replacing it with, 'I am.' Moreover, when asked about which was the higher path, life as a householder or that of an ascetic, he replied, 'Was not Rama spiritually advanced and was he not leading a householder's life?'

Nonetheless, the likes of Ramana are rare indeed. A teacher of such calibre only comes, some would say, every 500 years. Ramana himself spoke of the differences in absorption in the Self, which can be either temporary or permanent. *Nirvikalpa samadhi* Ramana likened to a bucket lowered into a well; the water in the bucket merges with the water in the well but the rope and bucket (representing ego and its attachments) still exist, meaning that the bucket can always be pulled out from the well, ending the total absorption. Meanwhile, *sahaja samadhi* he likened to a river flowing into an ocean, whose waters become inseparably merged. Ramana's *sahaja samadhi* happened spontaneously at the age of 17 – for me, is *nirvikalpa samadhi* all I can really hope for?

Ramana's teaching was not the beginning of a new religious movement nor did it spawn social and political upheaveal, bloodshed and war. Rather, it gave access to the simplest and most ancient of philosophical truths to those living in the modern world during the *Kali Yuga*, a period of profound spiritual darkness. Indeed, this echoes the prophecy of the Lord Sri Krishna in the *Bhagavad Gita*, when he tells Arjuna that, in times of human ignorance, he will reincarnate to restore the dharma.

Indeed, a guru is needed to dispel the illusion of ignorance, though in rare cases the guru does not necessarily need to be in human form: 'The outer guru gives the mind a push inwards and the inner guru pulls it,' Bhagavan said. Thus Ramana's presence was to initiate devotees on the path, either by his speech, his look or through sitting in silence. Accusations of inconsistency in his instruction have been made but these apparent contradictions highlight the way in which Ramana taught at the level of the understanding and emotional disposition of the aspirant. He employed two approaches to abiding in the Self – either *jnana marga*, the path of knowledge, through the method of *vichara* (Self Enquiry) or *bhakti marga*, the path of devotion and surrender. 'There are two ways: either ask yourself, "Who am I?" or submit,' he would say, knowing that intrinsically, *jnana* and *bhakti* lead to the same end. 'The eternal, unbroken, natural state of abiding in the Self is *jnana*. To abide in the Self you must love the Self. Since God is in fact the Self, love of the Self is love of God, and that is *bhakti*. *Jnana* and *bhakti* are thus one and the same.'

For the Western mind, intent on philosophical analysis and intellectual debate, Ramana prescribed Self Enquiry as the most effective path, though it is paradoxically deemed to be the harder of the two methods: first, owing to its simplicity and directness and second, because it breaks down the apparent veil of dualism (*dvaita*) that devotion and compassion between guru and devotee (from the point of view of the devotee) can bring about.

Fixing one's attention on the centre of consciousness in the body, the spiritual heart (which Ramana believed is on the right side of the chest and not the left, where the physical heart is located), a current of awareness of 'I' will arise. Through constant vigilance, when a thought arises, one should ask, 'Where did this thought come from, and why, and to whom?' This then leads to the final question, 'Who am I?' The answer will then be revealed but it will be beyond all words, concepts and thoughts: 'Self Enquiry is like the thief turning policeman to catch the thief that is himself.'

Bhagavan was quite specific about the need for constant spiritual effort: 'If you strengthen the mind, that peace will become constant. Its duration is proportionate to the strength of mind acquired by repeated practice.' Nevertheless, he also stated that events in one's life were attributed to one's *prarabdha*, karma that is to be worked out in this life: 'As beings reap the fruit of their actions in accordance with God's laws, the responsibility is theirs, not His.' Asked about this apparent contradiction between destiny and effort by a devotee, he replied: 'That which is called 'destiny', preventing meditation, exists only to the externalized and not to the introverted mind. Therefore he who seeks inwardly in quest of the Self, remaining as he is, does not get frightened by any impediment that may seem to stand in the way of carrying on his practice of meditation. The very thought of such obstacles is the greatest impediment . . . The best course, therefore, is to remain silent.' And again, he said, 'All the actions that the body is to perform are already decided upon at the time it comes into existence: the only freedom you have is whether or not to identify yourself with the body.'

Devoid of ritual and priestly hierarchy, cosmology and dogma, the teachings of Sri Ramana Maharshi are as appropriate for the man in the ashram as for the man in the office or home. Nevertheless, Self Enquiry is not for the faint hearted – it is for those who truly wish to go all the way home: 'It is intended only for ripe souls,' Bhagavan said, conceding that some devotees need to adopt less direct methods more suited to their spiritual development. Nonetheless, when a devotee asked for permission to drop the methods he had been using up until that moment, Bhagavan replied, 'Yes, all other methods only lead up to the *vichara*.'

I am halfway through my stay at the ashram. Whilst wandering around, I unexpectedly bump into Bharat. More synchronicity, I think. Just as he told me in our interview together, he has decided to stay in Tiruvannamalai for a while, hanging out and trying to decide where ultimately to settle down. I mention that I am hoping to walk up the hill and he offers to join me. So, next day, we set off early just after breakfast and start the climb up to the top. We take the gate at the back of the ashram, where steps have been made out of stone but soon the path levels off into one long steep path, which snakes its way ahead of us. A recent reforestation project has transformed parts of the lower terrain into beautiful areas of wooded glades and thick green carpets of grass. In Ramana's day, the hill harboured wild animals, most notably tigers, though I am assured they no longer live here. And yet, despite the safety of the surroundings and its sylvan beauty, my awareness is soon lost in the physically exhausting task in hand. As we climb higher and higher, there is no adequate shade to shelter from the morning sun, which beats relentlessly down on us. As I still don't feel physically well, not having eaten properly for days now, we have to stop and rest many times on the way.

As we make our way up and up, we start to talk about the different teachers I have met and Bharat asks me what conclusions I have come to. 'I am still finding this paradox difficult to get hold off,' I say, trying to catch my breath. 'Gangaji says you can choose to be free. Ramesh says it is in your mind-body programming whether you will be free or not.' Bharat laughs, understanding the familiar conundrum. 'Both exist,' he says as we stop to rest by some large red boulders and take a slug of water. 'You must make a commitment to the truth, 100 per cent. But at the same time, ask yourself whose destiny is it and who makes that commitment? It's about opposites co-existing . . . It's all there in the teachings of Ramana.'

I continue to reflect on all the many interpretations of the same non-dualistic truth I have heard. On the one, hand there is the more experiential approach of Papaji's messengers, choosing to *surrender* to what is. On the other hand, there is the intellectual rigour of Self Enquiry, principally coming from the Ramesh line, leading to an *understanding* of what is. And yet both approaches are accommodated within the teachings of Bhagavan. In him, seemingly everything is contained.

We set off again. A bare-chested sadhu wearing only a white dhoti, his naked torso the colour of beaten bronze, *namastes* to us as he passes by. His forehead is daubed with holy ash with a vermilion gash of paste blobbed between his eye brows. Further along the path, a young boy has set up a stall of small statues, which he carves by the edge of the path. He beams excitedly as we approach — would we like to buy a statue of Siva, Hanuman, the wheel of Kali, Ganesh? I examine one of the pieces, a small carving of the elephant god, delicately chiselled in grey-blue stone. I buy it from him and he returns the transaction with a wide smile of brilliant white teeth.

After nearly an hour of walking, the path plateaus out, affording a stunning view over Tiruvannamalai, which stretches for miles across the plain into the distance. And in the middle of this panoramic sea of buildings and urban sprawl, rises up the Temple of Arunachaleswar, a shrine to Ishwara, the personal god. It is probably the most breathtaking man-made structure I have ever seen in my life, our position on the hill rendering us even more of a spectacular view than that from the ground. Dating from the 11th century, its fortress structure has four large *gopurams* or towers, rising to over 60 metres high, like huge electricity pylons waiting to conduct the very force of God from the heavens above.

In India, worshipping God and his manifestion is part of everyday life. Hinduism is practised by approximately 80 per cent of the population, which represents more than 700 million people. To outsiders, it can appear to be a complex amalgam of conflicting philosophical theories as well as possessing a bewildering pantheon of goddesses and gods. At its heart however, there is a central belief — Brahman, impersonal awareness, manifested within itself to become Ishwara, the personal god. Ishwara has three aspects, the *trimurti*, namely Brahma (the Creator), Vishnu (the preserver, married to Lakshmi and reincarnating as Rama and Krishna) and Siva (the destroyer, married to Kali). Which god or goddess one chooses to worship is ultimately a matter of personal taste, tradition or caste, though, if sincerely practised, all ways lead to the ultimate state of absorption in the Self.

Finally, Bharat and I arrive at Skandasramam, a small dwelling on the side of the hill, looking out over the landscape. During the time that Ramana was living on Arunachala before finally taking residence at the foot of the hill, he stayed here in silence for seven years, between 1915 and 1922. This was also the time when his mother, Alagammal, came to join him both as maternal protector and disciple, cooking for him and tending to his needs.

We pass through a gate and slip off our shoes. Skandasramam is a small grove where there are steps of rock to sit on to bask in the visionary beauty laid out before us. Dragonflies flit here and there and the air is filled with the music of running water, coming from a small spring at the back of the courtyard. We take the opportunity to rest and gather our thoughts, or lack of them, under the shade of sheltering trees, where the light on the ground reminds me of drops of liquid gold, like daubs of cyan in the paintings of the Impressionists. How easy it would be to find liberation in this Garden of Eden, I think. Oh, how I want to step off the world and remain here for the rest of my life – renounce all my worldly responsibilities and just remain submerged in the arms of mother nature.

On the left of the dwelling is a small ante-room – above the doorway is a plaque which reads, 'The Holy Room / The Soul of Mother Attained Nirvana'. Outside the main building there is a verandah, protected by emerald-coloured grilles and a corrugated roof. Inside, we pass into a small cool room. The doorway is low and, forgetting my relative height, I knock my head against the lintel. On the walls are black and white photographs of Ramana. In front of us is a much smaller room, where a handful of people are kneeling or sitting in the lotus posture in front of a small shrine to Bhagavan. Once more, the modesty and understatedness move me indescribably. There is a photograph of Ramana in the centre, flanked either side by a picture of Arunachala and a small book revealing his teachings. Even the candle placed in front of him burns with a graceful humility. I kneel before Bhagavan and then return to the outer room, where I sit and experience the sanctity of this holy place. The silence is so palpable that even the thinking of a thought would be a deafening noise. Never before have I tasted such peace of mind, stillness of being and openness of heart.

There is a sadhu called Skandaswami who looks after the dwelling. He sits on the shaded verandah, fanning himself with reeds. I notice a pamphlet propped up in one of the window frames – it is *Who am I?*, Bhagavan's teaching and I start to copy out some of its contents. Skandaswami notices what I am doing and offers the booklet to me to keep. I am deeply touched, I motion with my hands, but decline – how could I possibly remove something from this sacred place?

Virupaksha Cave, Ramana's main residence for 17 years during his time on the hill, is a short descent from Skandasramam but the heat is rising as the morning sun climbs in the sky. Bharat and I decide therefore to return to the ashram in time for lunch. We hardly speak on our way back – there doesn't appear to be any need for words.

The following day, again shortly after breakfast, I take the same journey up the hill, this time accompanied by a South American girl, backpacking around India. We encounter bare-footed disciples, swamis and sadhus along the way. Then we pass by Skandasramam to the tapping of the statue seller's hammer and chisel and negotiate the path that leads down to Virupaksha Cave. We cross over the small stream that cascades down the hillside and descend down steep steps, past rocks and tropical foliage. We move around a huge boulder and there, in front of us, is the place where all my wanderings have led. My heart is pounding. There is a gateway into a courtyard surrounding a small white building, which looks out over Tiruvannamalai and Siva's Temple. Trees hang over the compound in which monkeys squabble and stare at me with their blushing faces. I take off my shoes and enter the dwelling under a plaque hanging over the door, which reads: 'Virupaksha Cave / Sri Ramana Maharshi stayed here from 1899 to 1916'.

A sadhu is resting inside and he rises silently to greet me. The floor is red and pink and on it there is an Indian mandala – a lotus flower surrounded in a circle, made from blue and grey stone. On the walls are black and white photographs of Ramana as a young boy and later as a swami. There is also a stone couch where he slept, indicated by the sadhu pointing first to it, then to a picture of Ramana and then putting his hands together under his cheek. The sadhu then escorts me into a dark room with a tiny doorway, where we have to duck right down to get through. It takes many moments for my eyes to adjust to the darkness. The sadhu leaves, returning with a cushion, indicating where I should sit. A handful of people seem to emerge from the darkness, all deep in meditation. Even my breathing seems to be a disturbance and I silently practise *pranayama* to steady my breath.

Where the building ends it is the rock of the cave. Part of the rock wall bulges into the room, forming a ledge on which there is a picture of Arunachala, surrounded by a garland of white flowers. There are also burning candles and a dish of holy ash. The sadhu beckons me towards him as he lifts a cloth covering the rock. He rubs it with his hand, generating a greyish powder. He smoothes it between his finger tips and then rubs it onto my forehead. I feel honoured by this simple ceremony, that my body has been baptized by the very earth of sacred Arunchala from the tomb of the great sage, Virpakshadeva, and where Ramana was absorbed in *sahaja samadhi*.

I return to my seat and immerse myself in deep meditation. The silence of the cave consumes me. But whereas the silence in Skandasramam embraced everything in the world around me – its sights and sounds and smells – it was the merging with the silence of Prakriti. And yet here, with my eyes closed in the darkness, the silence has a depth and profundity I have never experienced before. Everything has been absorbed back into a blankess, a void, into the unmanifest spirit of Purusha. At first it feels disconcerting and unfamiliar. The cave is damp and the faint smell of incense makes my head feel giddy.

As in my dream of a few nights back, the oily darkness seeps into my skin, filling up orifices and pores and I drown in a sea of blackness. But this is not the anaesthetized withdrawal into the unconscious that sleep brings. Now, I am fully present, fully awake – a witness to the withdrawal of creation happening within me. My thoughts and feelings have died and the world passes away. Time stops. The universe dies. Nothing remains. I exist no more.

After some time and for no apparent reason, the mind resurfaces and I decide to leave, so creep quietly out of the cave. The sadhu smiles and offers me a small garland of white jasmine, pointing to my hair. I *namaste* and attach the flowers to my hairclip. I then gesture to the sadhu to write down his name in my notebook. 'Subramanian', he writes in bold capital letters. He then beckons me to a side room, where there are some pots for cooking and washing. Subramanian lives in this room, whilst looking after the cave during the day. He reaches up to a pot on a shelf, from which he pours out some powder and wraps it in a piece of newspaper. *'Prasad,'* he whispers offering me the parcel whilst putting some of the powder onto his tongue. I do the same, cautiously dabbing the grey ash on my lips. But I am pleasantly surprised – it tastes like burnt sherbet. I try and convey to him how much I am grateful for his gift and kind hospitality. Once again, we *namaste.* As I prepare to leave, he lingers by my side. I realize that the etiquette now is for me to offer a financial donation. But this particular day, I have left all my money and valuables in the ashram safe and have absolutely nothing to give him. I try to explain that I want to offer him some rupees but that I don't have any on me. Suddenly, I feel quite wretched. Even though the ashram specifically states that one shouldn't give money to sadhus on the hill and that any donations should only go through the ashram cashier, I still feel I have committed some awful faux pas, taken kindness from this modest and benevolent sadhu without giving anything in return. He waves his hand to show me that he has understood and returns to his chair, looking despondently down at the floor.

The pangs of anxiety and regret linger in my heart the entire journey down the hill to the ashram. Indeed for days it plays on my mind and I consider whether I should go back to the cave to offer Subramanian a donation. But the two trips up the hill have left me physically exhausted and, reluctantly, I make the decision not to return.

The days pass, each one blending into the next. I spend many hours relaxing in my room, reading, writing and trying to recuperate from my sickness, somewhat hindered by the fact that I am bitten on my lower left leg by a scorpion, resulting in my skin turning an alarming shade of red. But for most of the time, I stay well within the ashram precincts, not venturing out into Tiruvannamalai. The bustle of the main street running past the ashram is enough for me to taste Southern Indian life. My favourite time of the day is tiffin, which is served in a room adjacent to the dining hall. I take two cups and an Indian man ladles a stream of milky tea into one of them. I discover the ritual is to continuously pour the tea from one cup to the other and the higher the distance between the cups the better, enabling the air to cool down the temperature of the tea. It is absolutely delicious.

It is my last evening in the ashram. Dinner is at seven-thirty. The Doctor helps out with the seating arrangements and when the food is distributed, Mr Ramanan serves everyone with ghee, which he pours over the rice. The food is particularly tasty this evening – soup, rice and vegetable curry, poppadums and pickle, followed by sweet rice, caramel papaya and a banana, curds and buttermilk.

I decide to spend the evening in the Old Hall, the main meditation room where Ramana lived and gave satsang between 1925 and 1949. It is a modest room, tucked under the shade of a frangipani tree with large yellow flowers. Inside there is a stone floor, green shutters and an elaborate ornamental dado running around the walls. I am shocked by the number of people I find inside since the silence is so loud you could hear a pin drop. I find a gap by the wall and sit against it and close my eyes. Everything is so still, I think.

The focus of the room is Bhagavan's couch, covered in Indian shawls, where he spent so many years dispensing his wisdom. A large framed hand-coloured black and white photograph of Ramana now resides in his place, depicting him reclining against some pillows with his long thin legs stretched out. It makes me smile to see this charming attempt to evoke the memory of his presence.

As peace overwhelms me, I hear the faint purring of the overhead fan and the pulse of the crickets in the outside grass. There is nowhere to go, nothing to do, I reflect once more. I then start to think about my journey home, re-entry into my so-called life. A sadness wells up in my heart – I don't want to leave this holy place. If only I could preserve this moment and carry it back with me forever. Then I think about what Ramana said when he was approached by a devotee, upset at her imminent departure from the ashram. 'Why do you weep?' he said to her, 'I am with you wherever you go.'

The following morning as I pack my things to leave, I reflect on something I have read in one of Ramesh's books that I have brought with me. First, there is a mountain, he says. It is perceived as being real because there is total involvement. Second, the next stage, is that there is no mountain because everything is seen as unreal, not having a self-subsistent reality. Finally, the last stage, is that there is a mountain. It is perceived as being real because consciousness is seen as manifesting as a mountain. It reminds me of something else I have long since read – a quote from the *Four Quartets* by T S Eliot:

> *We shall not cease from exploration*
> *And the end of all our exploring*
> *Will be to arrive where we started*
> *And know the place for the first time*

> *'Little Gidding', Four Quartets*
> T S Eliot

As my taxi pulls away taking me back to Chennai, I look back at Arunachala in all its splendour, reaching up into the brilliant blue sky. I close my eyes, trying to burn the image on the back of my eyelids. I then turn around and look out to the open road ahead of us. 'In the end everyone must come to Arunachala,' Bhagavan said. It is true, I reflect, for this is the end of my exploring and yet I shall never cease from my exploration of this most blessed life.

WHO AM I?

Bhagavan Sri Ramana Maharshi

Questions and answers, 1902, published in 1923

1. Sivaprakasam Pillai : — *Swami, Who am I? How is salvation attained?*

    Brahmana Swami : — *By incessantly pursuing within yourself the enquiry 'Who am I,' you will know your true Self and thereby attain salvation.*

2. S : — *Who am I?*

    B: — *The real 'I' or true Self is not any of the five senses, nor the sense objects, nor the organs of action, not the* prana, *(breath or vital force), nor the mind, nor even the deep sleep state when there is no cognizance of any of these.*

3. S : — *If I am not any of these, what else am I?*

    B : — *After excluding each of the above, saying 'This is not I,' that which remains alone is 'I'; and that is consciousness.*

4. S : — *What is the nature of that consciousness?*

    B : — *It is* satchitananda *(ie, reality, consciousness, bliss), where there is not even the slightest trace of the thought 'I' at all. This is also called* mowna *(silence),* atman *(Self). The only thing that exists is that. The three (world, ego, and God personal, Ishwara) if considered as separate entities, are mere illusions, like the appearance of silver in the mother-of-pearl. But God,* jivas *(egos) and the world are One,* Sivaswarupa *or the* Atmaswarupa *are Real.*

5. S : – *How are we to realize that real (or Sivaswarupa)?*

B : – *When the external objects* (drisya) *vanish, then the true nature of the seer or subject is realized (to be the real, the Absolute).*

6. S : – *Can we not realize that* (Sivaswarupa) *while we see objects also?*

B : – *No. Because, the seen (phenomena) and the seer (the noumenon) are like the rope and the appearance of a serpent therein. Unless you get rid of the superimposed illusion of a serpent, you cannot believe that what exists is only the rope.*

7. S : – *When will the external objects vanish?*

B : – *If the mind which is the cause of all thoughts and all activity vanishes, the external objects will vanish.*

8. S : – *What is the nature of the mind?*

B : – *Mind is merely thoughts. It is a form of energy. It manifests itself as all the objects (ie, the world). When the mind sinks within the Self ie, the Sivaswarupa, then the Self is realized. When the mind issues out, the world appears, and the Self is not realized.*

9. S : – *How will the mind vanish?*

B : – *Only by pursuing the enquiry 'Who am I?'. Though this enquiry is a mental operation, it destroys all other mental operations, and finally itself vanishes, just as the stick with which the funeral pyre is kindled, is reduced to ashes after the pyre and corpses are burnt. Then we attain knowledge or realization of the Self. Then the thought 'I' (personality) is dissolved; breathing and other other activities of* prana *(vitality) are subdued. Both personality and breathing (ie,* pranas*) have a common source. Whatever you do, do without egoism (ie,) without the feeling "I am doing this.' When one reaches that state, even one's wife will be seen by him as the Mother of the universe. True* bhakti *(devotion) is the surrender of one's ego into the Self.*

10. S : – *Are there not other methods to make the mind disappear?*

B : – *Except enquiry, there is no other adequate method. If the mind is lulled by other means, it keeps quiet for a while, and again jumps up and leaps back to its former activity.*

11. S : – *But these instincts and innumerable self-preserving and other latent tendencies* (vasanas) *in us, when will they be subdued?*

B : – *The more often you withdraw into the Self, the more these tendencies pale off; and finally they leave you.*

12. S : — *Is it indeed possible to root out all these tendencies, which have soaked into our mind, generation after generation?*

B : — *Never yield room for doubts of that sort in your mind. But firmly resolve and dive into the Self. The mind constantly directed by the above enquiry into the Self becomes dissolved, and transformed in the end into the Self. Whenever you feel any doubt, do not try to clear the doubt; but try to know him who feels the doubt.*

13. S : — *How long should one go on with this enquiry?*

B : — *It is needed so long as there is the least trace of tendencies in the mind to create thoughts. So long as your enemies occupy a citadel, they will be issuing out. If you kill each, as he issues out, the citadel will be captured by you in the end. Similarly each time thoughts rear their heads and issue out, crush them by the above enquiry. This process of crushing out all thoughts at their birth-place or place of origin is termed* vairagya *(dispassion). Hence enquiry is needful right up to the time of Self-realization. What is needed is a continuous and uninterrupted 'thought' of the real Self.*

14. S : — *Is not all this, the universe and all that takes place therein, the result of Ishwara's (God's) will; and if so why should God will thus?*

B : — *God has no purpose. He is not fettered by any action. The world's activities cannot affect him. Let us take the analogies of the sun and space to make this clear. The sun rises without any desire, purpose, or effort. But directly the sun rises, numerous activities take place on this earth. The lens placed in its rays produces fire in its focus; the bud of the lotus blossoms, water evaporates, and every living object on earth enters upon, maintains, and finally drops its activity. But, the sun is not affected by all such activity, as he merely maintains his nature, acts by fixed laws, has no purpose, and is, merely a witness. So it is with God. Again take the case of space or ether. Earth, water, fire and air are all in it, and have their motions and modifications therein. Yet none of these affects ether or space. The same is the case with God. God has no desire or purpose in his acts of creation, maintenance, destruction, withdrawal, and salvation, to which beings (jivas) are subjected. As beings (jivas) reap the fruit of their acts in accordance with His laws (the laws of karma etc,) the responsibility for such fruit is theirs, not God's. God is not affected or bound by any acts.*

BIBLIOGRAPHY

Ashtavakra Gita, (Tr. Hari Prasad Shastri), Shanti Sadan, 1992

Brahma Sutras, (Tr. & Ed. Swami Vireswarananda), Advaita Ashrama, 1996

The Collected Works of Ramana Maharshi, (Ed. Arthur Osborne),
Samuel Weiser, 1997

The Geeta, The Gospel of the Lord Shri Krishna, (Tr. Shri Purohit Swami),
Faber and Faber

Maharshi's Gospel, The Teachings of Sri Ramana Maharshi, T N Venkataraman, 1994

Ramayana, (Tr. C Rajagopalachari), Bharatiya Vidya Bhavan, 1987

The Republic, Plato, (Tr. Desmond Lee), Penguin, 1987

A Sourcebook in Indian Philosophy, (Ed. Sarvepalli Radhakrishnan &
Charles A Moore), Princeton University Press, 1989

The Ten Principal Upanishads (Tr. Shree Purohit Swami and W B Yeats),
Faber and Faber, 1988

Viveka-Cudamani (The Crest Jewel of Wisdom), (Tr. A J Alston), Shanti Sadan, 1997

Yoga Vasishtha (The World Within the Mind), (Tr. Hari Prasad Shastri),
Shanti Sadan, 1989

Balsekar, Ramesh, *The Final Truth, A Guide to the Ultimate Understanding*,
Advaita Press, 1989

    Consciousness Speaks, Advaita Press, 1992

    Pointers from Ramana Maharshi, Zen Publications, 1998

    Pointers from Nisargadatta Maharaj, Chetana, Mumbai, 1999

    Advaita, the Buddha and the Unbroken Whole, Zen Publications, 2000

    Sin & Guilt, Monstrosity of Mind, Zen Publications, 2000

Bharat, *Split Seconds*, Bharat Rochlin, 2001

Blackburn, Simon, *Think*, Oxford University Press, 1999

Brunton, Paul, *A Search in Secret India*, Sri Ramanasramam

Daniélou, Alain, *The Myths and Gods of India*, Inner Traditions International, 1985

Eliot, T S, *Collected Poems 1909-1962*, Faber Paperbacks, 1980

Ferguson, Margaret (Ed. et al), *The Norton Anthology of Poetry*,
W W Norton & Company, 1996

Frydman, Maurice (Tr), Dikshit, Sudhakar S (Rev. & Ed.),
I Am That, Talks with Sri Nisargadatta Maharaj, The Acorn Press, 1994

Gangaji, *You Are That! Satsang with Gangaji, Vol. I*, The Gangaji Foundation, 1995

   freedom & resolve, the living edge of surrender, The Gangaji Foundation, 1999

Godman, David (Ed.), *Be As You Are, The Teachings of Sri Ramana Maharshi*,
Arkana Penguin Books, 1985

   Papaji: Interviews, Avadhuta Foundation, 1993

Godman, David, *Nothing Ever Happened, Vol. I, II, III*, Avadhuta Foundation, 1998

Gyatso, Tensin (His Holiness the Dalai Lama), *Ancient Wisdom, Modern World:
Ethics for a New Millennium*, Little, Brown, 1999

Hinnells, John R (Ed.), *A Handbook of Living Religions*, Penguin Books, 1991

Honderich, Ted (Ed.), *The Oxford Companion to Philosophy*,
Oxford University Press, 1995

Huxley, Aldous, *The Doors of Perception*, Flamingo, 1994

Kerouac, Jack, *On the Road*, Penguin, 1991

Lucille, Francis, *Eternity Now: Dialogues on Awareness*,
Truespeech Publications, 1996

Marwick, Arthur (Ed.), *The Sixties: Mainstream Culture and Counter-Culture*,
The Open University, 1998

Moore, Roslyn (Ed.), *Meeting Papaji*, Do Publishing, 1999

Mudaliar, A Devaraja, *Day by Day with Bhagavan*, Sri Ramanasramam, 1995

Nagamma, Suri, *Letters from Sri Ramanasramam*, Sri Ramanasramam, 1995

Nobody (Ed.), *Wake Up and Roar: Satsang with H W L Poonja, Vol. II*, Pacific Center Publishing, 1993

Osborne, Arthur, *Buddhism and Christianity in the Light of Hinduism*, Sri Ramanasramam, 1996

    Ramana Arunachala, Sri Ramanasramam, 1994

    Ramana Maharshi and the Path of Self Knowledge, Sri Ramanasramam, 1997

Parsons, Tony, *The Open Secret*, The Connections, 1995

Penrose, Roger, *Shadows of the Mind*, Vintage, 1995

De Ruiter, John, *Unveiling Reality*, Oasis Edmonton, 2000

Swami, Narasimha B V, *Self-Realization: The Life and Teachings of Bhagavan Sri Ramana Maharshi*, Sri Ramanasramam, 1931

Tarnas, Richard, *The Passion of the Western Mind*, Pimlico, 1991

Tzu, Ram, *No Way for the Spiritually "Advanced"*, Advaita Press, 1990

Venkataramiah, Munagala, *Talks with Sri Ramana Maharshi*, Sri Ramanasramam, 2000

Watts, Alan, *The Culture of Counter-Culture*, Tuttle Publishing, 1999

Wilber, Ken, *One Taste: The Journals of Ken Wilber*, Shambhala Publications, 1999